CW00959614

the new

Scottish Terrier

the new

Scottish Terrier

cindy cooke

HOWELL
BOOK
HOUSE

Howell Book House
A Simon & Schuster Macmillan Company
1633 Broadway
New York, NY 10019

Copyright © 1996 by Cindy Cooke

All rights reserved. No part of this book may be reproduced or transmitted
in any form or by any means, electronic or mechanical, including photocopy-
ing, recording, or by any information storage retrieval system, without
permission in writing from the Publisher.

MACMILLAN is a registered trademark of Macmillan, Inc.

Library of Congress Catologing-in-Publication Data

Cooke, Cindy.
The New Scottish Terrier/Cindy Cooke.
p. cm.
ISBN 0-87605-307-X
1. Scottish Terriers. I. Title.
SF429. S4C66   1996
636.7'55—dc20   95-47430
                                         CIP

Manufactured in the United States of America
10 9 8 7 6 5 4 3 2 1

*To my parents who allowed me to have dogs despite the doctors'
warnings; and to Miriam "Buffy" Stamm, a great role model and a
dear friend.*

Contents

Ch. [Braedston] Dundee and Braedston Lorna. The original of this picture was given to Fayette Ewing by Robert Miller who handled Dundee in the show ring. The Braedston prefix was attached to Dundee's name after Captain W. W. Spelman purchased the dog.

Preface

When I agreed to write this book, I felt confident that I was pretty knowledgeable about the Scottish Terrier. Having finished the book, I have been humbled by how much I had to learn in order to finish it. We all know how wonderful our dogs are, but few of us are sufficiently aware of those who brought the Scottish Terrier to its present development. We owe a great debt to them all—the canny Scotsmen of the late nineteenth and early twentieth centuries who developed the modern breed, the wealthy patrons who paid to bring their foundation stock (and in some cases, their keepers) out of the highlands, the breeders of Great Britain who shared with us their finest bloodlines, and the pioneer American enthusiasts who labored so diligently to breed and perfect the Scottish Terrier as we know it. I think we owe a particular debt to those who wrote about the breed—McCandlish, Casperz, and Ewing, above all. These three people were dedicated to the preservation of the Scottish Terrier's finest qualities and to its improvement wherever necessary.

So much of what breeders and exhibitors do is evanescent. It is the writers who preserve our past for us. I hope this book will serve the fancy now and in the future as well as have the eloquent writings of the past.

Finally, no book such as this can be complete. To those whose achievements may have been overlooked in this work, my sincerest apologies. Recent and current canine history is, sadly, written in promotional advertisements appearing in the dog press. Those who do not or cannot advertise are often overlooked: a detrimental situation in many ways. I hope this book will inspire more lovers of the Scottish Terrier to write about our breed—its accomplishments, its needs, its problems. Then, perhaps, future historians will have a larger pool of more objective source material upon which to draw.

Ch. Anstamm Maid In America in a field of Texas bluebonnets.

Chapter 1

Early History
of the Scottish Terrier

The facts surrounding the origins of the Scottish Terrier are difficult to separate from a tangle of romantic tales and never-ending disputes. A contentious group, early fanciers could not settle on a name for the breed they loved, let alone agree on the breed's origins. At one time or another, Scotties were designated as "Skye Terriers," "Cairn Terriers," "Aberdeen Terriers," "West Highland Terriers," "Fox Terriers" and "Otter Dogs." In 1906, C. J. Davies, author of the very first book devoted solely to the Scottish Terrier, seriously speculated that Scotties were more likely descended from bears than wolves!

It is easy to understand why there would be disagreements in the ranks of the fancy at this time. The ancestors of our modern Scottish Terrier developed in the rugged Highlands of Scotland, where both dog and man faced numerous obstacles to survival: The weather is stormy; the land is rocky; the ocean is cold; and the wind blows fiercely. Highlanders, usually eking out the barest existence themselves, gave little thought to standardizing the appearance of their dogs. Their concern was the dog's ability to rid the harsh land of vermin.

In each glen, fox hunters and gamekeepers developed individual strains of Highland terriers to suit their personal tastes. A vivid portrait of the Scottish huntsmen of this era and their game little dogs appears in the journal of Capt. W. W. Mackie, often credited with bringing the Scottie to the attention of the world outside the Highlands. Capt. Mackie's childhood dog was "a grizzly-looking wee beggar" named Bobby, brought from Banffshire by Mackie's father. Having grown up with Bobby and his successor, "a snarling, snapping, wiry-looking article from the same locality," Capt. Mackie suffered from what he described as "terriers on the brain." In the late 1870s or early '80s, he embarked on a walking tour of western Scotland to see the terriers and meet the men who kept them. Here are some excerpts from his journal:

> Almost all the tod [fox]-hunters that I have met say that *they* are the only possessors of the good old sort. M'Corkindale, of Hell's Glen, has had the same blood for the past forty-eight years; Robinson, of Lochlomondside, has had them for sixty years; Cameron of Glenorchy, about thirty years; M'Gregor, living in a wee cottage at the south end of the Black Mount has had them for fifty years; Cameron, of the Black Corries, had them from his predecessor twenty years ago; while on the Black Mount, Kinloch-More, throughout Morven, Ardramurchan, and, in fact, all the shires west of a line drawn from the Mull of Galloway to John o'Groat's, Fox terriers— as they are known—have existed from time immemorial. I have listened to how Donnachie Bhan's wee "butch" killed the big dog-fox; and the manner in which John Buha's "Dobhran" . . . went into the badger, and both were dug out dead a fortnight afterwards, having killed each other. I have also heard how Ian Dhu's "Cavack" caught the otter under water, brought it ashore, and carried it home alive, "alive, oh!" These and similar tales I have listened to, and pretended to believe, to keep friendship with the tellers.

The writer goes on to describe meeting Robinson, the tod-hunter for Laird McMurich. Mackie met Robinson at an inn where the old tod-hunter, none too sober, invited them to meet him at daybreak at the Laird's. The following morning, Mackie and a companion were shown to the kennel, where they saw four terriers.

> The terriers stood about the height of the modern Fox Terrier. Their coats were a bit open and rough looking, but still hard enough to satisfy a fancier's wish; they had foxy-looking heads, semi-erect or half-cock ears, gaily carried tails; in colour they were a sort of rusty grey, and each had one or more white feet . . . The weight of his terriers would be from seventeen to twenty pounds.

The tod-hunter showed up late and hung over. He explained the white feet by saying that he had, some twenty or thirty years earlier, a particularly game dog that he used extensively for breeding. In each litter sired by this dog, there was always a puppy or two with white feet, and those were the ones favored by the old man. Robinson claimed that his dogs had flatter ribs and longer legs than the terriers of his youth, but that he wished they were lower to the ground. He claimed his dogs had killed forty-seven foxes in one spring.

The remainder of the journal describes a diverse group of dogs, mostly grizzled, brindled or sandy in color, all weighing in the neighborhood of seventeen to twenty pounds. Most had erect or semi-erect ears; big heads; large jaws and teeth; short, stout legs; and harsh, unkempt coats. Capt. Mackie purchased several dogs from those he had seen at the time, which formed the nucleus of his kennel.

THE BEGINNINGS OF DOG SHOWS

Not until the late 1800s did anyone make a serious effort to standardize names and breeds. The first English dog show to include a class for Scottish Terriers was the Birmingham show of 1860. There was, as yet, no Standard for the Scottish Terrier so virtually any dog that was not too large, had some length of coat, a smart expression and a willingness to kill rats was allowed to compete in the breed classes. Some shows offered divided classes. The 1863 Cremone show offered prizes for white, fawn, blue, Skye, and Dandie Dinmont "Scottish" Terriers, while in London, the dog classes were divided by weight—over and under seven pounds.

In 1877, dogs now considered ancestors of our modern Scottish Terrier were exhibited as Skye Terriers at several shows. Judges, however, were inclined to regard the long-haired terrier as the true "Skye" Terrier. Two years later, when the Kennel Club offered classes for *"Scotch Terriers,"* an entry numbering fifteen appeared. Among these were many of the same dogs previously exhibited as Skye Terriers, including the bitch Splinter II, the foundation matron of the modern Scottish Terrier.

The name "Aberdeen" became linked with a variety of Highland terriers at about this same time. According to D. J. Thompson Gray, author of *The Dogs of Scotland* (1891), there was a breed of prick-eared, hard-coated terriers exhibited in Aberdeen between 1873 and 1880. Mr. William Lort, having judged the breed on one occasion, dubbed it the "Aberdeen Terrier." In 1881, he offered prizes for two classes of Aberdeens at the Birmingham show. When the breed judge failed to appear, Mr. Lort stepped in and judged the classes himself. Sadly, the merits of the entry failed to meet his standards, and he withheld the prizes. The name "Aberdeen" continues to this day to be associated with the Scottish Terrier, but if there ever was a truly distinct strain of "Aberdeen Terriers," it long ago merged with the other Highland strains that make up today's Scottish Terrier.

Meanwhile, although the essential physical characteristics of the Scottish Terrier were long established, no written Standard existed yet. Controversy raged in the various livestock journals until, in 1880, Mr. J. B. Morrison responded to the requests of fanciers by drawing up the first written Standard of points for the breed.

The Morrison Standard served as the official breed Standard until the formation of the Scottish Terrier Club of England in 1887, and the Scottish Terrier Club of Scotland the following year. The English and Scottish Standards were nearly identical, varying only slightly in the value assigned to certain points. The Morrison Standard, the first Scottish Standard, and all subsequent English and American Standards appear in Chapter 11.

With the advent of a written Standard, the quality of the entries at the shows began to improve. At the 16th Kennel Club show at the Crystal Palace in 1881, Mr. Payton Piggott took first prize with a dog named Tartan, while Mr. H.J. Ludlow's Bon Accord went unplaced. Both would go on to great success in the show ring, but their place in breed history would be assured because both would sire litters from Mr. Piggott's Splinter II, the aforementioned foundation matron of the modern Scottish Terrier.

Mr. Piggott jumped into the Scottish Terrier fancy with both feet. He brought sixty terriers out of the Highlands from Gordon Murray. One of these was the bitch Splinter II. Mr. Piggott was in and out of the terrier game before he accomplished much, and he sold Splinter II to a more dedicated breeder, Mr. H.J. Ludlow.

No written description of Splinter II exists, although Mr. Ludlow described her as "a lovely little bitch." For whatever reason, early breeders linebred on this bitch to the virtual exclusion of all others. Mated to Tartan, she produced Worry, the dam of four champions. Rambler, her son by Bonaccord, sired the two founding sires of the breed, Ch. Dundee (out of Worry) and Ch. Alistair (out of a Dundee daughter). The prepotency of Splinter II's descendants can be seen in the pedigree of Heather Prince, born in 1892 and one of the top sires of his day.

The founding fathers of the breed were Ch. Dundee and his half-brother/grandson, Ch. Alistair. These two were rivals, in the show ring and for the affections of the leading brood bitches of the day. Dundee was a brindle dog, described as having large, well-placed ears, a good body and legs, great character and, according to one report, "a coat so hard it might have been borrowed from a hedgehog." Dorothy Caspersz claims that Alister was black, but the first Scottish Terrier studbook describes him as a steel gray brindle.[1] Writers of the day acclaimed Alister's nearly perfect head, ears and eyes, depth of chest and well-ribbed body.

Despite their close family relationship, Dundee and Alister were said to be of different types. Dundee was higher on the leg, shorter-bodied, and generally more refined than Alister, who was longer-bodied, heavier boned, and closer to the ground. For decades, breeders claimed that each dog threw his "type," and they claimed to be able to distinguish between their descendants on this basis. Nearly fifty years after the death of these twin pillars of the breed, Dr. Fayette Ewing wrote:

---

[1]*There are three possible explanations for this discrepancy. One is that Ms. Caspersz was mistaken. A second possibility is a mistake in the studbook (not the only one—Dundee's sire and dam are also incorrect). A third possibility is that Alister was black in his youth but had grayed with age. He was nearly ten years old when the studbook was assembled.*

Let me call your attention to the fact that today in Scottish Terriers are to be found at least two predominant types—the Dundee and the Alister. The Dundee is more refined, finer in bone, shorter and more leggy. The Alister is lower, somewhat longer, heavier, bigger-boned, and coarser. The Alister type is mostly the favorite of the modern fanciers.

The next influential sire was Ch. Rascal, a dark, brown-brindle grandson of Dundee, born in 1889. Eight of his grandparents were out of Splinter II. We are fortunate enough to have his precise measurements taken when he was 5 years old. He was 11½ inches tall, measured at the withers, and weighed twenty-three pounds. His head was nine inches long, measured from occiput to tip of nose. His body, measured from occiput to set-on of tail, was nineteen inches long.

Rascal's grandson, Seafield, and Heather Prince were the leading sires as Great Britain entered the twentieth century. It was also about this time that the first Scottish Terriers emigrated to the New World.

Seafield was alleged to have been a shy dog, but his son, Seafield Rascal, neither exhibited nor perpetuated this defect. His breeder Andrew Kinnear sold him for the princely sum of £250 to Mrs. Hannay, the first woman breeder and exhibitor of Scottish Terriers. Breeders were apparently not reluctant to double up on this dog in their pedigrees. The great sire, Laindon Lockhart, was the product of breeding Seafield Rascal's son, Bonaccord Jock, to a Seafield Rascal daughter, Eng. Ch. Bonaccord Nora.

Heather Prince, whose pedigree appears on page 6, was the first of many leading sires to carry the Heather prefix. Prince was a big-boned, big-ribbed

Eng. Ch. Dundee.

2 Prince Alexander
- 3 Whinstone
  - 4 Ch. Alister
    - 5 Rambler
      - 6 Bonaccord
      - 6 Splinter II
        - 7 Rambler
          - 8 Bonaccord
          - 8 Splinter II
        - 7 Worry
          - 8 Tartan
          - 8 Splinter II
    - 5 Ch. Lorna Doone
      - 6 Ch. Dundee
        - 7 Bonaccord
        - 7 Splinter II
      - 6 Bitters
        - 7 Bonaccord
        - 7 Splinter II
  - 4 Heather Belle
    - 5 Ch. Dundee
      - 6 Rambler
        - 7 Tartan
        - 7 Splinter II
      - 6 Worry
        - 7 Bonaccord
        - 7 Splinter II
    - 5 Glengogo
      - 6 Rambler
        - 7 Tartan
        - 7 Splinter II
      - 6 Worry
        - 7 Bonaccord
        - 7 Splinter II
- 3 Nettle
  - 4 Flegg Tartan
    - 5 Ch. Alister
      - 6 Rambler
        - 7 Bonaccord
        - 7 Splinter II
          - 8 Rambler
            - 9 Bonaccord
            - 9 Splinter II
          - 8 Ch. Dundee
            - 9 Tartan
            - 9 Splinter II
      - 6 Ch. Lorna Doone
        - 7 Ch. Dundee
          - 8 Worry
        - 7 Bitters
          - 8 Bonaccord
          - 8 Splinter II
    - 5 Flegg Thistle
      - 6 Tartan
        - 7 Bonaccord
        - 7 Splinter II
      - 6 Bitters
        - 7 Bonaccord
        - 7 Rambler
          - 8 Bonaccord
          - 8 Splinter II

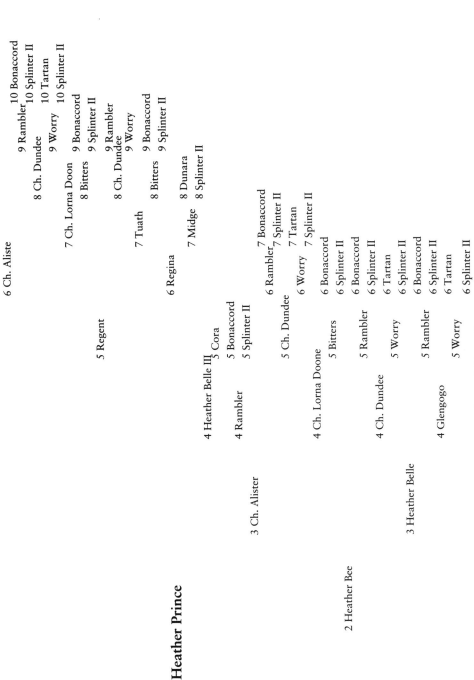

Heather Prince

2 Heather Bee

3 Ch. Alister
3 Heather Belle

4 Heather Belle III
4 Rambler
4 Ch. Lorna Doone
4 Ch. Dundee
4 Glengogo

5 Cora
5 Bonaccord
5 Splinter II
5 Ch. Dundee
5 Regent
5 Bitters
5 Rambler
5 Worry
5 Rambler
5 Worry

6 Ch. Aliste
6 Regina
6 Rambler
6 Worry
6 Bonaccord
6 Splinter II
6 Bonaccord
6 Splinter II
6 Tartan
6 Splinter II
6 Bonaccord
6 Splinter II
6 Tartan
6 Splinter II

7 Ch. Lorna Doon
7 Tuath
7 Midge
7 Bonaccord
7 Splinter II
7 Tartan
7 Splinter II

8 Ch. Dundee
8 Bitters
8 Ch. Dundee
8 Bitters
8 Dunara
8 Splinter II

9 Rambler
9 Worry
9 Bonaccord
9 Splinter II
9 Rambler
9 Worry
9 Bonaccord
9 Splinter II

10 Bonaccord
10 Splinter II
10 Tartan
10 Splinter II

Splinter II appears twenty-seven times in ten generations of this pedigree.

Eng. Ch.
Alister.

dog with a short, thick head and a large, round eye. Notwithstanding these faults, he sired six English champions. As was so often the case, it was Heather Dirk, his nonchampion son, who carried his name into future pedigrees. Dirk's grandson, Eng. Ch. Claymore Defender, bred to Eng. Ch. Bonaccord Nora (a Seafield Rascal daughter) produced the sensational brothers, Eng. Ch. Bapton Norman and Bapton Noble. This particular breeding points out the absurdity of assigning dogs to the Dundee or Alister clans. Seafield is considered to be a Dundee dog, while Heather Prince is called an Alister dog. By this point in history, the two lines had been so thoroughly blended that any distinctions were, practically speaking, imaginary.

It was about this time, just after the turn of the century, that William McCandlish moved from Edinburgh to Bristol and established his famous Ems Scottish Terriers. He produced an unprecedented four champion bitches in direct descent, beginning with Eng. Ch. Seafield Beauty, her daughter Ems Cosmetic, her granddaughter Ems Vanity, and her great-granddaughter Ems Mode. McCandlish also has the honor of producing the breed's first wheaten champion, Ems Morning Nip, whose coat was described by Dorothy Caspersz as the color of ripe corn tipped with black. McCandlish served as the Secretary of the Scottish Terrier Club of England from 1903 until 1914 but was most influential as a writer. His book, *The Scottish Terrier* (1909), did much to bring the breed to the attention of the general public. World War I, however, brought an end to McCandlish's breeding program and curtailed those of many others.

Two of England's most successful breeder-entrepreneurs, however, came through the war relatively unscathed: A.G. Cowley and Robert "Bobby" Chapman. Both men had a long history in Scotties. Chapman's father,

Bonaccord, whelped
about 1882.

Eng. Ch. Seafield Rascal,
whelped about 1906.

Robert Sr., was the breeder of Heather Prince, the most prominent sire in
England between 1894 and 1900. Prince's son, Ch. Heather Bob, out of the
great brood bitch Ch. Sunray, was a successful show dog and an influential

sire. Robert Jr., known as Bobby, inherited his father's dogs, his famous name, his eye for a dog, and his talent for breeding. The Chapmans were sort of the local *lairds* and virtually every tenant in the countryside around the Chapman home in Glenboig raised Scottish Terriers for them.

A.G. Cowley began breeding and exhibiting in 1909, but had his greatest success in the years following World War I. Cowley was a "crocker" during the war, providing horses to the English Army. Unlike the majority of other British breeders, Cowley had an adequate supply of dog food in the form of condemned horses.

While other breeders were drastically cutting back their numbers of dogs, Cowley was buying every worthwhile dog available. In 1951, the normally matter-of-fact Dorothy Caspersz wrote of Cowley:

Eng. Ch. Heather Bob, whelped July 28, 1898.

Eng. Ch. Ems Vanity, Eng. Ch. Ems Cosmetic and Ems Symphony.

No one taking an interest in Scottish Terriers at the shows from about 1909 onwards could fail to be impressed by the frequent recurrence of the name Albourne in the news and the prize lists. To Mr. A.G. Cowley, who owned this prefix, belongs the distinction of making a record number of champions in the breed. In all, he made forty-three, and the total of British champions actually bred by him is recorded as twenty-two. Small wonder he was alluded to as the "Albourne wizard" and deserved the title . . . Probably only once in a century is such a being born.

The years between World War I and World War II proved to be a turning point for the Scottish Terrier, largely because of the efforts of Chapman and Cowley and the nearly simultaneous appearance of three stud dogs and one fabulous brood bitch. The three dogs were Ch. Albourne Barty, Ch. Heather Necessity, and Marksman of Docken. The bitch was Marksman's sister, Albourne Annie Laurie. These four Scottish Terriers, often referred to as *The Four Horsemen,* established the modern type of Scottie, longer in head, shorter in body, and lower to the ground than their ancestors.

Ch. Albourne Barty was a black dog, described as short in body, low to the ground, and substantial in bone. His head was somewhat thick and short and his eye somewhat round, although dark. Barty sired eight British champions, three in one litter out of Albourne Annie Laurie. In 1928, there were thirty-eight CCs awarded in England—Barty's get won thirteen of them. His daughters and granddaughters produced the best offspring from Barty's rival, Ch. Heather Necessity.

Necessity, also black, was described in detail by Dorothy Caspersz:

That this dog represented a definite advance towards a type breeders were seeking seemed to be generally conceded. His critics maintained that such exaggerated length of head allied to such a short thick body verged upon the grotesque. His tail was absurdly out of proportion, a wee rudder like an inverted carrot and carried always stiffly erect, even when the dog was sitting. He had a head of excessive length for those days, but of good shape; adorned by neat little ears well placed, and small dark eyes set well under the brow. His neck would be considered short in the light of modern criticism, but was at least strong and muscular which is more than can be said of some present-day attenuations. His chest was the right breadth, with his body well swung between his straight heavily boned forelegs. The quarters were very strong but a trifle tied in at the hock, with insufficient bend at the stifle. Consequently what he gained in substance and compactness he lost in agility. One could not picture him doing any of the work for which the breed was originally intended. His jet black coat was dense and double, although somewhat too profuse. It tended to be soft on face and legs, but he had arrived at a time when exhibitors were cultivating more growth of hair on these parts and calling them furnishings, so he lent himself

Eng. Ch. Albourne Barty.

			Eng. Ch. Laindon Luminary
		Albourne Joe	
			Eng. Ch. Laindon Lightsome
	Eng. Ch. Albourne Adair		
			Eng. Ch. Albourne Beetle
		Eng. Ch. Albourne Dinkie	
			Albourne Young Gyp
Eng. Ch. Albourne Scot			
			Eng. Ch. Ruminantly Raven
		Binnie Boy	
			Abertay Maud
	Fragments		
			Baltimore
		Florida	
			Albourne Finesse
ENG. CH. ALBOURNE BARTY			
(Whelped 9/17/1925			Abertay Brigadier
Breeder: A.G. Cowley)		Eng. Ch. Laindon Luminary	
			Abertay Luna
	Eng. Ch. Laindon Lumen		
			Claymore Commandant
		Eng. Ch. Laindon Lightsome	
			Abertay Bliss
Albourne Jennifer			
			Eng. Ch. Albourne Adair
		Eng. Ch. Albourne Adonis	
			Albourne Matron
	Albourne Free Love		
			Eng. Ch. Albourne Adair
		Eng. Ch. Albourne Alisa	
			Albourne Huffy

Eng. Ch. Heather Necessity.

				Albourne Joe
			Eng. Ch. Albourne Adair	
		Eng. Ch. Albourne MacAdair		Eng. Ch. Albourne Dinkie
			Albourne Matron	Ruminantly Rocket
	Harton Highlander			Albourne Snap
			Loyal Boy	Biddick Boy
		Harton Holdfast		Loyal Ann
			Glenbrae Betty	Claymore Conqueror
ENG. CH. HEATHER NECESSITY				Monnyruy
(Whelped 9/14/1927			Ornsay Chieftain	Romany Monk
Breeder: Mr. Walker)				Tantallon Vixen
	Eng. Ch. Ornsay Brave			Misty Morning
			Eng. Ch. Bellstane Lassie	
	Skerne Scotch Lass			Meadow Lass
			Abertay Aristocrat	Romany Bishop
		Meg (2)		Abertay Darkie
			Fanny (2)	Abertay Brigadier
				Tattle (2)

admirably to being put down in show condition all the year 'round, as indeed he was. . . . He was considered too big, but he could, and did, look a model standing still, and his ring demeanour was always faultless. Definitely a great personality, he was dignified yet friendly to all admirers who approached his bench at a show, and in the ring his regal bearing and imperturbability under all circumstances did much to convince the majority that not only was his type a new one but a desirable one as well.

Necessity won a record number of Challenge Certificates and sired an amazing eighteen British champions.

			Albourne Linnson
		Eng. Ch. Albourne Beetle	
			Chandos Pearl
	Eng. Ch. Albourne Andy		
			Albourne Linnson
		Jealous Joyce	
			Ornum Clementine
Albourne MacAndy			
			Albourne Linnson
		Eng. Ch. Albourne Beetle	
			Chandos Pearl
	Albourne Mode		
			Laindon Lockhart
		Albourne Glendalyne	
			Albourne Pearl
Albourne Annie Laurie			

Marksman Of Docken

			Barlae Leader
		Eng. Ch. Barlae Proof	
			Barlae Sunshine
	Willowdale Rab		
			Romany Monk
		Chance Shot	
			Dornoch Gipsy
Eng. Ch. Mischief Of Docken			
			Eng. Ch. Bapton Norman
		Romany Monk	
			Romany Lydia
	Chance Shot		
			Cambus Corker
		Dornoch Gipsy	
			Dornoch Lassie

Albourne Annie Laurie (originally Melody of Docken) was a hard-coated, red-brindle, a little long in body with a head somewhat too short. Her quality was undisputed, but because of her indifferent showmanship, she changed hands three times. Her breeder, Miss Wijk, first sold her to Cowley. He managed to win two Challenge Certificates with her before breeding her. Her three-champion litter sired by Barty included Chs. Albourne Brigand,

Albourne Annie Laurie.

Marksman of Docken.

Reveller, and Braw Lass. Cowley then sold Annie Laurie, a decision he always regretted, to Richard Lloyd, for whom she produced two more champions, including the great Necessity son, Ch. Sandheys Silvertip.

Annie Laurie's brother, Marksman of Docken, was a silver-gray dog, somewhat soft-coated, described by Dorothy Caspersz as "a great dog in every sense of the word, grandly proportioned throughout. . . . His greatest handicap was his size, for he was built on a very large scale." Marksman had a long, elegant headpiece and, despite his longish body, carried his ribs well back into a strong, short loin. Unlike his sister, he had a perfect temperament. Although he sired no great sons, his daughters and granddaughters proved outstanding producers.

On both sides of the Atlantic, the influence of Necessity and Barty widened as their descendants continued to prosper. In England, Barty's son, Ch. Albourne Reveller, accidentally bred a bitch named Albourne Circe. The product of this mating was given the appropriate name of Albourne Binge Result. Bred to his half-sister, Binge Result sired Ch. Albourne Admiration,

Eng. Ch. Albourne
Admiration.

described by Dorothy Caspersz as one of the greatest show dogs the breed
has ever possessed. Admiration finished his championship just after his
first birthday and went on to win twenty Challenge Certificates, the last of
which was won when he was eight years old. Cowley sold Admiration to
Captain G. Bohun de Mowbray, who set the dog's stud fee at ten guineas,
twice that of any of the Heather stud dogs. This extravagant fee necessarily
limited the number of bitches brought to Admiration. Through his grandson, Ch. Malgen Juggernaut, however, Admiration is behind many of the
great Walsing dogs.

Eighteen sons of Necessity, many out of Barty daughters and granddaughters, were exported to the United States and stamped their type—lower to
the ground, heavier in body, shorter in back, and longer (and somewhat
coarser) in head—on the breed forever. It is interesting, however, that the
most important of Necessity's sons were two who never left England:
Eng. Chs. Heather Ambition and Heather Fashion Hint.

Ambition was a black dog, similar in type to his sire and he produced
seven English champions. His influence on the breed was soon overshadowed
by that of Fashion Hint. Luckily for American breeders, Ambition's grandson, Heather Asset, was imported by Deephaven Kennels where he produced
sixteen American champions. Most importantly, Heather Asset carried the
wheaten gene and is, in large measure, responsible for the extraordinary
quality of wheaten Scottish Terriers in America.

Robert Chapman considered Eng. Ch. Heather Fashion Hint the
paradigm of the modern Scottish Terrier. He named the dog Fashion Hint
because he expected the dog to set the type of the future. In many ways,
Fashion Hint was a clone of his sire, Necessity, only smaller. Dorothy Caspersz,
who was ambivalent about the new type of Scottie, described Fashion Hint:

Eng. Ch. Heather Realisation.

Heather Fashion Hint may be aptly described as a marvel when standing still; marvelous, inasmuch as he is a living instance of two modern crazes carried to excess: excessive length of head with almost unbelievable shortness of body, on a short-legged dog results not only in what is, to my way of thinking, an animal entirely out of proportion, but also—unavoidably—hampers the free movement of such an animal.

Despite Caspersz's misgivings, Chapman's predictions about Fashion Hint were proved true in short order as he sired thirteen English champions. His most celebrated champion son, Heather Realisation, made his first appearance in September 1934. This sensational puppy, described as a dark gray, thick-set, low to ground dog with a long head and a hard coat won two Challenge Certificates at the age of eight months, beating the four-year-old Eng. Ch. Albourne Admiration, who was then in his prime. Realisation was the dog who made Chapman's predictions about Fashion Hint's long-range impact on the breed come true. Despite having to compete with the great Admiration, Realisation went on to win forty-three Challenge Certificates, a record that would stand until 1984 when it was broken by his descendant, the great Eng. Ch. Mayson Monopoly. Sadly for all concerned, Realisation died shortly before his fourth birthday. Fortunately for the American Scottish Terrier fancy, Realisation left three sons, Heather Herald and the litter brothers Heather Benefactor (originally named Walsing Wonder) and Eng. Ch. Walsing Warrant, who would carry the Necessity-Fashion Hint-Realisation line forward in this country.

The revolution in breed type that started with Barty, Necessity, Annie Laurie and Marksman was complete on both sides of the Atlantic. The postwar Scottie was shorter in body, lower to the ground and more substantial than his turn-of-the-century ancestor. His head was longer but slightly more coarse. Not until the arrival in the 1960s of the Bardene stud dogs, the so-called Three Bs, would the Scottish Terrier fancy be so dramatically influenced by such a small group of dogs again.

Ch. Heather Fashion Hint.

				Eng. Ch. Albourne Adair
			Eng. Ch. Albourne MacAdair	
		Harton Highlander		Albourne Matron
				Loyal Boy
			Harton Holdfast	
Eng. Ch. Heather Necessity				Glenbrae Betty
				Ornsay Chieftain
			Eng. Ch. Ornsay Brave	
		Skerne Scotch Lass		Eng. Ch. Bellstane Lassie
				Abertay Aristocrat
			Meg (2)	
ENG. CH. HEATHER FASHION HINT				Fanny (2)
(Whelped 6/2/1929)				Eng. Ch. Laurieston Leaper
Breeder: J. Donald)			Eng. Ch. Laurieston Landseer	
		Laurieston Ladeside		Garnqueen Gertrude
				Garnock Bertie
			Carmel Kate	
Innerkip Irma				Carmel Betty
				Ornsay Ranger
			Garnock Bob	
		Innerkip Nanette		Garnock Jean
				Ornsay Bannock
			Garnock Ura	
				Garnock Kate

Chapter 2

The Scottish Terrier in America—From the Turn of the Century to World War II

The first Scottish Terriers shown in the United States were imported by Mr. John Naylor of Mt. Forest, Illinois. Naylor was described by his friend, Dr. William Bruette, as

> Not a large man but what he lacked in size he made up in personality. He had a world of it. His unusually dark eyes looked out from under the heaviest and most bristling of brows and there was an engaging frankness and sincerity about him that always commanded attention.

Naylor, an immigrant from Scotland, never forgot the Scottish Terrier of his youth, old Glenlyon. He described Glenlyon in a letter to Dr. Ewing as "a semi-prick eared dog with a well put-up body, and the best coat I ever saw." Naylor told Dr. Bruette that Glenlyon had—

> The stoutest heart, the best nose, and the most unquenchable love for sport of any dog that he had ever owned and that he was perfectly trained and would retrieve from land and water, handle well with the gun and was perfectly disposed toward the ferret or other working terriers.

Like most enthusiasts, John Naylor was eager to share the object of his enthusiasm with others. To that end, he went to considerable lengths to obtain the best representatives of the Scottish Terrier. It was not easy. This was at about the time that Capt. Mackie was still combing the Highlands

Mr. John Naylor's Tam Glen.

Tiree, the first American champion Scottish Terrier.

for his foundation stock, so good specimens were rare, even in Great Britain. When Naylor did finally obtain his first imports, Tam Glen (sometimes spelled Glenn) and Bonnie Belle, he showed them for three years at all the important shows.

At this time, there was no American Kennel Club established to register dogs or oversee and standardize dog shows. The purebred dog registry predating the American Kennel Club was the American Kennel Register, privately published by *Forest & Stream* magazine. At most shows, there were no classes for "Scottish Terriers." Naylor was usually obliged to show his dogs in the "Rough-haired Terrier" class, where the competition consisted of Dandie Dinmont Terriers, Skye Terriers, Yorkshire Terriers and any other hard-coated mongrel with "attitude."

Undaunted by these obstacles, Naylor lived up to his nickname, "Diehard" Naylor. He showed his dogs as far north as Boston, as far south as New Orleans, and as far west as St. Louis. When Capt. Mackie refused his offer to buy Dundee, Naylor bought a great young Dundee son, Niel Gow. Sadly, Niel Gow disappeared May 25, 1896, from Mr. Naylor's kennel. Niel Gow's description here is taken from the handbill printed by Mr. Naylor:

He is sandy-colored with very faint brindle markings, ears pricked, sharp pointed and covered with velvety hair. Tail not cut, carried up but not over back. Forelegs very slightly bent. Long head, eight inches from nose to occiput, small eyes, rather long body and flat ribbed. Weight about sixteen pounds.

Naylor's enthusiasm for the Scottish Terrier was not shared by the public and he retired from breeding in 1889. In the summer of 1891, Henry Brooks returned to Boston from a trip to England with two Scottish Terriers, "Kilbar" and "Brunhilde," purchased from H.J. Ludlow. The following year, Brooks hired an English kennelman and went into partnership with Oliver Ames using the kennel name, Wankie. Brooks and Ames imported numerous Scottish Terriers and soon dominated the breed in the American show ring.

In 1893, they purchased Tiree, an Alister son, from the famous dog importer, George Steadman Thomas. Tiree was a twenty-pound dog, black in color, described by Dr. Bruette as "good at both ends with wonderful shoulders and legs. He was full of terrier character but would have been better for more refinement in head." Tiree, the first AKC registered American champion, was a sensation in his day, winning Best in Show at Philadelphia in 1893.

At first, it seemed as if Brooks and Ames's lavish spending and untiring labors were generating real interest in the Scottish Terrier. There were fifty-five Scotties entered at Westminster in 1895. However, sixteen of those dogs belonged to the Wankie Kennels, and they won fifteen of the nineteen prizes. With competition so one-sided, it is little wonder that each succeeding year, fewer exhibitors were willing to take the field against Brooks and Ames. Three years later, the Westminster entry had dropped to nine and public interest was so low that Brooks and Ames could not even give away young dogs. Shortly afterward, Wankie Kennels were closed, and what little demand there was for the breed at the turn of the century was satisfied by James Little of Newcastle Scotties.

Little usually declined to compete in the show ring with the free-spending Wankie establishment, but he bought two influential dogs: the gray brindle Ch. Ashley Crack, linebred on Alister; and the black Whinstone son, Ch. Bellingham Bailiff.

Popularity, however, continued to elude the Scottish Terrier. It was probably for this lack of favor with the public that Dr. Fayette Ewing was able to buy two Scotties, one an English import, for the paltry sum of fifty dollars from a professional handler at the St. Louis dog show in 1897. Dr. Ewing was a successful eye doctor, but from that day until his death in the early 1950s, he would use all of his resources to promote the Scottish Terrier.

Dr. Ewing's resources proved to be formidable: his profession, which afforded him sufficient capital to pay the high costs of importing quality dogs; his writing talent, which led to a weekly Scottish Terrier column in

Popular Dogs magazine; and his energy, that never deserted him throughout his long career.

In 1898, he purchased Romany Ringlet from J.N. Reynard, secretary of the Scottish Terrier Club of Scotland. Ringlet, a puppy sensation at the shows in Scotland, was the first Scottie bitch to attain an American championship. Ringlet was a granddaughter of Eng. Ch. Rascal and Heather Prince. Dr. Ewing's next imports were Loyne Ginger, the first wheaten Scottish Terrier to become a champion, and her half-brother, Loyne Ruffian. Ruffian sired Nosegay Sweet William, the first American-bred Scottie to take Winners Dog at Westminster.

Although Dr. Ewing imported and bred many more outstanding Scotties, it was not his style to dominate the show ring, choking out all competition as was the case with his predecessors, Brooks and Ames. Ewing was a missionary for the Scottish Terrier and his goal was to convert all who had eyes to see and ears to hear. He extolled the virtues of the Scottish Terrier in every dog-oriented publication of the day. His out-of-print weekly column in *Popular Dogs* is still one of the best sources for information about the Scottie. Dr. Ewing's *Book of the Scottish Terrier,* published in 1931, was the first breed book in America.

Ch. Nosegay Forget-Me-Not, the first American-bred Scottish Terrier champion, was the daughter of Ch. Romany Ringlet. Forget-Me-Not was bred and owned by Dr. Fayette Ewing.

Dr. Ewing's Nosegay Scottish Terriers were exhibited in all parts of the country, not in an effort to garner honors to their owner, but to introduce the breed to new fanciers. A true breed pioneer, he demanded that show superintendents offer classes specifically for Scottish Terriers and refused to show in general rough-haired terrier classes.

Brooks, his sister Miss Fanny Brooks, Ames, and Little had formed a Scottish Terrier Club of America in 1894, but according to Miss Brooks, the club never held a meeting. In 1900, Dr. Ewing and his friends, Mrs. Jack Brazier and Mr. J. Steele Mackenzie, formed the Scottish Terrier Club of America that is still in existence today. They held their first Specialty on Saturday, September 17, 1904, in conjunction with the Bryn Mawr Kennel Club show.

Dr. Ewing's work swiftly began to show results. Every year entries grew larger as new fanciers, many introduced to the breed through Ewing's relentless stream of articles and correspondence or by seeing his dogs on show benches throughout the country, joined his crusade. In 1906, Francis G. Lloyd established Walescot Kennels in New Jersey. Lloyd was an active fancier, serving as president of the Scottish Terrier Club of America (STCA), and a successful exhibitor, dominating the eastern show rings with his imported and homebred champions. Lloyd is reported to have paid $2,500 for Ch. Clonmel Invader, renamed Walescot Invader. When Lloyd passed away in 1920, he was honored by the STCA with the establishment of the Francis G. Lloyd Memorial Trophy, the most prestigious trophy offered by the club.

In 1911, the breed got another boost when the famous Tickle 'Em Jock won Best In Show at Westminster. Jock began life in England as a butcher's dog. He was spotted following the butcher's cart by the canny dog importer George Steadman Thomas, who purchased the dog on the spot and resold him to America for $500, a princely sum in those days. Jock had a sensational show career and retired to leave virtually no mark on the breed as a sire.

Lloyd's chief competitors included Walter Stern, Richard Cadwalader, Jr., and Henry Bixby. Walter Stern established his Earlybird Kennels in 1912. He followed what had now become a fairly standard pattern of importing

Francis G. Lloyd and his Walescotts on the lawn of his home in Bernardsville, New Jersey.

Ch. Buillthistle Of Nosegay. *Leon Price*

Tickle 'Em Jock, Best in Show winner at the Westminster Kennel Club show in 1911, the first Scottish Terrier so honored. *Hedges*

top English dogs and knowledgeable English kennel men to breed and exhibit them. Mr. Stern was fortunate enough to obtain Bert Hankinson, formerly employed in England by Dean Willis of Bapton fame. Stern imported large numbers of outstanding dogs during the five years that he exhibited actively, among them the great show bitch, Ch. Bapton Beryl, and Ornsay Blackwatch, sire of three champions. When Stern retired in 1917, Hankinson took his expertise to Walescot where he kept Lloyd's dogs at the forefront of the fancy until Lloyd's death in 1920. Hankinson then established his own successful breeding program under the kennel name of Scotshome.

Richard Cadwalader, Jr., of Philadelphia founded his famous Fairwold line with the imported Eng. Ch. Albourne Beetle, Cowley's first English champion. Beetle, a descendant of the prepotent sire, Laindon Lockhart, was the winner of the first Lloyd Trophy in 1921. Another of Cadwalader's top stud dogs was Ch. Ornsay Bill, originally imported to Canada by Donald McKeller. Renamed Ch. Fairwold Ornsay Bill, he finished his American championship quickly, despite his propensity to bite anyone attempting to examine his mouth. Henry Bixby's Boglebrae Kennels were based primarily on the offspring of Albourne Linnson, sire of Cadwalader's Beetle.

Another name to be reckoned with was Prentice Talmadge, who was better known as a buyer of great dogs than as a breeder. Among his successful imports were Ch. Bentley Cotsol Lassie, winner of the Lloyd Trophy in 1923 and 1924. Lassie was so admired that a study of her head was used at the top of the official Scottish Terrier Standard. She preferred indoor shows to the extent that she occasionally had to be dragged before moving in grass. Lassie's kennelmate was the great stud dog, Ch. Albourne Adair, the great grandsire of Eng. Ch. Heather Necessity and grandsire of Ch. Albourne Barty.

Int. Ch. Bentley Cotsol Lassie.

Ch. Heather Essential of Hitofa.

Adair had a ring of gray hairs around his tail which regularly appeared in his progeny and can still be seen today in many Scottish Terriers.

Talmadge also imported Ch. Albourne Vindicated, who was the only one of the many Scottish Terriers imported during these years to return to his homeland. Cowley sold the young Vindicated to Talmadge for £600, or about $2,000. Talmadge resold the dog to Z.B. West (Malibu Kennels) in California where he was bred to over sixty bitches. In the meantime, Vindicated's daughter, Cheer of Corse, was drawing raves from all who saw her in the English show ring. Robert Chapman, always looking to add talent to his already formidable stud force, bought Vindicated from the Wests, replacing him with Heather Ambassador, a son of Barty and the great Albourne Annie Laurie. Chapman kindly allowed Vindicated to stand at stud at William McBain's Diehard Kennels for a few months before shipping him home. This allowed eastern breeders one last opportunity to use the dog. A sad footnote to the story of the beautiful Cheer: she was sold to Dr. Ewing and bred to Ch. Nosegay's Solomon's Seal. She whelped seven puppies, only to have all but one die from hookworm infestation or accident while Ewing was on vacation. After whelping her second litter, Cheer herself died suddenly of infection.

Reading the columns of Dr. Ewing and his correspondence with breeders from all over the world, it is apparent that, by the 1930s, the Scottish Terrier was becoming well established in the United States. Although most of the top Scottish Terrier breeders of the period were located in the Northeast, outstanding Scotties were being produced all over the country. From California, Caswell Barrie's homebred, Ch. Ballantrae Wendy became the first top-winning Scottish Terrier not bred on the Atlantic seaboard. She won the

Lloyd Trophy in 1929 and 1930. In Milwaukee, Charles Schott's imported Ch. Bellstane Laddie was the leading sire of the day, having produced seven American champions by 1934. In Michigan, Robert McKinven made the most of the blood of Ch. Albourne Adair, breeding fourteen champions from Adair's sons, Chs. Ardmore Wallace and Ardmore Skipper and his daughter, Ardmore Jewel. Ch. Ardmore Rowdy was an influential sire for Mrs. Clarence Stanley's Eagle Creek Scotties in Indianapolis.

What is almost unapparent in Ewing's columns was that the United States, and indeed, most of the world, was experiencing a depression. There may have been bread lines and soup kitchens elsewhere, but those who attended the Scottish Terrier Club of America banquet in February, 1930, feasted on strawberries, lobster, oysters, shrimp, fish, steak, chicken and ice cream a la mysterieuse. Scottie registrations climbed fairly steadily during the 1930s, peaking in 1936 at over 8,000. New breeders sprung up every month, and nearly every one, it seemed, had to have an English import.

Three of the most influential imports of the pre-World War II years were Frank Spiekerman's Eng. & Am. Ch. Heather Essential of Hitofa, S.S. Van Dine's Ch. Heather Reveller of Sporran and Edward F. Moloney's Ch. Heather Gold Finder. Essential's most important contribution to the breed was through his son, Ch. Hillcote Laddie, bred by John Hillman. Laddie sired fifteen champions, the most important being Theodore Bennet's Ch. Deephaven Warspite.

Reveller made his mark in the show ring, winning the 1933 Lloyd Trophy. His owner, S.S. Van Dine, was a popular author whose mystery novel, *The Kennel Murder Case,* featured the names of many prominent Scottie fanciers and their dogs. Van Dine had very strong theories about breeding, but only managed to produce one homebred champion during his period of activity in the breed. Reveller was the sire of five champions, including Diehard Reveller, sire of the first homebred Barberry Knowe champion. Heather Reveller's daughter, Henshaw's Gloaming, was the dam of Ch. Hillcote Laddie.

Eng. & Am. Ch. Heather Gold Finder proved to be a much more successful sire than his half-brother, Heather Reveller, producing nineteen American champions. He was the foundation for Edward F. Moloney's Goldfinder Kennels which produced a series of top winners for nearly twenty years. Moloney won the Lloyd Trophy in 1950 with Ch. Goldfinder's Admiral, a son of Ch. Deephaven Red Seal.

Before discussing the American records of the descendants of the great English dogs of the 1930s and 1940s, it is necessary to discuss the English system of classifying pedigrees by lines and families. In her book, *The Scottish Terrier,* published in 1906, C.J. Davies proposed that the Bruce Lowe figure system (originally proposed to classify the pedigrees of race horses) be applied to Scottish Terrier pedigrees. The top line of the pedigree is the tail-male descent, referred to as a male line. The bottom line of the pedigree is the tail-female descent, referred to as a female family.

Ch. Heather Reveller of Sporran.

Ch. Heather Gold Finder.

As an example, most Scottie chronicles reflect that Eng. Ch. Heather Ambition, who sired five English champions, owes his place in American Scottish Terrier history to his two grandsons, Heather Asset and Ch. Heather Criterion, and his great-grandson, Ch. Ortley Ambassador of Edgerstoune. These three influential sires are credited to Ambition's line. All three dogs, however, are also descendants of Eng. Ch. Heather Fashion Hint through lines other than the *tail male*. From a genetic point of view, Ambition and Fashion Hint are equally likely to have contributed to the genetic makeup of Asset, Criterion and Ambassador. The line and family method of classification is simple to understand and use, but it bears little relationship to the actual genetic makeup of any dog. For that reason, few references to this system appear in this book.

The years from 1930 to the beginning of World War II were golden ones for Scottish Terriers. British enthusiasts bred some of the most outstanding and influential Scotties in the breed's history during this era and Americans were willing to spend outrageous sums to buy them—everyone was wild to have the new Necessity-Barty type. As it became apparent that war was inevitable, British breeders were forced to part with dogs that would otherwise never have left the land of their birth. It was inevitable that, with such a good foundation, the quality of American-bred Scottish Terriers would soon equal that of the British dogs.

Chapter 3

The Scottish Terrier In America—The Postwar Years

During the decade preceding World War II, registrations and show entries soared in both England and the United States. From 1930 to 1935, 54 percent of American Scottish Terrier champions were British imports and 80 percent of American champions were sired by British stud dogs. Only 20 percent had two American parents. It was almost unheard of at that time for an American breeder to develop a line of even three generations of purely American-bred dogs. That would change drastically, in part because World War II forcibly weaned American breeders from depending on the output of their British counterparts. In the five years following the end of the war, only 5 percent of American champions were imports and 18 percent were sired by English dogs. Seventy percent were American bred. Imported British Scottish Terriers would never again so completely dominate the American dog show scene.

That is not to say, however, that England was quite done colonizing on these shores. The descendants of a single English dog, Walsing Wizard, would eventually fan out across the United States providing the winners and producers of postwar America. Walsing was the prefix of W. Max Singleton, whose dogs would have an extraordinary impact on British and America postwar bloodlines. He bought his foundation bitch, Walsing Whisper, from Miss Wijk for a mere £3. Whisper was a daughter of Eng. Ch. Heather Necessity and Twinkle of Docken, whose pedigree was intensely linebred on Laindon Lockhart. Whisper finished her championship in 1932, winning five Challenge Certificates. Heather Benefactor and Eng. Ch. Walsing Warrant were Whisper's great-grandsons, and Whisper's sister, Malgen Starshine, was their great-great-grandmother. Whisper's great-granddaughter, Walsing

29

Walsing Wizard.

				Eng. Ch. Heather Necessity
			Eng. Ch. Heather Fashion Hint	
		Eng. Ch. Heather Realisation		Innerkip Irma
				Eng. Ch. Sandhey's Silvertip
			Gaisgill Sylvia	
Heather Benefactor				Gaisgill Ling
				Albourne Samson
			Eng. Ch. Malgen Juggernat	
	Eng. Ch. Walsing Wellborn			Malgen Jerusha
				Eng. Ch. Albourne Barty
			Walsing Waitress	
Walsing Wizard				Eng. Ch. Walsing Whisper
				Eng. Ch. Radical of Rookes
			Randolph of Rookes	
	Walsing Waiter			Bowood Speculation
				Eng. Ch. Albourne Barty
			Walsing Waitress	
Walsing Woven				Eng. Ch. Walsing Whisper
				Eng. Ch. Heather Necessity
			Rosehall Rip	
	Walsing Watercress			Rosehall Rosalind
				Eng. Ch. Albourne Barty
			Walsing Wicker	
				Eng. Ch. Walsing Whisper

Wizard's Influential Male Descendants

A1 Walsing Watch Tower
    B1 Walsing War Loan
        C1 Rosehall Enchanter
            D1 Eng. Ch. Rosehall Edward
                E1 Eng. Ch. Wyrebury Wonder
                    F1 Eng. Ch. Wyrebury Welldoer
                        G1 Wyrebury Weathercock
                            H1 Hargate Happy Boy
                              I1 Eng. Ch. Happy Kimbo
                                J1 Ch. Bardene Boy Blue
                                J2 Bardene Blue Star
                                  K1 Bardene Blue
                                        Starlite
                                L1 Ch. Bardene
                                        Bingo
                      G2 Glendoune Gay Boy
                      G3 Ch. Wyrebury Worthwhile
A2 Westpark Masterpiece
    B2 Ch. Reimill Radiator
        C2 Ch. Glad-Mac's Rolling Stone
    B3 Eng. Ch. Westpark Rio Grande
        C3 Eng. Westpark Romeo
            D2 Eng., Am. Ch. Westpark Derriford Baffie
        C4 Eng., Am. Ch. Wyrebury Wrangler
            D3 Ch. Wyrebury Wilwyn
                E2 Ch. Special Edition
    B4 Ch. Trevone Tartar Of Bothkennar
        C5 Ch. Fran-Jean's Bokor
            D4 Ch. Cantie Captivator
                E3 Ch. Balachan Agitator
         C6 Ch. Tartar's Bo-Pete
            D5 Ch. Clan Ebon Beau Brummel

Woven, was one of the last English champions to finish before World War II brought dog shows to a halt in England.

Woven, bred to Heather Benefactor, would produce the preeminent wartime sire, Walsing Wizard. Wizard would seem to have been born unlucky. Championship dog shows were canceled during the war, so he was denied the opportunity to gain his title. Even worse, government regulation severely restricted the keeping and breeding of dogs, so his breeding opportunities were limited. Despite these obstacles, Wizard's progeny would dominate the breed during the next two decades, in the 1950s through his son, Westpark Masterpiece, and in the 1960s through his son, Walsing Watch Tower. A close look at his pedigree explains the prepotency of this remarkable dog.

A large number of the most successful postwar American breeders entered the fancy just prior to the start of World War II. In the six years between 1935 and 1941, the following famous kennel names appeared for the first time:

Barberry Knowe (Mr. and Mrs. Charles Stalter), Shieling (Mr. and Mrs. T. Howard Snethen), Marlu (Maurice Pollak), Deephaven (Theodore Bennett), Relgalf (Mrs. Jean Flagler Matthews), Edgerstoune (Mrs. John G. Winant), Kinclaven (Marie Stone), Bothkennar (Bryce Gillespie) and Carnation (E. H. Stuart).

Barberry Knowe

Of all of these, the most influential and enduring was Barberry Knowe. The first Scottish Terrier at Barberry Knowe was purchased by Helen Stalter as a gift for her husband, Charles. When that puppy did not develop into a show prospect, they purchased Diehard Reveller who became their first champion. In 1933, they imported a Necessity daughter who, bred to Reveller, produced their first homebred champion, Barberry Knowe Reveller.

Over the next 50 years, the Stalters bred or owned 105 champions. Among their many winners were: Ch. Barberry Knowe Barbican, winner of the Lloyd Trophy in 1951 and 1952; the imported Ch. Walsing Wild Winter of Barberry Knowe, winner of the Lloyd Trophy in 1962 (and a descendant of Walsing Wizard on his dam's side); and the two famous daughters of Ch. Barberry Know Merrymaker, Ch. Carmichael's Fanfare and Ch. Balachan Naughty Gal. Fanfare, won thirty-two Bests in Show, including Westminster in 1965. Ch. Balachan Naughty Gal, bred by Dr. and Mrs. T. Allen Kirk, Jr., was the last great standard-bearer for Barberry Knowe Kennels. Although edged out for the Lloyd Trophy by her English rival, Ch. Gosmore Eilburn Admaration, Naughty Gal was three times Best of Breed at the STCA Specialty Show at Montgomery County between 1970 and 1972, a feat that has not been repeated. She also carried off the supreme honor at the February 1973 STCA Winter Specialty in New York. The Stalters had the benefit of guidance from some of the leading professional terrier handlers of the day. The Prentice family, William and his son and daughter, Phil and Florence, handled the Barberry Knowe dogs and guided the breeding program. Later Johnny Murphy took over until he retired in 1968. Stephen Shaw and Barbara Kingsbury shared the handling honors until the death of Mrs. Stalter in 1978.

Shieling

Howard and Molly Snethen started their Shieling kennels in the early 1930s with two bitches bred by Charles Schott of Milwaukee, Wisconsin. Luckie Nancy and Dark Maid were granddaughters of Ch. Sandhey's Silvertip, a son of Necessity and Annie Laurie. From these two half-sisters, the Snethens produced nearly fifty champions. Of these, seven were owner-handled Best In Show winners! The most well known, of course, was Ch. Shieling's Signature, who was Best In Show at Westminster in 1945, the second Scottish

Ch. Barberry Knowe Merrymaker, owned by Mr. and Mrs. Charles C. Stalter, is shown here winning BOB at the Scottish Terrier Club of Pennsylvania Specialty under judge Edward Danks. *William Brown*

Ch. Barberry Know Barbican is shown here in a 1950 BOB presentation with handler Phil Prentice, Mrs. John G. Winant and judge, George Hartman.

Terrier and the first American-bred to achieve this honor. This feat has never been repeated by any owner-handled Scottie. Signature was somewhat of a long shot to even win the breed at the Garden, let alone Best in Show. He had been beaten the previous day at the Scottish Terrier Club of America Specialty by a class dog, Heather Commodore of Edgerstonne.

Howard Snethen, however, was one of the first owner-handlers whose grooming skills rivaled those of the most talented professional handlers, and he was a fierce competitor in the ring. While showing Signature for that historic Westminster Best in Show, he dropped the lead while moving the dog down and back. Signature never missed a beat, turning at the end of the mat and walking the whole long way back to the judge.

The judge later described Signature as "a well-balanced terrier and most nearly reached perfection among the dogs entered." In 1954, family problems led to the dispersal of the Shieling dogs. Three years later, the reunited Snethens started over again, importing two dogs, Ch. Glenview Grand Duke and Ch. Kentwelle Kadet, and a bitch, Ch. Reanda Rheola. Grand Duke was undoubtedly one of the breed's most tightly linebred champions. My Ideal of Glenview was his only great-grandsire, Glenview Glennis was his great-granddam three times and the fourth great-granddam was a daughter of My Ideal! Ch. Kentwelle Kadet was a son of Eng. Ch. Reanda Roger Rough, 1957's Dog of the Year in England.

Very early in her legendary show career, Ch. Carmichael's Fanfare was BOB from the classes at the 1961 STCA Specialty under judge John Marvin, handled by breeder Ruth Johnson. *Evelyn Shafer*

Ch. Balachan Naughty Gal was BOB at the STCA Specialty under judge T. Howard Snethen, handled by R. Stephen Shaw. The trophy presenter is Anthony Stamm.
Evelyn Shafer

Marlu

Maurice Pollak lost no time in establishing his Marlu Scottish Terriers as a force, both as show dogs and producers. His second champion, Marlu Milady, was Best of Breed at the 1937 spring National Specialty from the classes and won the Lloyd Trophy that same year, handled by Bob Braithwaite. Milady and her descendants produced over twenty Marlu champions, many sired by the outstanding stud dogs acquired by Pollak: Eng., Am. Ch. Walsing Warrant, Ch. Deephaven Warspite, and Ch. Deephaven Red Seal. Warrant's career as a progenitor of American champions parallels that of Wizard in England. This is not surprising since Warrant was a full brother to Heather Benefactor, the sire of Walsing Wizard.

Deephaven

Warspite and Red Seal were bred by Theodore Bennett of Minneapolis, Minnesota. Bennett, like most Scottie fanciers of his day, built a kennel and intended to hire an English kennel manager to oversee his breeding program. Instead, he hired an American, a former real estate businessman named Frank J. "Bob" Bartos, Jr. Bartos was an immensely talented groomer, and he was also blessed with a breeder's eye. Without ever going to England to select dogs, Bartos acquired, first for Bennett and later for Carnation Farms, some of the most influential sires of the breed. Bennett's Deephaven Scots were founded on a Scotsward bitch and the first of many successful imports, Eng. Ch. Crich Certainty. Certainty was considered one of Heather Necessity's greatest sons, but Bennett and Bartos were able to buy him because he had developed a hematoma and became unshowable as a result. He sired some of the best of

Ch. Shieling's Signature, owned and bred by Mr. and Mrs. T. Howard Snethen, BIS at the Westminster KC, 1945.

Ch. Marlu Milady.

the Deephaven bitches. Heather Asset was another noteworthy sire imported by Deephaven. Asset was unable to complete his championship after a case of trench mouth resulted in the loss of several teeth. He sired a total of sixteen champions, but his greatest contribution was his influence on the wheaten color phase of the Scottish Terrier. He sired one wheaten son, Ch. Bramshire Blazing Sun, but it was his nonwheaten descendants who were most important in transmitting the recessive wheaten gene: the brindles, Carnation Revelation, Ch. Deephaven Fixed Asset, Ch. Deephaven Dividend, Ch. Kinclaven Tabasco and the black Ch. Deephaven Superman.

During Bartos's tenure as kennel manager, Bennett bred twenty-four champions, the most important of which were Ch. Deephaven Warspite and the great Ch. Deephaven Red Seal. Bartos traded Warspite to Maurice Pollak in return for Pollak's Ch. Marlu Crusader, and Red Seal, a son of Crusader, was sold to Maurice Pollak when he was one year old. In 1948, Red Seal won the Lloyd Trophy for Marlu Farms, handled by Johnny Murphy.

Carnation Farms

E.H. Stuart of Carnation Farms became interested in Scotties in the mid-1920s through his friendship with Marie Stone. He began breeding in 1932, but was hardly setting the world on fire with his early efforts. He finished three champions between 1938 and 1946. In 1947, however, he hired Bob Bartos away from Deephaven Kennels, and for the next twenty years, Carnation Farms was a powerful force in the breed. The first thing Bartos did was import Reimill Radiator, a son of Westpark Masterpiece and a grandson of Walsing Wizard. In England, Masterpiece was siring some of the finest postwar champions, and at Carnation, his son, Radiator, proved to be both an outstanding showman and a prepotent sire. On June 4, 1949, Bob Bartos got a special birthday gift: Ch. Deephaven Red Seal came to Carnation from Marlu Farms. For the next six years, Radiator and Red Seal led the Carnation stud force, with Red Seal ultimately siring twenty-five champions.

Carnation's connection to Deephaven, and thereby, to Heather Asset, has been responsible for many of the breed's outstanding wheatens. Ch. Carnation Golden Girl, a double great-granddaughter of Asset, was the first wheaten Scottish Terrier to win a Best In Show, and she did it from the Open class!

In 1955, Alfred James, who began breeding shortly before the start of World War II, was closing his famous Westpark Kennels in England. James was the breeder of the great Walsing Wizard son, Westpark Masterpiece. Masterpiece proved to be an outstanding sire, producing seven English champions, and in the first decade of postwar dog shows, his descendants at Westpark won over 150 Challenge Certificates. His son, Eng. Ch. Westpark

Ch. Deephaven Red Seal.

```
                                                    Eng. Ch. Heather Fashion Hint
                                  Eng. Ch. Heather Realisation
                                                    Gaisgill Sylvia
              Ch. Walsing Warrant
                                                    Eng. Ch. Malgen Juggernaut
                                  Eng. Ch. Walsing Wellborn
                                                    Walsing Waitress
        Ch. Marlu Crusader
                                                    Eng. Ch. Fashion Heather Hint
                                  Eng. Ch. Dandy of Docken
                                                    Brilliant of Docken
              Ch. Marlu Milady
                                                    Scotshome Humorist
                                  Roseneath Miss Muffet
                                                    Sandridge Sabula
CH. DEEPHAVEN RED SEAL
(Whelped 6/26/1945                                  Heather Asset
Breeder: Deephaven              Ch. Kinclaven Tabasco
Kennels)                                            Ch. Carioca
              Ch. Kinclaven Classic
                                                    Eng. Ch. Heather Realisation
                                  Ch. Gleniffer Leading Lady
                                                    Gleniffer Gaiety
        Deephaven Mary
                                                    Nosegay Buckwheat
                                  Deephaven Sir Galahad
                                                    Fraochen Bittersweet
              Mac's Welton Gold Penny
                                                    Faraway Sandy of Mt. Tuck
                                  Mac's Welton Hope
                                                    Clarksdale Anne
```

Rio Grande and great-grandson, Eng. Ch. Westpark Derriford Baffie were hugely successful, both as show dogs and as sires. Rio Grande sired twelve English champions while Baffie produced seven. Baffie racked up a remarkable thirty-five Challenge Certificates, a record at that time and second only to that of Eng. Ch. Heather Realisation. James contacted Bartos at that time and offered him Rio Grande and Baffie. To the dismay of many English fanciers, both dogs left England for careers at Carnation Farms.

The seven-year-old Rio Grande went on to sire twenty-one American champions. As a show dog, Baffie went undefeated in the breed at fifty all-breed shows, winning thirty-nine Group Is and twenty-two Bests In Show. He also won four Specialty Bests of Breed and brought Carnation Farms their first Lloyd Trophy in 1958. Baffie sired twenty champions, six for Carnation out of Red Seal daughters.

In 1964, Bartos imported the unforgettable Eng. Ch. Bardene Bingo. His story, however, must be told later in conjunction with those of the other famous Bardene dogs.

Kinclaven

Marie Stone was an exceptional woman for many reasons. First of all, she was divorced at a time when divorce was rare in upperclass social circles. The Scotties were apparently her hobby since she took the dogs with her when she parted from her well-to-do businessman husband. Second, in an era when owner-handlers were uncommon, and female owner-handlers were rare, Marie Stone successfully showed her own dogs. She bred over thirty champions, including some of the most beautiful wheatens anyone had seen up to that time. Her Kinclaven Wild Oats was the first American-bred wheaten champion. Another wheaten, Ch. Kinclaven The Stooge, was a Best In Show

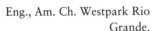

Eng., Am. Ch. Westpark Rio Grande.

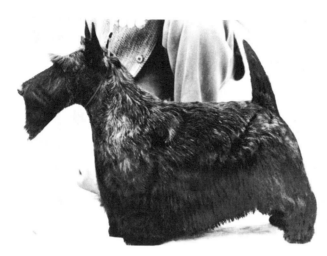

Eng., Am. Ch.
Westpark
Derriford Baffie.

winner. Sadly, the Kinclaven dogs were dispersed in 1951 after Mrs. Stone was diagnosed with cancer.

Edgerstoune

Another influential woman of this era was Mrs. John G. Winant of Edgerstoune fame. Mrs. Winant was already a successful breeder of West Highland White Terriers, but when her husband was appointed the wartime Ambassador from the United States to the Court of St. James, she took the opportunity to acquire some outstanding Scottish Terriers. Later, when Mr. Winant was serving as governor of New Hampshire, a reader of Dr. Ewing's column in *Popular Dogs* wrote him describing a sign outside the governor's mansion advertising Westie and Scottie puppies for sale! Mrs. Winant imported extensively, concentrating on the progeny of Heather Ambition, Fashion Hint and Realisation. Her first homebred champion, made up in 1941, was Ch. Edgerstoune Benefactor, sired by a Fashion Hint son out of a Realisation daughter. Mrs. Winant's most famous dogs were the imported Wizard great-grandson, Ch. Walsing Winning Trick of Edgerstoune and his son, Ch. Edgerstoune Troubadour. Trick, handled by Phil Prentice, had a remarkable show career. Over a three-year period, he was shown only forty times and at only the most important shows. He was undefeated in the breed and failed to win only three of the Terrier Groups in which he competed. He won twenty-eight Bests in Show, including Westminster in 1950, the third Scot to be so distinguished.

Rebel

Trick's son, Ch. Edgerstoune Troubadour, was sold as a youngster to Dr. and Mrs. W. Stewart Carter. Although he won several specialties and Bests

In Show, Troubadour's show career was cut short because the Carters wished to give his sons greater opportunities to compete in the show ring. One of those sons, Ch. Rebel Invader, a double grandson of Winning Trick, won the 1954 Lloyd Trophy for the Carters. Invader's brother, Ch. Rebel Raider, was the sire of Ch. Gaidoune Gorgeous Hussy, the first of many top-producing Gaidoune bitches. Troubadour sired a total of thirty-five champions, a record for that time. Troubadour's best known son was Richard and Eileen Weaver's Ch. The Laird of Scots Guard, sire of thirteen champions.

Seagraves

Goldie and John Seagraves started with a Trick son and daughter, Ch. Rag-A-Bash Dunstaffnage and Rag-A-Bash Bridget. After this first litter, the Seagraves apparently decided their kennel name was too complicated because all their subsequent champions bore the Seagraves prefix. Linebreeding to Trick through his son Troubadour, John and Goldie bred many top winners and producers. The best known were the father and son, Ch. Seagraves Heather Rogue and Ch. Seagraves Rogue's Image, owned and shown by Ann and Helen Harbulak. Rogue's Image was Best of Breed at Montgomery County in 1974. He went on to sire eight champions, including the top-producing sisters, Ch. Am Anger of Glendale Star and Ch. Am Anger Starlight, each the dam of eight champions. Another Rogue's Image daughter, the Group-winning Ch. Carus Quite A Doll, was the dam of five champions and the foundation bitch for Jeanne and Axel Pearson.

Todhill

Edgerstoune bitches provided the foundation stock for the Sheirburns's short-lived Friendship Farm, and for Robert and Claribel Graham's more influential Todhill Kennels. Ch. Friendship Farm Diplomat was a grandson of Edgerstoune Larkspur and linebred on Ch. Deephaven Red Seal through his son, Ch. Goldfinder's Admiral. The Grahams purchased Diplomat and bred him to their Edgerstoune Pepper daughter, Todhill's Beeswing, to produce their first homebred champion, Todhill's Cinnamon Bear. Cinnamon Bear was the sire of the brothers, Ch. Gaidoune Great Bear and Ch. Gaidoune Grin and Bear It. The Grahams' stud force included some of the top sires in the East. In addition to Cinnamon Bear, Todhill was home to Ch. Friendship Farm Diplomat, Ch. Special Edition of Todhill, and, for the last six years of his life, Ch. Walsing Winning Trick of Edgerstoune. Diplomat, Cinnamon Bear and Special Edition sired a total of forty-five champions. When added to the champions produced by Trick in his last years, it is apparent that Todhill was one of those rare kennels whose impact on the breed resulted from a powerful stud force rather than top-producing bitches.

Ch. Walsing Winning Trick of Edgerstoune, handled by Phil Prentice, going BIS at Westminster in 1950 under judge George Hartman (second from right). *Willam Brown*

Relgalf

Jean Flagler, later Matthews, founded her Relgalf kennels in 1932 with several imported Scottish Terriers, including the Fashion Hint son, Ch. Radical Of Rookes. After her marriage, she moved her dogs to Rye, New York, built a large, modern kennel, and added Welsh, Airedale and Fox Terriers to her establishment. Russell Openshaw handled her Scotties and was among the first professional handlers to travel extensively with his string of dogs. Mrs. Matthews's Relgalf Scotties won more Lloyd Trophies than any other kennel in the history of the breed, starting with the first in 1936 (Ch. Flornell Soundfella, a Necessity son), then six consecutive wins between 1938 and 1943 (Ch. Flornell Sound Laddie 1938–39, Ch. Bradthorn Bullion 1940, Ch. Relgalf Ribbon Raider 1941–1943), and three more consecutive wins in 1945 through 1947 with Ch. Relgalf Rebel Leader. The Relgalf juggernaut was halted abruptly in 1949 when Openshaw, along with three other professional handlers, was suspended by the AKC. Mrs. Matthews believed that Openshaw's suspension was not only meant to halt her winning streak, but was also in reprisal for her successful election as President of the STCA in 1946. Disgusted, Mrs. Matthews closed her kennels, dispersed all her dogs and resigned from the STCA. Some of her best dogs went to Mr. and Mrs. Richard Koch. Ch. Relgalf Rebel Dictator was the sire or grandsire of all their Strathkirk champions.

Ch. Edgerstoune Troubadour, owned by Dr. and Mrs. W. Stewart Carter and handled by Jake Terhune, was a great winning son of Winning Trick. He is shown winning BIS at the Chagrin Valley KC in 1952 under judge T. H. Carruthers III. *Evelyn Shafer*

Bothkennar

Bryce Gillespie was a noted California breeder under the prefix Bothkennar from the late 1920s until the end of World War II. His first champion, finished in 1936, was a son of Fashion Hint out of the imported bitch Rosehall

Ch. Special Edition, a Montgomery County BOB winner owned by Robert and Claribel Graham, shown with handler John Murphy.

Ch. Todhill's Cinnamon Bear with handler John Murphy.

Ret. Ch. Bothkennar Spitfire, his top-producing sire, was a grandson of Mrs. Winant's Ch. Ortley Ambassador of Edgerstoune. Gillespie passed away shortly after he imported his best known dog, Ch. Trevone Tartar Of Both-kennar, a son of Westpark Masterpiece. Gordon Campbell took over the Bothkennar dogs, including Tartar who went on to sire sixteen champions. His name appears in the pedigrees of many top-winning California dogs, and his son, Ch. Fran-Jean's Bokor, was an influential sire in the Mid-west. Bokor was the sire of the 1956 Lloyd Trophy winner, Ch. Cantie

Confident, and Ch. Sandoone Missy Lou, the first homebred champion for Betty Malinka.

Tartar figured largely in the breeding program of Constance Swatsley who bred a dozen champions between 1958 and 1968. Her foundation bitch, Ch. Scotbart Serenade, was a Tartar daughter. Mrs. Swatsley linebred on Tartar and Winning Trick, adding some Niddbank in 1962 when she bred Niddbank Fairy to Ch. Niddbank Topic. Her most successful Scottish Terrier was Ch. Revran Reprise who won Best in Show from the classes over more than 3,000 dogs at the Beverly Hills summer show in 1967.

Blanart

One of the most eminent postwar breeders slogged away through the 1930s and 1940s with little success. For fifteen years, Blanche Reeg could not even win a blue ribbon, either with her Airedales (her first breed) or her Scottish Terriers. Mrs. Reeg later blamed her lack of early success on a rather helter-skelter breeding program that consisted of breeding her best bitches to the top-winning dogs of the day. Finally, her good friend Dorothy Clawes gave her a puppy bitch named Hi-Scott's Clipper, who happened to be a grand-daughter of Blanart Bomber, an unshown dog bred some years earlier by Mrs. Reeg. On the advice of Mrs. Seth Malby, Mrs. Reeg bred Clipper to Cabrach Caliper, a dog with strong Diehard bloodlines, and produced her first home-bred champion, Blanart Barcarolle. In an interview published in the August 1984 STCA magazine, *The Bagpiper*, Mrs. Reeg described what it was like to be a woman owner-handler competing with professionals in the Scottish Terrier ring during the 1930s and 1940s:

Ch. Trevone Tartar of Bothkennar.

Ch. Flornell Sound
Laddie.

Yes, you couldn't do it. They wouldn't let you . . . [T]hey ganged up on us.
They would give us no help whatsoever. They wouldn't give you advice on
how to handle, condition, or trim. In fact, on the subject of trimming, they
would show you *the wrong way*. And, I would just go in the ring . . . in
those days the entry fee was $3.50 . . . and I would park next to one of
them . . . Johnny Murphy or Frank [Brumby] or somebody else, to see how
they trimmed. Each time I would study how they trimmed something
different, for example, behind the tail . . . because they wouldn't tell me.
That is one of the reasons why it took me so long!

Apparently, Mrs. Reeg's fifteen years of observing the top terrier
handlers were not wasted. When she finished Barcarolle in 1949, she became
the first woman in the East to handle a Scottish Terrier to its championship.

In breeding Barcarolle, Mrs. Reeg followed a maxim that would become
her first and last commandment: *Give back to the sire the best blood of
his dam.* In other words, she began to linebreed. She bred Barcarolle, a
great-granddaughter of Diehard Fashion, to Diehard Toby, a double great-
grandson of the same dog. Together, Toby and Barcarolle produced four
champions, including Blanart Barrister, himself the sire of fourteen
champions. Barrister later went to Francis Gannon in Indiana where he
produced several Fran-Gan champions and provided the foundation stock
for Betty Malinka's Sandoone Scotties. Altogether, Barcarolle produced ten
champions sired by six different stud dogs. Her top-producing son was Ch.
Blanart Bolero, sired by Ch. Barberry Knowe Rascal, a grandson of Ch.
Diehard Reveller. Her top-producing daughter, Blanart Barcee, dam of five
champions, was the product of breeding Barcarolle to her son Barrister.

In 1957, the year that Barcarolle passed away, Mrs. Reeg bred a Barrister daughter to Bolero to produce her greatest-winning Scottish Terrier ever, Ch. Blanart Bewitching. Shown by Mrs. Reeg at thirty-six all-breed shows and thirteen Specialties, Bewitching won twenty-seven Bests of Breed, nine Bests of Opposite Sex, seven Bests in Show, twenty Group Is, five Group IIs, two Group IIIs, and thirteen successive Specialty Bests of Breed, including five nationals. Bewitching won the Lloyd Trophy in 1959 and 1960 and twice won the Terrier Group at Westminster. Altogether Mrs. Reeg bred fifty-seven Blanart champions, and her line was hugely influential, particularly in the East. By the early 1970s, Barcarolle's name appeared in the pedigrees of well over 200 champions. Blanart also supplied foundation bitches for a number of successful breeders, including Mr. and Mrs. Frank Brumby, who bred nineteen Rannoch-Dune champions from their Ch. Blanart Bouquet, and Cornelia Crissey, whose 1961 Lloyd Trophy winner, Ch. Crisscot Carnival, was a son of Ch. Blanart Bellflower.

A woman who persevered without success for fifteen years was clearly a person of strong character. In addition to her late-blooming but impressive career as a breeder-exhibitor, Mrs. Reeg was also not one to sit back and accept just any hand she was dealt. When she felt the Scottish Terrier Club of America was not providing enough support to breeders, she formed the Scottish Terrier Breeders' Association. She and Jane Moloney were influential

Blanche Reeg with her great homebred, Ch. Blanart Bewitching.

Ch. Blanart Bolero.

in persuading the American Kennel Club to offer the Bred By Exhibitor class for dogs bred and owned by the person handling them.

In January 1951, an ad appeared in *Diehard Dope*, a newspaper catering to Scottish Terrier fanciers, announcing with great fanfare the arrival of Eng. Ch. Rosehall Toryglen Tam O'Shanter, Best in Show winner and sire of two English champions in one litter. Notwithstanding his quality or his pedigree (he was a son of Eng. Ch. Rosehall Edward, progenitor of the great Wyrebury dogs), Tam O'Shanter sired no champions in the United States. He left behind in England, however, a family that would strongly influence two of the most successful postwar kennels: Helen Gaither's Gaidoune and Tom and Evelyn Kirk's Balachan Scottish Terriers.

Balachan

Tam O'Shanter's most famous son in England was Eng. Ch. Glendoune Gauntlet, later exported to Canada. The Kirks acquired a black Gauntlet daughter named Fran-Jean's Bridie Mollie from Hosea Bayor in Indiana. Mollie's mother was an English granddaughter of Tam O'Shanter. The Kirks' second bitch, the imported Ch. Glendoune Gwenda, was a Gauntlet granddaughter, and her mother was another English-bred Tam O'Shanter granddaughter. Bridie Mollie was not the showgirl in the family. While Gwenda was winning Specialties, Groups, and Bests in Show on both coasts, Bridie Mollie was producing the Kirks' first homebred champions, Balachan Aggressor and his more famous brother, Balachan Agitator, sired by Mary German's Ch. Cantie Captivator. Agitator was the top-winning male Scottie in 1960, handled by Clifford Hallmark. He was just aced out of winning the Lloyd Trophy that same year by Blanche Reeg's Bewitching. Bridie Mollie went on to produce a total of seven champions sired by three dogs, while Gwenda produced six. Gwenda's daughter, Ch. Balachan Gibson Girl was the dam of the 1968 Lloyd Trophy winner, Ch. Balachan Night Hawk (by

Agitator), and the great show bitch, Ch. Balachan Naughty Gal. Tom and Evelyn became popular judges and gradually cut back on their breeding program to accommodate the growing demand for their services. Tom Kirk is remembered as a successful breeder, exhibitor and judge of Scottish Terriers and was the author of two books important to any student of Scottish Terrier history, *Pedigrees of American Scottish Terrier Champions* and *This Is The Scottish Terrier.*

Gaidoune

In 1955, Dr. Nancy Lenfesty and her husband, Tom, went to England to find a Scottie bitch for Helen Gaither. They settled on Glendoune Gaibonnie, a daughter of Gauntlet's litter mate, Ch. Glendoune Gipsy, sired by Glendoune Gayboy, a son of Eng. Ch. Wyrebury Welldoer. From this bitch and her prolific daughters and granddaughters came a string of ten all-breed Best in Show winners and a dozen Specialty Best of Breed winners in less than fifteen years. Gaibonnie's top-producing daughter was Ch. Gaidoune Gorgeous Hussy, sired by Ch. Rebel Raider. Hussy produced a total of twelve champions out of fourteen offspring. This record was equaled by her daughter, Ch. Gaidoune Gisele, and surpassed by Gisele's daughter, Ch. Gaidoune Tinsel Glow, dam of fourteen champions. Hussy's son from her third litter, Ch. Gaidoune Great Bear, was the first of a long line of Gaidoune Bears. Great Bear was born on the day that Bill Mazeroski hit the winning home run for the Pittsburgh Pirates in the 1960 World Series, so Maz became his call name. Maz won fifteen all-breed Bests and three Specialties, including Best of Breed from the classes at Montgomery County in 1962. He went on to break the producing record of his great-grandsire, Troubadour, by siring fifty-nine champions. Other top Gaidoune sires included Great Bear's brother, Ch. Gaidoune Grin and Bear It and Ch. Gaidoune Bicentennial Bear. Over 100 champions bore the Gaidoune prefix before Mrs. Gaither went into semiretirement. Most of Dorothy Morris's Scots Delight dogs and the Kirk Nor Scotties of Judith Bonaiuto were tightly linebred to Gaidoune. Today, the Gaidoune name can still be found on Scotties handled by Mrs. Gaither's friends, Linda and Gene Hains and Alice Watkins.

On the West coast, the descendants of Westpark Masterpiece were more influential than those of Walsing Watch Tower, particularly during the 1950s. This was largely due to the presence at Carnation Farms of the Masterpiece sons, Ch.'s Reimill Radiator and Westpark Rio Grande, and grandson, Ch. Westpark Derriford Baffie.

Masterpiece's line was also strongly represented in the West by Bryce Gillespie's previously mentioned import, Ch. Trevone Tartar of Bothkennar. Another strong line from Masterpiece came down through his grandson, Ch. Wyrebury Wrangler, imported in 1955 by Fayette C. Ewing IV grandson

Ch. Gaidoune
Gorgeous Hussy.

of the breed's founding father in the United States. Ewing also imported
Ch. Wyrebury Water Gypsy (a Wrangler daughter), in whelp to Eng.
Ch. Wyrebury Wilwyn (a Wrangler son). This litter produced three
champions, and Wrangler's success as a sire resulted in his English breed-
er, William Berry, being named breeder of the year for 1957 in the United
States!

Glad-Mac's

Irene Robertson bred her first litter of Glad-Mac Scotties in 1949 when she
took her pet bitch to Ch. Reimill Radiator. She kept a bitch from that breeding but soon realized that Glad-Mac's Buttons 'n' Bows was not the
quality she had wanted. Through *Dog World* magazine, she began to corre-
spond with Mrs. Dudley Jones who was handling a wheaten bitch named
Golden Princess, bred by Mrs. Howard McComb. Mrs. Robertson purchased
Golden Princess and later, a wheaten male named Cedar Root Gaydes Gold.
Like virtually all wheatens, these two were linebred on Heather Asset through
his sons Ch. Deephaven Dividend and Deephaven Superman. Mrs. Robertson
traveled from her home in the state of Washington all the way to Memphis,
Tennessee to spend three weeks with Mrs. Jones learning to trim and handle.
She also became friendly with Robert Sharp of Seaglen Scotties across
the border in Canada. Sharp generously offered her one of his best bitches,
Leading Wren of Seaglen, with the condition that she be bred to Ch. Reimill
Radiator and that a dog and a bitch puppy from the litter be returned to
him. The two males from that breeding were Sharp's Am., Can. Ch. Glad-
Mac's Sailor of Seaglen and Mrs. Robertson's top-producing sire, Ch.

Ch. Gaidoune Great
Bear.

Glad-Mac's Rolling Stone. Rolling Stone finished handily but his specials career was cut short when a kennel fight resulted in his loss of seven teeth. Rolling Stone's top-winning get were the Group winners, Ch. Glad-Mac Masterpiece, out of a daughter of Ch. Glad-Mac Sailor of Seaglen, and Ch. Gayclan Glamour Girl, out of a double granddaughter of Ch. Deephaven Red Seal. Mrs. Robertson's first Best in Show winner was the owner-handled Ch. Glad Mac's Show Girl, a granddaughter of Glad Mac's Buttons 'n' Bows, her first homebred puppy.

Mrs. Robertson was still going strong into the 1970s and 1980s when she acquired two Sandgreg stud dogs, Ch. Sandgreg's Mr. Hot Shot a Group-winning wheaten, and Ch. Sandgreg's Square Deal, a Specialty Best of Breed and Group winner, and a great-great-great grandson of Rolling Stone and Glamour Girl. Square Deal carried the wheaten gene and surpassed Rolling Stone's record with thirty-four champions. These include the Best in Show winner, Ch. Sandgreg's Sweet Luv, her sisters, Ch. Sandgreg's Sweet Charity and Ch. Wychwyre Liberty, and Pat and Tony Gruda's Ch. Glad Mac's Globetrotter, a Specialty Best of Breed winner from the classes. Mrs. Robertson bred over seventy champions before retiring from breeding.

Glenby

Bertha Russell bred on a very small scale, accounting for just six champions in the six years she was active. She was very interested in obedience, however, and two of her champions also sported obedience titles. She was instrumental in forming a Scottish Terrier obedience drill team that was a popular attraction at dog shows and even made appearances on early television programs. Limited scale did not mean lack of quality in the Glenby Scotties, however. Her Ch. Glenby Captain missed winning the 1950 Lloyd Trophy by just eight points and two Captain daughters

Ch. Glenby Captain.

Ch. Marlorain Dark Seal.

would provide the foundation for the well-known Marlorain Scotties of Martha Melekov and Lorraine Davis. Mrs. Russell would also provide guidance and inspiration for Christine and Fred Stephens, who would make the Glenby name prominent again.

Marlorain

The great sire Ch. Deephaven Dark Seal passed away in September of 1954, just two weeks before Ch. Mariglen Blythe Spirit presented Martha and Lorraine with his son, Ch. Marlorain Dark Seal, one of the two "founding fathers" of Marlorain. The other was an import, Ch. Wychworth Windfall, a son of the Grahams' Special Edition, so tightly linebred that Eng., Am. Ch. Wyrebury Wrangler was his triple great-grandfather. Dark Seal daughters bred to Windfall produced a series of top winners and producers. A bitch of this breeding, Ch. Marlorain Silver Spoon, was the dam of Ch. Bardene Bingo's top-producing American-bred son, Ch. Marlorain Rainmaker. He produced eight champions in only three years at stud before succumbing to cancer. In the early 1970s, Martha and Lorraine purchased Marlorain Alfie of Anstamm, a Bobby Dazzler son. Alfie's grandson, Ch. Marlorain Beau Brummel, out of a Rainmaker daughter, was a Group and Best in Show winner. When Martha died in 1975, Marlorain Kennels was dispersed, but the fifty Marlorain champions and the many descendants from Marlorain stock exerted tremendous influence on the breed.

Young's

A Red Seal granddaughter, Ch. Silver Eve's Anastasia, provided the foundation for Elaine and Karl Young's breeding program, which produced some of the breed's loveliest wheatens. By carefully linebreeding to Rio Grande sons and grandsons, the Youngs set a type that combined good conformation with rich, wheaten color. After breeding nearly a dozen champions, including Ch. Young's Grand D'Or (a Group winner from the Puppy class), Mrs. Young elected to concentrate her energies on judging rather than breeding and exhibiting. Two of her last champions, Young's Rowdy Red Of Passmores and Young's Cat Ballou, provided the foundation for seven generations of Jeannie Passmore's breeding.

Gilkey

Ann Gilkey lived in Wisconsin when she bought her first Scottie from Irene Garthright and named her Ann's Own Kiltie. Kiltie's daughter, bred to a son of Ch. Kinclaven My Bill, produced the first Gilkey champion, a male with the unlikely name of Gilkey's Fancy Tammie. Tammie sired Mrs. Gilkey's sensational Ch. Gilkey's Johnny Come Lately, a black dog who sired nineteen champions, including many of the breed's most beautiful wheatens. Johnny Come Lately missed winning the 1961 Lloyd Trophy by a single point. He is behind many of the top winners of Bob and Mildred Charves and the Sandgreg Scots of John and Barbara DeSaye.

R.D. "Dave" Linton

No overview of this period in the history of the Scottish Terrier could fairly omit one of the breed's most colorful characters, R.D. "Dave" Linton. Linton made two significant contributions to the breed. First, during World War II, he cared for a number of Max Singleton's Walsing dogs in order to preserve this important bloodline. Second, between 1949 and 1953, he published a monthly newspaper called *Diehard Dope*. The first issue appeared in March 1949. Printed on legal-size paper, front and back, it consisted of eighteen pages of news and opinions about Scottish Terriers and the fanciers of the breed.

On the masthead appeared Linton's motto: *Give the Fanciers Light and They Will Find Their Way*. In this introductory issue appeared a story that would be the first of many exposés written in a style that can only be described as righteous indignation: the story of the disbanding of Relgalf kennels. By 1951, the newspaper was typeset and ran photographs as well as articles. Linton identified many problems and offered solutions, often many years before his contemporaries acknowledged that he was right. He noted, for example, in 1949 that the entire membership of the Board of Directors of the Scottish Terrier Club of America lived in metropolitan New York and insisted that the Club needed better geographical representation. He decried the artificial coloring of show dogs and proposed a solution that has yet to be put in to place. Like the breed he loved, he could be relentless in pursuit. When a breeder-judge named C.B. Van Meter was accused of corruption, Linton published story after story of Van Meter's wrong doing until, after two years, the American Kennel Club finally acted to suspend him.

Linton's publication was pugnacious in style, but it also contained all of the elements of great drama. There was comedy, as in the tale of Ch. Barberry Knowe Barbican, having an off-day in the ring. An employee of show superintendent George Foley was seen outside the ring with a wildly out-of-control Scottish Terrier on lead. The Foley boy, as these men were collectively known, was trying to follow outside the ring as Barbican moved around inside the ring. Linton's description of this attempt at double

Ch. Young's Samantha with owner-handler Elaine Young.

Ch. Kinclaven Wild
Oats.

handling is hilarious. There is also tragedy in the classical sense in his accounts of Phil Prentice's suspension—a great terrier man brought down by alcoholism. Linton was not always in high dudgeon, however. His accountings of the deaths of his beloved Scotties are tender and poignant. Linton made a lot of enemies with this newspaper—a prophet without honor in his own land. His health began to fail and, since *Diehard Dope* was always on the financial edge, he was forced to stop publishing in 1953. It was a great loss to all friends of the breed.

Chapter 4

The Bardene Story

*T*his Dog Is A Famous British Champion. Handle With Care. Whoever wrote this warning on a Pan Am Air bill on May 31, 1961, probably never knew just how famous this particular British champion would be in his new American home. It had been nearly a year since Miriam "Buffy" Stamm opened her 1960 Scottish Terrier Club of England Yearbook, saw the photo of Eng. Ch. Bardene Boy Blue, and fell in love. The language of the ad—"Offers have come from all over the world for this lovely dog"—led her to believe that he was not for sale. In an article published in the January 1986 *Bagpiper,* Mrs. Stamm described her reaction to the ad:

> The picture somehow managed to project "Simon's" personality all the way across the Atlantic and into my living room. Never had I seen such a dog. Not only had he caught my attention; he had also captured my heart. I was hopelessly hooked. We had been looking for a stud outside our lines who could bring in new blood to complement and improve our stock. Here was just the dog, but he was not available. It was too depressing. I mooned over his picture the way a lovesick teenager would over her favorite rock star. I even took the Yearbook to work with me and placed it, open to his picture, just inside my desk drawer, where I could look at it several times during the day. Finally, at the suggestion of my husband, and knowing I had nothing to lose, I composed a carefully worded letter to the Palethorpes. After complimenting them on their magnificent dog, I concluded by asking that if ever, in a moment of madness, they felt they could part with Simon, would they consider giving us first chance to buy him.

This letter began several months of friendly correspondence. Then came a surprising proposition—Walter Palethorpe told her to make an offer for Boy Blue. Neither she nor her husband had any idea what would be fair. On the one hand, the dog was four years old; on the other, he was in high

Eng., Can., Am. Ch. Bardene Boy Blue.

			Eng. Ch. Wyrebury Welldoer
		Wyrebury Weathercock	
	Hargate Happy Boy		Eng. Ch. Wyrebury Witching
			Eng. Ch. Rosehall Edward
		Wyrebury Wintergreen	
Eng. Ch. Happy Kimbo			Eng. Ch. Desert Czarina
			Eng. Ch. Walsing Watchlight
		Folknor Firewatch	
	Bardene Barley Sugar		Folknor Fuchia
			Medwal Meteor
		Bidfield Barbola	
Eng., Can., Am. Ch. Bardene Boy Blue			Bidfield Barleycorn
			Eng. Ch. Wyrebury Wonder
		Eng. Ch. Wyrebury Welldoer	
	Bardene Beau Brummel		Wyrebury Dream Of Dockingdee
			Eng., Am. Ch. Reimill Radiator
		Bardene Belindo	
Bardene Beau Peep			Ryeland Right Again
			Eng. Ch. Westpark Masterman
		Eng. Ch. Westpark Beau Geste	
	Bardene Blackbird		Westpark Penelope
			Eng. Ch. Wyrebury Welldoer
		Bardene Benefactress	
			Ryeland Innerkip Isobel

demand. She was also worried that Mr. Palethorpe might consider an offer that fit within the Stamms' budget insultingly low. Finally, she took the plunge and offered $400.

For weeks the Stamms endured the uncertainty. Mrs. Stamm was sure that their offer had been rejected and was angry at herself for not offering more. At last, a letter arrived advising them that they were to be the new owners of Boy Blue. Tony Stamm described that day as follows:

> The arrival of Bardene Boy Blue was an event of major proportion to the folks at Anstamm—a holiday for both of us and an early afternoon trip to Detroit to await the arrival of Eng. Ch. Bardene Boy Blue. What a thrill it was to see a blue kennel with the Union Jack on the side come out of the Pan Am plane. The thrill was even greater when we opened the door and this striking dog stepped forth, head and tail up, displaying no sign of fear or nervousness. After clearing customs, we headed homeward with Boy Blue sitting calmly on the seat between the two of us.

It is hard to imagine a time when the Bardene name was virtually unknown in the United States, but that was the case in 1961. Boy Blue changed all that. He was a remarkable blend of substance and elegance, a big, black-brindle dog with a long, aristocratic head and a longer body to balance the head. Few breeders were neutral on the subject of Boy Blue—they either loved him or they did not like him at all. Among those who liked him immediately was the great terrier handler, Jake Terhune, who saw Boy Blue in October, 1961 at the Scottish Terrier Club of Kentucky Specialty. Boy Blue had arrived in a coat that was long by American standards and the Stamms had been unable to get him in good condition. Despite this, Terhune wanted to handle Boy Blue, telling the Stamms he considered Boy Blue one of the greatest Scotties he had ever seen. Terhune brought Boy Blue out the following spring and finished his championship with two Group Is.

Boy Blue, with his free-flowing gait and nonstop showmanship, was a big hit at the all-breed shows but the Specialty wins eluded him—he was still one of a kind, too different from the competitors. Jake Terhune experienced heart trouble in the fall of 1962, was hospitalized and his recovery was considered doubtful. As a result, Boy Blue went to Lena Kardos, a well-known California-based Scottish Terrier handler. She took Boy Blue on the Florida circuit that January and on to Westminster. Terhune, whose recovery after a short convalescence had surprised his doctors, watched from the sidelines and cried as Lena piloted Boy Blue to Best of Breed. A month later, Terhune succumbed to another heart attack, putting Boy Blue's show career permanently in the hands of Lena Kardos.

Together, Lena and Boy Blue brought his show record to two Bests In Show and sixty-seven Group Is. Mrs. Kardos was influential in the California Scottish Terrier fancy and encouraged breeders to use Boy Blue while she had him. As a result, Boy Blue offspring were seen on both coasts relatively soon after his arrival. Like Necessity, he had the gift of stamping what came to be known as "the Bardene look" on his puppies. He sired forty-one champions, breaking the record of Ch. Edgerstoune Troubadour.

Just four weeks after Boy Blue left England, a breeder named George Young passed away, leaving behind two litters of Scottie puppies, one sired by Boy Blue and the other by a dog known as Bardene Blue Starlight. Young had been breeding for about fifteen years, but ill health kept him out of the show ring. He was in the habit of running both litters together, so when he died and when the puppies were just a few weeks old, his widow did not know which puppies were which. Young and Palethorpe had been friends and the puppies were all Bardene-bred, so Young's widow asked Palethorpe to help her sort the puppies into the correct litters. Years later, Palethorpe said he was convinced that one of those puppies had been assigned to the wrong litter—he believed that Bardene Bingo was sired by Boy Blue. If so, it would enhance Boy Blue's already secure place in breed history.

Boy Blue's successes as a show dog and a sire brought the Bardene name to the attention of the American Scottie fancy. When the Stamms' second import, Bardene Black Jewel, made her American debut by winning a Best in Show from the classes, it only intensified interest in the Bardene Scots. In 1962, Bardene Bingo was a puppy sensation in England, winning his first Best in Show before he was a year old. All-breed judge Percy Roberts awarded that honor and when he returned to the United States, he made no secret of his admiration for the little black Scottie. Palethorpe was well aware of the growing interest Bingo was generating in America. As Bingo's honors grew, Palethorpe encouraged several American breeders, including the Stamms and the Stalters, to believe that Bingo might be sold to them.

Bob Bartos was one of the few who was *not* trying to buy Bingo. He had contacted Palethorpe about some bitches when Palethorpe proposed the sale. Bartos only agreed to take Bingo because a good young dog of his had recently died. Bingo arrived at Carnation Farms on August 29, 1964. After four weeks of conditioning, Bartos took him to the Tacoma KC for a blue ribbon to qualify Bingo for entry at Westminster. He did a little better than qualify—he went Best in Show! Bingo was not shown again until just before Westminster, 1965.

Bartos took him to the Portland show for a little extra training and again Bingo won Best in Show from the classes. Bob Bartos's hopes to finish him by winning Best in Show at Westminster, however, were thwarted by the great Ch. Carmichael's Fanfare. Bingo had to be content with Best of Opposite Sex to her BOB "Mamie," then went on to win the Terrier Group under the

Eng., Can., Am. Ch. Bardene Bingo.

```
                                              Hargate Happy Boy
                              Eng. Ch. Happy Kimbo
                                              Bardene Barley Sugar
              Bardene Blue Star
                                              Bardene Beau Brummel
                              Bardene Breezandi
                                              Bardene Blackbird
      Bardene Blue Starlite
                                              Eng. Ch. Westpark Masterman
                              Eng. Ch. Westpark Beau Geste
                                              Westpark Penelope
              Bardene Blackbird
                                              Eng. Ch. Wyrebury Welldoer
                              Bardene Benefactress
                                              Ryeland Innerkip Isobel
Eng., Can., Am. Ch. Bardene Bingo
                                              Wyrebury Weathercock
                              Hargate Happy Boy
                                              Wyrebury Wintergreen
              Eng. Ch. Happy Kimbo
                                              Folknor Firewatch
                              Bardene Barley Sugar
                                              Bidfield Barbola
      Bardene Blue Cap
                                              Eng. Ch. Westpark Masterman
                              Eng. Ch. Westpark Beau Geste
                                              Westpark Penelope
              Bardene Blackbird
                                              Eng. Ch. Wyrebury Welldoer
                              Bardene Benefactress
                                              Ryeland Innerkip Isobel
```

celebrated Scottie authority, Heywood Hartley, and on to collect the most coveted Best in Show in the American dog fancy; this under Robert Kerns.

Amazingly, Bingo was shown at only eight all-breed shows and two Specialties in 1965, winning four Bests in Show and BOB at both Specialties. He joined an already dynamic stud force at Carnation Farms where, almost immediately, he had access to some of the finest bitches in the country. Like Boy Blue, he was a potent sire and his forty-eight champion offspring bore

Eng., Can., Am. Ch. Bardene Bingo, owned by E. H. Stuart, is shown here with hand-ler Bob Bartos immediately following his 1967 Westminster BIS win under judge Percy Roberts. *William Gilbert*

his stamp. His first champion son, Carnation Casino, finished in 1966 with a Best in Show from the classes. Bingo was the top-winning Terrier of 1966, but, despite success at such important shows as Beverly Hills and Santa Bar-bara, the Breed win at Westminster again eluded him. Finally, in 1967, Bingo achieved his goal, becoming the fifth Scottish Terrier to win Best in Show at Westminster. The Terrier Group judge on this occasion was yet another great friend of the Scot, Cyrus K. Rickel, and Percy Roberts, the man who awarded Bingo his first English Best in Show, put him to the top at the Garden.

In June 1963, one of the coldest, wettest summers in English history, Buffy and Tony Stamm went to England to visit the Palethorpes and tour some of the other Scottish Terrier kennels. While there, they put a deposit down on a

Am., Can. Ch. Bardene
Bobby Dazzler.

```
                                                              Eng. Ch. Happy Kimbo
                                        Bardene Blue Star
                                                              Bardene Breezandi
                   Bardene Blue Starlite
                                                              Eng. Ch. Westpark Beau Geste
                                        Bardene Blackbird
                                                              Bardene Benefactress
        Eng., Am. & Can. Ch. Bardene Bingo
                                                              Hargate Happy Boy
                                        Eng. Ch. Happy Kimbo
                                                              Bardene Barley Sugar
                   Bardene Bluecap
                                                              Eng. Ch. Westpark Beau Geste
                                        Bardene Blackbird
                                                              Bardene Benefactress
Am., Can. Ch. Bardene Bobby Dazzler
                                                              Int. Ch. Westpark Romeo
                                        Eng. Ch. Westpark Derriford Baffie
                                                              Derriford Tam O'Shanter
                   Ryeland Raffie
                                                              Rosehall Enchanter
                                        Ryeland Innerkip Isobel
                                                              Innerkip Iris
        Bardene Barefoot Contessa
                                                              Eng. Ch. Wyrebury Welldoer
                                        Bardene Beau Brummel
                                                              Bardene Belindo
                   Bardene Breezandi
                                                              Eng. Ch. Westpark Beau Geste
                                        Bardene Blackbird
                                                              Bardene Benefactress
```

puppy out of a two-week old litter by Bingo. That puppy, Bardene Bobby Dazzler, was the third of the so-called *Three Bs* and he went to the Stamms in 1965. On a visit to Anstamm, Mrs. Kardos asked Mrs. Stamm, "What's he like?" When Mrs. Stamm indicated that he was as good a dog as Boy Blue and that his head was equally dramatic, Mrs. Kardos conveyed her skepticism without speaking. They went to the kennel for Mrs. Kardos to examine him. At first, she said nothing. Mrs. Kardos finally communicated her opinion with a single word, "Wow!"

Bobby Dazzler made his debut at Montgomery County in 1965, where he was Winners Dog and Best of Opposite Sex under British authority Muriel Owen. He completed his championship twenty days later by winning two Group Is. Though he lacked Boy Blue's great showmanship, he had better size, and was more compact; they both had the same dramatic head and hard-bitten expression. By 1966, judges were more accustomed to the Bardene type since Boy Blue, Bingo and the Boy Blue son, Ch. Anstamm Dark Venture, had already produced a number of champions. As a result, Bobby Dazzler was more successful at Specialty shows than Boy Blue and won the Lloyd Trophy for 1966. He was Bingo's top-producing son with thirty-two champions.

It would be hard to overstate the influence of these three dogs on the breed. By 1970, half of all Scottish Terrier champion pedigrees traced back to one or more of this trio. The modern history of the breed has been written *almost* exclusively by the Three Bs' descendants. These include: Every Lloyd Trophy winner for the past twenty-five years; all but three of the last twenty-nine National Specialty winners (covering fifty-two Specialties); and all but two of the breed's top twenty American sires. Naturally, breeders in the Midwest, home of Anstamm, and the West, home of Bob Bartos and Lena Kardos, were first to use these dogs and these regions still show their strongest influence.

Another change was taking place at about the same time—less dramatic, perhaps, but just as influential. The big breeding kennels, owned by wealthy fanciers and employing full-time kennel managers, were giving way to another type of breeder. By the 1970s, the majority of Scottie breeders were from the economic middle class who usually started with a pet and gradually upgraded as they learned more. Top-winning owner-handlers, virtually unknown in many terrier breeds, are routine in the Scottish Terrier ring at shows all over the United States. We will profile many of them in the following chapter.

Chapter 5

The Contemporary
Scottish Terrier in America

The story of the last quarter century of the Scottish Terrier cannot be told in the same format as earlier history, since it is impossible to
predict which dogs and breeders will persevere to influence the breed into
the next century. For that reason, and because important breeders and dogs
tend to be more influential in their home regions, this chronicle is presented
geographically rather than chronologically.

THE NORTHEAST

The death of Helen Stalter in 1975 ended Barberry Knowe's part in active
competition, but the influence of the line she and her husband, Charles,
established is still very powerful, particularly in the Northeast. Ron Schaeffer
and Kathi Brown are good examples of contemporary breeders who, while
keeping very few dogs, have consistently bred top-winning stock based on
Barberry Knowe bloodlines.

Schaeffer

Ron Schaeffer was introduced to Scotties by Florence and Phil Prentice,
kennel managers and handlers for Barberry Knowe. His foundation bitch,
Fashion First Impression, bred by John Murphy, was an Ch. Edgerstoune
Troubadour granddaughter. First Impression, bred to a Boy Blue grandson,
produced Ch. Schaeffer's Sky Rocket, sire of eight champions, including the
Group-placing bitch, Ch. Schaeffer's First Impression. Sky Rocket's top-
producing son, Schaeffer's Dark Avenger, sired seven champions. Among them
was Ch. Schaeffer's Calling Card, BIS and five-time Specialty BOB winner,
including BOB at Montgomery County, 1979. In 1985, Schaeffer arranged

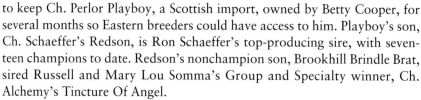

to keep Ch. Perlor Playboy, a Scottish import, owned by Betty Cooper, for several months so Eastern breeders could have access to him. Playboy's son, Ch. Schaeffer's Redson, is Ron Schaeffer's top-producing sire, with seventeen champions to date. Redson's nonchampion son, Brookhill Brindle Brat, sired Russell and Mary Lou Somma's Group and Specialty winner, Ch. Alchemy's Tincture Of Angel.

One way that Schaeffer has been able to limit his numbers of dogs is to work with other breeders. At various times, Schaeffer has co-owned or co-bred dogs with Lyn Zurl, Karen Hansen, and Carol and Harold Ames. Among those who have either started with Schaeffer bitches or have followed his guidance in their breeding programs are Gary and Susan Carr (Whiskybae Yanky), Harold and Carol Ames (Amescot), Shirley and Nick Karas (Karascot) and Luis Arroyo (Brookhill).

Whiskybae

Although Gary and Sue Carr live in "Barberry Knowe country" they acquired their Barberry Knowe-bred foundation stock from relatives in Texas, Richard and Carla LaCoe of Whiskybae Scottish Terriers. The Carrs purchased Whiskybae Ginger Bear (bitch) and Whiskybae Connecticut Yanky (dog), who combined the old Barberry Knowe lines with the newer Bardene inheritance through Ch. Meeder's Discord. Ginger Bear produced three champions, including Whiskybae Yanky Bagpiper, the foundation for Carol and Harold Ames's Amescot Kennels. The Carrs, however, bred all of their top winners from her nonchampion daughters, Whiskybae Anne Of Ballynoor and Whiskybae Yanky Ginger Snap. Anne's daughter, Ch. Whiskybae Yanky Go Lightly, was another top ten rated bitch. Following Ron Schaeffer's advice, Go Lightly was bred first to Ch. Schaeffer's Calling Card, then to Ch. Perlor Playboy, and finally, to the Playboy son, Ch. Schaeffer's Redson. She produced one champion in each litter: Ch. Whiskybae Yanky Hit Man, Ch. Whiskybae Yanky Anchor Man and Ch. Whiskybae Yanky Earth Angel. Ginger Snap was also the dam of three champions, Whiskybae Yanky Minute Man, Whiskybae Yanky Magpie and Whiskybae Yanky Stunt Man. After winning the National Sweepstakes at Montgomery County in 1984, Stunt Man was sold to Bob and Jane Phelan, where he became the first big winner for the Caevnes Scots. Magpie's son, Strutfire's Gingerbred Man, is the sire of Donna Cone's BIS winner, Ch. Whiskybae Yanky Andy's Kandy.

Amescot

Ch. Whiskybae Yanky Bagpiper was co-owned by Carol and Harold Ames and is behind their Amescot Scotties. Piper's daughter, Ch. Amescot Piper's High C, by Ch. Ashton's Renaldo Aristocrat, was the first of three Scots owned or co-owned by the Ames to win Sweepstakes at Montgomery County. The other two were Schaeffer's Cracklin' Rosie and Whiskybae Yanky Stunt Man.

Ch. Alchemy's Tincture of Angel.

Ch. Brookhill Morning Edition, bred by Luis Arroyo and owned by Marjory Carpenter, is shown here in 1991, with handler Peggy Brown, winning her second consecutive BIS at Montgomery County under Italian judge, Dr. Giuseppe Benelli.

Nancy Walthers handled several of the most successful Amescot dogs, including Ch. Amescot's Lotta Talk, who finished by going Winners Dog at the 1992 Rotating Specialty. Lotta Talk's sister, Ch. Amescot's She's A Charmer, is the dam of Mrs. Walther's Specialty winner, Ch. Great Scot's What A Hot Shot.

Brookhill

Probably the biggest Cinderella story of recent years is that of Ch. Brookhill's Morning Edition. Breeder Luis Arroyo bought "Lola's" grandmother from the Ames as a pet. Ron Schaeffer encouraged Luis to breed her to the 1979 Montgomery County BOB winner, Ch. Schaeffer's Calling Card. The pick of this litter was a bitch given the unlikely name Mac Pooch Ms. Michie. Ron

Schaeffer handled Ms. Michie to her championship, and she produced one champion from each of three litters. Her most successful daughter, Ch. Brookhill's Morning Edition, was by Ch. Sandgreg's Second Edition. Sold to Marjorie Carpenter at the age of twelve weeks, Lola's puppyhood was spent as a therapy dog working with the elderly. In 1989, at ten months, Lola was Best of Winners at Devon and Montgomery County. She was BIS at Montgomery County in 1990 and 1991 and won the Lloyd Trophy in 1991.

Motherwell

Bill Berry and his mother, Marie, got their first Scottish Terrier from Shirley Morris in 1978. A brindle son of Ch. Barberry Knowe Spitfire, Mirriemoor Cheeky Charlie became their first champion. Their next champion was Eilburn Empress, an English import, co-owned with Betty Cooper. Empress was Best of Winners at the 1985 STCA Rotating Specialty. It was not, however, until the Berrys acquired Yellow Iris Windflower from Leslie Blanchard and Miguel Braschi that their breeding program took off. Windflower produced five champion bitches, all sired by Ch. Perlor Playboy. The Berrys' most recent standard-bearer is multiple Specialty winner, Ch. Brookhill Matador, a repeat breeding of Lola, co-owned with professional handler Peggy Brown.

Raab Hill

Like Ron Schaeffer, Bob and Betty Marshall started with a bitch bred by Johnny Murphy. Ch. Fashion Felicity was by Special Edition out of a Baffie granddaughter. She produced six champions, five by Ch. Barberry Know Merrymaker and one by Ch. Barberry Knowe Blizzard. One Merrymaker daughter, Ch. Raab Hill Merry Poppins, was the tail-female foundation for Dick and Jackie Seelbach's three generations of Ram Tree "Merry" champions.

Duff-De

A Merrymaker-Felicity son, Ch. Raab Hill Rollingstone was the grandsire of Bill and Kathy DeVilleneuve's Ch. Duff-De Fireworks, a daughter of Ch. Schaeffer's Sky Rocket. Aptly named, Fireworks was the first big winner for this young couple since she started with a bang, winning several Groups and two Specialty Bests of Breed. Her grandson, Ch. Duff-De Pac Man, had a successful specials career in the mid-1980s earning 100 Bests of Breed in seven years as a special. In 1986, the DeVilleneuves imported Killisport Charisma of Scarista, a litter sister to Eng. Ch. Killisport Rox at Scarista. Charisma, a multiple Group winner produced seven champions, all sired by the venerable Ch. Duff-De Pac Man.

Another Merrymaker daughter, Ch. Fashion Merry Star, bred by Johnny Murphy, provided foundation bitches for two more Eastern kennels: Wychwood and Gren Aery.

Wychwood and Gren Aery

Fred and Jean Ferris founded their Wychwood Scottish Terriers with Ch. Am Anger Glendale Star, sired by Ch. Seagrave's Rogue's Image. Glendale Star was a novice breeder-exhibitor's dream. She was rated among the top ten Scottish Terriers from 1974 to 1976, winning numerous Groups and placing BOS at Montgomery County in 1973, all owner-handled by her relatively inexperienced owners. She produced eight champions, five in her first litter by Ch. Barberry Knowe Conductor. Her daughter, Ch. Wychwood Sea Nymph, was a Specialty winner and a top-ranked Scot in 1978. Ch. Wychwood Beau Geste was her top-producing son with fourteen champions to his credit. Glendale Star's sister, Ch. Am Anger Starlight, produced seven Gren-Aery champions for Joan Eagle, most sired by her Schaeffer's Sky Rocket son, Ch. Gren-Aery Edward.

Sparwyn

Ch. Wychwood's Beau Geste was the sire of two Sparwyn champions for Debbie Mackie. One of these, Ch. Sparwyn Chip Off The Old Block, is the sire of Ms. Mackie's biggest winner, Ch. Sparwyn Speak N Spar, ex Ch. Hughcrest Strut N Spar. Speak N Spar was BOS at Montgomery County in 1991.

Blueberry Hill

Another beneficiary of the Barberry Knowe legacy is Kathi Brown of Blueberry Hill and her partner, Geraldine Pondrier. They started with Ch. Blueberry Thistle, a granddaughter of Ch. Barberry Knowe Conductor. Carefully linebred to Barberry Knowe studs, Thistle produced five champions, including Ch. Blueberry's Colonial Caper, who finished as a puppy and was a Specialty and Group winner. Kathi and Gerry also bred the Group and Specialty winner, Ch. Blueberry Born To Boogie, owned and shown by Merle and Carolyn Taylor. More recent Blueberry champions have resulted from crosses to Glenby lines.

Stonehedge

Tom Natalini and Don Massaker managed a successful breeding program, producing Specialty and Group winners, while running a boarding kennel, handling dogs professionally and working full-time. They started with Ch. Raab Hill Rockette, and her half-brother, Ch. Raab Hill Special Delivery, who were BOS and BOW respectively at the 1969 Rotating Scottish Terrier Club of America Specialty. To their predominantly Barberry Knowe Lines, Natalini and Massaker introduced Ch. Marlorain Lolita, a Bobby Dazzler granddaughter out of a Boy Blue daughter. Bred to the Rockette son, Ch. Stonehedge Bandmaster, Lolita produced three champions. One, Ram Tree

Stonehedge King Arthur, went on to a successful specials career siring eight champions. As a professional handler, Natalini has shown many dogs to their championship, including Chris Hepler's Ch. Anstamm All American, BOB from the classes at Montgomery County in 1982.

In 1987, Irwin and Ilene Hochberg commissioned Natalini to help them import a good Scottish Terrier from England. Never one to do anything by halves, Natalini brought home England's number one Scottish Terrier, Eng. Ch. Killisport Rox At Scarista *and* his daughter, Suzanna of Scarista. Rox and Suzanna came to the United States after Rox's BOB win at Crufts. Both finished quickly, but in America, Suzanna shone. She was BOB at Devon in 1988 and at Hatboro in 1989. An all-breed BIS winner, Suzanna was number four Scottish Terrier (*Terrier Type* System) in 1988 and 1989. Natalini's partner, Don Massaker, always favored Rox. Sadly, Massaker passed away just before Rox won BOB at Westminster in 1990. Rox is the sire of thirty-four champions. His top-winning offspring is the multiple BIS winner, Ch. Stonehedge Galaxy, co-owned by Natalini and Jim and Marjorie McTernan. Rox's best-known champion son is Thom and Mary Parotti's Eng., Can. and Am. Ch. Scarista's Rocky, the sire of twelve champions.

Selkirk and Coleco

Scarista breeding has provided the foundation for Chuck and Anita Knirnschild's Selkirk Scotties and Sheila Coe's Coleco Scots. The Knirnschilds went to Scotland to select their foundation bitch, Ch. Selkirk Heather of Scarista. Sheila Coe started with Ch. Motherwell Starlight Express, a Ch. Perlor Playboy daughter, bred by Bill and Marie Berry. Later, Mrs. Coe imported two Scarista-bred bitches, Ch. Auchenscot Learig at Scarista and Ch. Scarista Sure Gold. The Knirnschilds and Mrs. Coe both bred first to Rox. The Knirnschilds then bred their Scarista bitch to Ch. Coleco's Stand-Up Comic, a son of Rox ex Starlight Express. The combination has been successful, producing nearly a dozen champions.

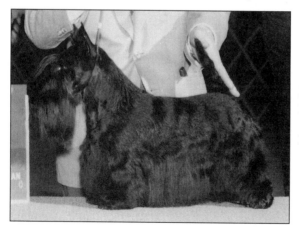

Eng., Am. Ch. Killisport Rox At Scarista, owned by Irwin and Ilene Hochberg. *John Ashbey*

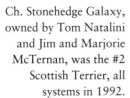

Ch. Stonehedge Galaxy, owned by Tom Natalini and Jim and Marjorie McTernan, was the #2 Scottish Terrier, all systems in 1992.

THE SOUTH

The climate of the Southern states is generally inhospitable to the coat and skin of the Scottish Terrier, but successful breeders have managed to raise dogs that thrive despite the heat, humidity and external parasites. Tom and Evelyn Kirk, of the Balachan prefix, provided much of the foundation stock for, and were mentors to, many southern breeders. Gail Gaines, once their protegée, is now the doyenne of Southern breeders.

Neidfyre

Gail Gaines started in the late 1960s with a Bingo granddaughter, Balachan Natie Nittack, a half-sister of Ch. Balachan Naughty Gal, by the Kirk's imported Ch. Viewpark Red Hackle. Natie Nittack soon gained her championship and was the foundation for Gail's Neidfyre Kennels. Natie Nittack produced four champions, and for the next fifteen years, Gail developed a successful line based on this bitch, using primarily Balachan, Viewpark and Barberry Knowe stud dogs. Her Group-winning Ch. Neidfyre Doon Agape and Neidfyre Folksinger, 1976 Montgomery County Winners Dog, were among her most memorable winners.

Glenlivet

Miss Caroline Reid of Glenlivet Scotties began with bitches combining Viewpark, Gaidoune, Balachan and Woodhart bloodlines. She bred numerous champions, the best-known being the great-producing bitch, Ch. Glenlivet Heather-Bell and the Best-in-Show winning Ch. Glenlivet Gordon of Jaudon. Heather-Bell was a double granddaughter of Ch. Viewpark Red Hackle. Gordon was out of Caroline's first champion, Ch. Glenlivet Christina, and the BIS-winning Heather-Bell son, Ch. Jaudon's Highland Jester.

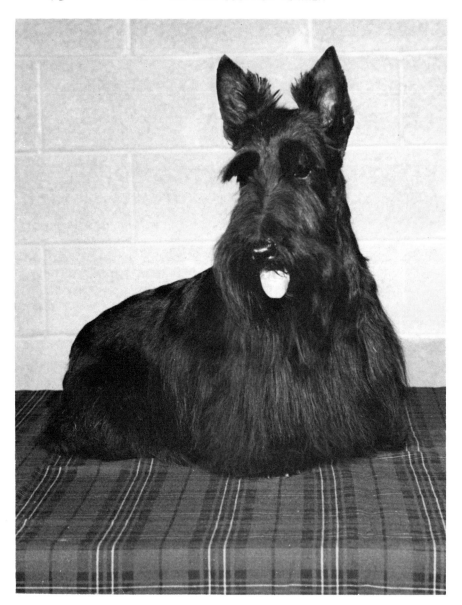

Ch. Glenlivet Heather-Bell, bred by Caroline Reid and owned by Ron and Judy Barker, is the breed's all-time top-producing bitch with nineteen champions out of twenty-one offspring.

Jaudon

Jaudon was the kennel name of Ron and Judy Barker, the young couple who were fortunate enough to purchase Heather-Bell as their foundation bitch. Heather-Bell was a double granddaughter of Ch. Viewpark Red Hackle. The

Ch. Glenlivet Gordon of Jaudon, owned by Caroline Reid, was a 1976 BIS winner. Gordon is shown with handler A. D. "Pete" Clay and judge Mrs. Evelyn Tingle. *Earl Graham*

Barkers handled Heather-Bell throughout her successful show career and finished most of her offspring. Her first three litters were by Jaudon's Guid Brigadier, a son of Betty Munden's Ch. Gadiscot Guid Giftie. In her first litter, Heather Bell produced three champions, including the BIS winner, Ch. Jaudon's Highland Jester. All five in her second litter and all six in her third also finished. Heather Bell produced four champions in her fourth litter, by Ch. Gillsie Prince William. Her final champion was alone in a litter by Ch. Bear-Bee's Bit of Dunbar.

Edina

Another couple who started with a Glenlivet bitch was Joanne and Eddie Ingram of Edina Scottish Terriers. Their Ch. Glenlivet Fiona, a half-sister to Heather Bell, was the top Scottie bitch in 1975, and was ranked second mid-year in 1976 when she died suddenly. She had only one litter, by Ch. Jaudon's Highland Jester, but produced four champions. The Ingrams bred nine champions before they retired from showing.

Aerie

Herb and Linda Quarles understood the importance of a good foundation— they started with *two* quality bitches. Their first champion, Kirk Nor Sitting Pretty, was a daughter of Judith Bonaiuto's BIS and Specialty winning

Ch. Kirk Nor Outrider and a granddaughter of Ch. Gaidoune Great Bear. Sitting Pretty was a Specialty winner before retiring to produce five champions. Among these were 1975's top-ten ranked Ch. Kirk Nor Rhymes and Reasons, 1977's Montgomery County Winners Dog, Ch. Aerie Poem, Prayer and Promise, and Ch. Aerie Almost Heaven. Another Topper, Almost Heaven eclipsed the records of her predecessors at Aerie by winning five BIS, numerous Groups and Specialty BOBs. In the middle of her show career, Almost Heaven was bred back to her sire, Ch. Gaidoune Bicentennial Bear, and produced a litter of four champions. Throughout her show career, Almost Heaven was entirely owner-handled.

The Quarles's second foundation matron, Ch. Scattergood Magic Moments, also combined Gaidoune and Scots Delight bloodlines. Magic Moments was the Quarles's second top-10 rated Scottie in 1975. In her second litter, sired by Ch. Gaidoune Bicentennial Bear, Magic Moments produced four champions, including the 1979 Montgomery County BOW, Aerie Beneath the Golden Sun.

When Herb and Linda Quarles divorced, the fancy wondered if their successful Aerie name would fade away. Herb had always showed their dogs. Linda, a consummate groomer, was such a behind-the-scenes person that many exhibitors had no idea what she looked like. By 1987, Linda had remarried and moved with her new husband, Gene Hains, to Indiana. Since Gene was completely new to the dog world, Linda had to overcome her apprehension about going into the ring herself. She was starting over almost from scratch, bringing one bitch from her old life, Aerie Heart To Heart. A striking silver-brindle bitch, Heart To Heart had the frustrating habit of balking when Linda tried to move her. Once Linda finally convinced her to move out in the ring, Heart To Heart finished by going Winners Bitch at the 1988 STC of Western Virginia. Meanwhile, new husband Gene was earning his spurs as an exhibitor by learning to show Anstamm Leading Man. "Cary"

Ch. Aerie Almost Heaven, bred and owned by Herb Quarles and Linda Hains, is shown here with owner-handler, Linda Hains, winning the Terrier Group at James River Kennel Club in 1983. The Group judge is Dr. T. Allen Kirk, successful breeder and author of *This Is the Scottish Terrier. Sherry*

did not make life easy for Gene, either. Cary objected to standing still, on the ground or on the table, and his preferred gait was the caper! Gene was determined, however, and finished Cary with back-to-back Specialty wins in 1988 at Michigan and Western Virginia.

Linda had given up the Aerie name when she divorced Herb. Helen Gaither, a longtime friend of Linda's, offered to let Linda and Gene share her distinguished Gaidoune prefix. The foundation for these new Gaidoune "Bears" came from Mrs. Carl Leathers, John Caspers and the Hebrides breeding of Dame Catherine Carpender and Jeff and Lori Teague. From Mrs. Leathers, the Hains obtained a bitch, Lorilyn Allabear, and a dog, Lorilyn Bearitone. They also bought two other bitches, Manderley Meadowsweet from John Caspers, and Gaidoune Debutante from Catherine Carpender and the Teagues. Gene and Linda handled Bearitone and Meadowsweet to Winners Dog and Winners Bitch, respectively, at the 1989 Chicago Specialty. Bearitone went BOB at the Western Virginia Specialty the same year. Gaidoune Debutante, a Group winner from the classes, finished her championship at the 1990 Louisville Specialty and, one week later, was BOB at the Michigan Specialty.

Dame Catherine Carpender, the co-breeder of Gaidoune Debutante, got her first Scottish Terrier as a pet in 1930. Her first show dog was Ch. Camyscot Miss Pepper, from the first-ever American litter of six Scottish Terrier champions. In recent years, Dame Carpender has shared her "of the Hebrides" kennel name with Jeff and Lori Teague. Their Canna of the Hebrides produced three champions, sired by Ch. Aerie Windstar.

Redoubt's

Although Carol Plott had shown Scotties as a child, it was not until the early 1970s that she and her husband Don decided to buy a show bitch. They chose Wayridge Becky Nic-Bobby, out of a Bobby Dazzler daughter by a Bingo son. Becky finished quickly and, bred to Ch. Anstamm Happy Venture, produced Redoubt's Salute to Anstamm, a top-producing Happy Venture son. The Plotts also acquired Ch. Schwer's Happy Melody and Ch. Schwer's Dynamic Happy Boy, BIS at Montgomery County, 1973. Carol soon gained a reputation as one of the best groomers in the breed and was always willing to share her skills. Many of today's successful exhibitors in the Maryland area learned to trim from Carol. She and Don always kept a small number of dogs, but by working together with Lee and Elaine Lawrence of Gaelwyn Scottish Terriers, both couples were able to increase the size of their gene pool without becoming "overdogged." In recent years, the constraints of Don's job made it nearly impossible for them to breed and show actively.

Gaelwyn

Lee and Elaine Lawrence's foundation bitch, Don-John's Wee Bonnie, had a pedigree that was to prove very successful in the 1970s and 1980s. She was

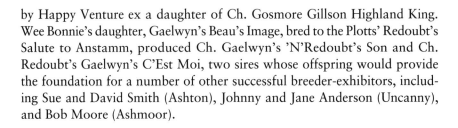

by Happy Venture ex a daughter of Ch. Gosmore Gillson Highland King. Wee Bonnie's daughter, Gaelwyn's Beau's Image, bred to the Plotts' Redoubt's Salute to Anstamm, produced Ch. Gaelwyn's 'N'Redoubt's Son and Ch. Redoubt's Gaelwyn's C'Est Moi, two sires whose offspring would provide the foundation for a number of other successful breeder-exhibitors, including Sue and David Smith (Ashton), Johnny and Jane Anderson (Uncanny), and Bob Moore (Ashmoor).

Ashton

Sue and David Smith purchased Reality Symbol in 1976 from Ed and Blanche Nutter. Symbol also combined the inheritance of Happy Venture and Highland King. She was by Ray and Hilda Bigelow's BIS-winning Happy Venture son, Ch. Dunbar's Distinction, ex Ch. Anstamm King's Tribute, by Highland King. Symbol was bred to a son of the Plotts' Redoubt's Salute to Anstamm and produced four champions, including Ch. Ashton's All Spice, the 1980 Montgomery County Best in Sweepstakes. Going back to Blanart and Carmichael lines gave the Smiths Ch. Ashton's Adamant, the 1979 Montgomery County Winners Dog. The Smith's last special, Ch. Ashton's Debonair, combined Adamant's Carmichael and Blanart lines with Symbol's Anstamm breeding.

Uncanny

Johnny and Jane Anderson ignored conventional wisdom and started with a dog instead of a bitch. The dog, a littermate of Sue Smith's Especially Me, was Ch. Redoubt's Ashton. Despite their inexperience, the Andersons conditioned and handled Ashton to Group and Specialty wins in 1980. Ashton sired only two champions for the Andersons before his untimely death. The Andersons very successfully brought Gaidoune lines into their breeding program when they bred their Ch. Uncanny's A Little Night Music to the Quarles's Ch. Aerie Deal with the Ladies. The resulting offspring, Ch. Uncanny's Go Your Own Way, finished with two Specialty Bests. Within a month of finishing, this lovely bitch won her first Group.

The Andersons' bitches were not prolific; Mrs. Anderson complained constantly that her bitches had small litters, but nearly all her homebreds finished, most with at Specialty wins. Perhaps because of those small litters, the Andersons joined forces in 1987 with Joan Duke of Balgair Scots. Until then, joining forces with the Andersons, Ms. Duke's most successful campaigner was the multiple Specialty-winning bitch, Ch. Balgair's Redoubt's Take A Bow, co-owned by James and Elizabeth Boso.

The combination of Uncanny and Balgair worked well. Ms. Duke had a knack for breeding, and Mrs. Anderson contributed her grooming and handling talents. They bred Ms. Duke's Balgair's Timely Token to Ch. Uncanny's Against All Odds. One of the two champions from this breeding, Ch. Uncanny's

Balgair's Chances R, sired their top-winning bitch, Ch. Uncanny's Starlight Express. Campaigned only eight months in 1989, Starlight Express won two Groups and was the number three ranked Scottish Terrier (Terrier Type System).

Balgair

Joan Duke started with a pet shop Scottie and took on the challenge of obedience training. After putting the CDX degree on her dog, Ms. Duke became interested in conformation showing. She then acquired her foundation bitch, Vauntie Glaikit, a granddaughter of Ch. Kirk Nor Out Rider and Ch. Gadiscot Guid Giftie. Glaikit produced three champions, and her daughter, Ch. Balgair's Duhallow Jen, and granddaughter, Ch. Balgair's Center Stage, have each, in turn, produced three champions. Ms. Duke linebred to Gadiscot and Camyscot lines until the early 1980s when she outcrossed to the Plotts' Ch. Redoubts' Gaelwyn's C'Est Moi. This breeding produced Ch. Balgair's Redoubt's Take A Bow, BOW at the STCA Specialty at Montgomery County, 1985, and her brother, Ch. Redoubts' Front Row Center, a Group winner from the classes.

In October 1988, Joan Duke handled Balgair's Encore, a young home-bred dog, to Best in Sweepstakes at Montgomery County under breeder-judge Gail Gaines. She and the Andersons planned an exciting future for Encore, and he soon proved he was ready for it. In April 1989, handled by Jane Anderson, he won back-to-back five-point majors at the New England Specialty and the Rotating National Specialty. Like all breeders with an exciting young dog, Joan and the Andersons dreamed of finishing Encore at Montgomery County. They decided to take the chance, so they pulled his coat down and waited for October.

On the day, Encore did everything right, but the dream did not come true. Encore was Reserve Winners Dog. Ms. Duke and Mrs. Anderson took their disappointment like champions, and Encore finished the next week by going BOW at the Washington D.C. Specialty. Encore began his specials career in 1990 by winning a Group under Betty Munden. Unfortunately, he was retired shortly afterward when Jane decided to quit showing dogs. Ms. Duke continued to breed, but infrequently, due to family obligations. Only one Scottish Terrier bore the new kennel name that she and the Andersons had planned to use—Ch. Balcanny's Stairway To Heaven, owned by Betty Gooch, was a Group winner in 1992, campaigned by Mark and Sally George.

Ashmoor

Like the Andersons, Bob Moore's first show dog was a male, Ch. Glendale Happy Hooligan. Hooligan, a Happy Venture son, finished quickly and was retired after a successful specials career. In 1982, Hooligan came out again at age nine and quickly moved to the number four position in the top ten.

Moore, with Carol Plott, acquired Ch. Reality Tassie Lynn, litter sister to Sue Smith's Reality Symbol. Tassie Lynn, bred to the Plotts' Redoubt's Salute to Anstamm, produced Moore's next big winner, Ch. Ashmoor At the Ritz, BOB at the 1983 STCA Rotating Specialty. Moore's most recent special was a young dog bred by Lee and Elaine Lawrence, Ch. Ashmoor Huck Finn of Gaelwyn. Huck Finn was tightly linebred to Happy Venture through the Plotts' Redoubt's Salute to Anstamm and the Lawrences' Don-John's Wee Bonnie. Before he was two, Huck Finn was a multiple Group and Specialty winner.

Hughcrest

Chris and Judy Hughes's meteoric fifteen years in Scottish Terriers started in 1975, after a successful association with Miniature Schnauzers. The Hughes had the good fortune to base their program on two of the breed's all-time top-producing bitches, Ch. Sonata Serenade and Fitzwilliam's Fancy. They purchased Serenade from Mike and Sharon Lowman. Serenade was by Happy Venture out of the Lowmans' great English producer, Ch. Reanda Razziella. Serenade finished quickly and in 1976, she was the number two Scottie in the country, winning two BIS, ten Group Is, and thirty other placements. If a pedigree can be said to predict success in the whelping box, Serenade was bound to be a great brood bitch. Her father was the breed's all-time top producer, and her mother was the dam of ten champions. True to her lineage, Serenade produced six champions, including her top-producing son, Ch. Hughcrest Home Brew, by Ch. Bardene Bookmark. The other bitch purchased by the Hughes was Fitzwilliam's Fancy. Fancy was Bardene-bred to the bone, by Ch. Anstamm Dazzler Dynamic out of a double Bobby Dazzler

Ch. Hughcrest Daiquiri Doll with breeder-owner-handler Judy Hughes. Daiquiri Doll was Best in Sweepstakes and Best of Breed from the classes at the STCA Specialty with Montgomery County in 1986 under English breeder-judge Susan Gaskell.

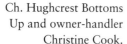

Ch. Hughcrest Bottoms
Up and owner-handler
Christine Cook.

granddaughter. The Hughes bred four champions from Fancy, all by Happy Venture, before sending her to Miriam Stamm in return for a puppy they wanted.

From these two bitches and their descendants, the Hughes produced over thirty champions. The Hughes's dogs were particularly strong at Specialty shows. Hughcrest bitches were especially successful at Montgomery County: Hughcrest Bottoms Up was Winners Bitch and BOS in 1978; Hughcrest Hellzapoppin duplicated those wins in 1980; Hughcrest Jigger O Gin (a Bottoms Up daughter) was Winners Bitch and BOW in 1981; Hughcrest Daiquiri Doll swept the boards in 1986, going Best in Sweepstakes and BOB from the classes; and Hughcrest Intoxication was Reserve Winners Bitch in 1988.

Bar-None

Michael and Christine Cook founded their successful Bar-None line on three Bardene-bred bitches. The first was Anstamm Dazzling Dierdre, a Bobby Dazzler daughter out of a Boy Blue granddaughter. Dazzling Dierdre is best remembered as the grand-dam of the great Ch. Braeburn's Close Encounter and the great-grand-dam of Ch. Deblin's Back Talk.

The Cooks' second foundation bitch was also their first champion, the English import, Ch. Gaywyn Nelda. Nelda was a Group and Specialty winner but only produced one champion. Her place in breed history is as the dam of Bar-None's Forget-Me-Not, the dam of eight champions, including two national Specialty BOB winners, Ch. Hughcrest Daiquiri Doll and Ch. Hughcrest Sparklin' Burgundy. Forget-Me Not's daughter, Ch. Bar-None's Reflection, produced three champions, as did Reflection's daughter, Bar-None's Lasting Impression. Lasting Impression's son, Ch. Anstamm Flashback, sired BOW at both 1994 STCA Specialties.

The Cooks' top-winning producer and most prolific bitch was Ch. Hughcrest Bottoms Up. Bottoms Up was by Ch. Dunbar's Democrat of Sandoone out of a Happy Venture—Fitzwilliam's Fancy daughter. The Cooks bought her after her big win at Montgomery County in 1978. With them she embarked on her long, successful specials career. For the next seven years, Bottoms Up dominated the Specialty scene, winning fourteen BOBs and ten BOSs—three at Montgomery County. In 1985 Bottoms Up crowned her illustrious career by winning BOB from the Veterans' class at Montgomery County. At just over eight years, she was the oldest Scottish Terrier to win this honor. Bottoms Up still holds the record for the most Specialties won by an owner-handled Scottie bitch. She produced nine champions, four in her last litter, by Ch. Enchanter of Eilburn.

Deblin

Debbie McGrory Brooks and Lynn Struck drew favorable attention from their earliest appearances in the show ring. Their first homebred, Ch. Deblin's Small Talk, was a daughter of Michael and Christine Cook's Ch. Bar-None's Dazzling Ad-Venture. It was Small Talk's son, however, who put Debbie and Lynn on the map. Ch. Deblin's Back Talk, sired by the 1982 Montgomery County breed winner, Ch. Anstamm All American, came early to stardom. He was BOB from the 6–9 puppy class at the 1985 Baltimore Specialty, the first of fifteen Specialty Bests, still the record for an owner-handled Scottish Terrier.

In 1987, Back Talk was BOB at Montgomery County, and is one of the breed's top sires, with forty-eight champions to date. Many of his offspring finished at Specialties, including his son, Deblin's Pep Talk, Winners Dog at Montgomery County 1990. Back Talk's litter sister, Ch. Deblin's Sweet Talk had to be spayed after her only litter, by Ch. Sun-Ray's Summer Sun. Sweet Talk's daughter, Ch. Deblin's Double Talk, is also the dam of five champions.

Quercus

Antonella Visconti Di Madrone and her husband moved to Quercus Farms outside Atlanta in 1979. Antonella's first imports included Ch. Denibi Aristocrat, a son of Eng. Ch. Gaywyn Landmark, and Ch. Offshore Tidal Race, a Landmark daughter out of a Kennelgarth bitch. Her third import, Eng., Italian and Am. Ch. Enchanter of Eilburn, a grandson of Ch. Gosmore Eilburn Admaration, was her top-producing sire with twenty-three champions. One was the 1985 Lloyd Trophy winner, Ch. Simonsez Charlie the Charmer. Duchess Visconti's Scottish Terriers are top producers in this region with over seventy champions carrying her Quercus prefix. Her top-producing bitch, with nine champions, was Ch. Woodmansey Wait For It, BOS at Montgomery County, 1981. Duchess Visconti has continued to import from England and Italy. Her most recent acquisition was Eng., Am. Ch. Kirthorn Lancelot, by Eng. Ch. Mayson Monopoly. Lancelot has proven to be a prolific sire in the United States.

Ch. Deblin's Back Talk.

```
                                                            Ch. Anstamm Dark Venture
                                        Ch. Anstamm Happy Venture
                                                            Ch. Fitzwilliam's Happy Girl
                    Ch. Anstamm Ruff-Me-Tuff Rowdy
                                                            Ch. Ruff-Me-Tuff Roustabout
                                        Ruff-Me-Tuff Demistuff
                                                            Ch. Sandoone Ruff-Me-Tuff Stuff
        Ch. Anstamm All American
                                                            Eng. Ch. Brio Fair'N'Square
                                        Ch. Gaywyn Square Deal
                                                            Cass of Cainedale
                    Ch. Anstamm Fancy That!
                                                            Ch. Anstamm Dazzler Dynamic
                                        Fitzwilliam's Fancy
                                                            Fitzwilliam's First Lady
Ch. Deblin's Back Talk
                                                            Ch. Anstamm Dark Venture
                                        Ch. Anstamm Happy Venture
                                                            Ch. Fitzwilliam's First Lady
                    Am. & Can. Ch. Bar-None's Dazzling Ad-Venture
                                                            Ch. Bardene Bobby Dazzler
                                        Anstamm Dazzling Deirdre
                                                            Ch. Anstamm Bright Promise
        Ch. Deblin's Small Talk
                                                            Ch. Seaforth's Kelly MacHamish
                                        Ch. Seaforth's Andrew MacHamish
                                                            Su-Et's Ginger Snap
                    Su-Et's Disney Girl
                                                            Ch. Schwer's Dynamic Happy
                                                                Fellow
                                        Su-Et's Happy Beth
                                                            Seaforth's Carrie Beth
```

Vikland

Bill and Kathy Bowers of Vikland Kennels started with a daughter of the top-producing Ch. Sandoone Prairyhill Rebecca. Their Ch. Prairyhill's Top O' The Morning finished quickly and produced four champions. The Bowers acquired two young stud dogs from the Midwest, Ch. Vikland's King Richard of Dunbar, by Ch. Dunbar's Democrat of Sandoone; and Ch. Sandgreg's Gemini O'Vikland, a son of Ch. Sandgreg's Editorial. By combining the lines of these two dogs with their Democrat daughter, Ch. Vikland's Top O' The Morning, the Bowers have successfully bred more than twenty champions. In 1985, they acquired Redoubts' Front Row Center, the littermate to Joan Duke's Ch. Balgair's Redoubts' Take A Bow. Front Row Center has sired four champions for the Bowers. One, Ch. Vikland's Curtain Call, is the fifth champion for the Bowers's top-producing bitch, Vikland's Shades O'Carbon.

FLORIDA

Florida may be a retirement haven, but most Scottie fanciers in the state are relatively new. Much credit for developing these new people belongs to the late Pete and Alice Clay. The Clays bred Scottish and Wire Fox Terriers in central Florida for years. Pete was a professional handler who piloted the BIS winner, Ch. Glenlivet Gordon of Jaudon. In 1986, Clay bought Ch. Blue Heather's Side Kick, a son of English import Ch. Make My Day of Mayson, Side Kick was a Group winner from the classes. The Clays most significant contribution, however, was not as breeders but as mentors. They were the driving force behind the formation of the regional club in the Tampa area.

Suncoast

Linda Terry grew up with Sealyham Terriers. When she decided to get a Scottish Terrier, she asked professional handler and Sealyham breeder, Marjorie Good, to find her a foundation bitch in England. Linda started her breeding program with Pendlehill Kelly who finished in 1988. Kelly is the dam of Linda's first homebred champion, Suncoast Runaway At Sunrise, by English import Ch. Kentwella Solo of Gaywyn. Linda went back to Pendlehill for another bitch and got Pendlehill Eve's Pride, a half-sister to Kelly. Ch. Pendlehill Eve's Pride finished in 1989, winning a Group enroute. Kelly and Eve's Pride have each produced two champions. An Eve's Pride daughter, Ch. Suncoast Nuit De Noel, owned by Donna Cambron, earned a major, like her dam, by winning a Group from the classes.

Thistlepark

Margo Park moved from California to Florida, bringing with her the litter brothers, Ravenscraig Rhythm and Ravenscraig Walk In The Park, bred by Al and Jeannie Jennings. Margo finished both boys, almost simultaneously.

The Parks then acquired two bitches: Heather's Maggie McGregor, out of Ch. Blue Heather Sidekick; and Ch. Charthill Patent Pending, by Bosworth out of a Hughcrest bitch. From Patent Pending came the Parks' most successful dog, Ch. Thistlepark Seas The Moment, Winners Dog at Montgomery County in 1993, and a Specialty, Group and BIS winner.

Other exhibitors active in Florida include Lois Bolding (Boldmere), Marilyn Finn (Finjolyn's), Charlene Hallenbeck (Lochnel), Ani Kramer (Remark), Harold and Bonnie Lamphear (Prodigee), Pat Silc (Silclanan), and Armando and Berenda Perez-Gili (Peregil).

THE MIDWEST

The influence of the Bardene dogs was most immediate in the far West (because Bingo lived there and because Boy Blue and Bobby Dazzler were shown there) but the Midwest was where they really made their mark. Boy Blue and Bobby Dazzler spent the major portion of their careers as stud dogs at home in Michigan where they and their descendants made Anstamm Kennels one of the most successful and influential in breed history.

Anstamm

Anthony Stamm began breeding Scottish Terriers in the late 1940s with dogs from Marie Stone's Kinclaven Kennels. Later, he added some Seaglen dogs from Robert Sharp in Canada. The best known of these was the Reimill Radiator grandson, Ch. Rear Admiral of Seaglen, who finished second in the competition for the Lloyd Trophy in 1957. Tony Stamm married Miriam Wise in 1955, and for the next five years, they bred and exhibited with some degree of success. They were, however, clearly dissatisfied with the results as each year they purchased one or two dogs of different lines. Although primarily known for blacks today, the Stamms were among the early breeders of wheatens out of their wheaten bitch, Ch. Gilkey's Golden Fantasy. It was not until the arrival of Boy Blue and Bobby Dazzler that the Stamms established a distinct line and "stamp" within the breed.

Boy Blue's first champion son, Ch. Anstamm Dark Venture, won the 1964 Lloyd Memorial Trophy and became the only sire with two Lloyd Trophy-winning offspring, Ch. Mar-De's Dark Felicia in 1967, and Ch. Anstamm Happy Venture, who won the trophy in 1972 and 1973. By this time, Miriam had retired and was handling all the dogs, including the champions, for over a decade. As Boy Blue, Dark Venture and Bobby Dazzler began to make their marks as sires, an increasing number of dogs bearing the Anstamm prefix were "stud puppies," that is, puppies bred by others using Anstamm studs and given to the Stamms in lieu of a stud fee. The great sire, Ch. Anstamm Happy Venture, was one such. Bred by Mary and Wilfred Schwer, Happy Venture's pedigree reflected a superb blend of the "Three B's" through some of their finest get. His dam, Ch. Fitzwilliam's Happy Girl, was out of Ed and

Am., Can. Ch. Anstamm Happy Venture.

```
                                                    Hargate Happy Boy
                                 Eng. Ch. Happy Kimbo
                                                    Bardene Barley Sugar
              Eng., Can. Am. Ch. Bardene Boy Blue
                                                    Bardene Beau Brummel
                                 Bardene Beau Peep
                                                    Bardene Blackbird
       Ch. Anstamm Dark Venture
                                                    Glendoune Gay Boy
                                 Ch. Sandbark Stalwart
                                                    Ch. Glendoune Gaytime
              Anstamm Paragon
                                                    Ch. Glad-Mac's Rolling Stone
                                 Ch. Galley Wren of Seaglen
                                                    The Black Wren of Seaglen
Am. & Can. Ch. Anstamm Happy Venture
                                                    Bardene Blue Starlite
                                 Eng., Can., Am. Ch. Bardene Bingo
                                                    Bardene Bluecap
              Ch. Bardene Bobby Dazzler
                                                    Ryeland Raffie
                                 Bardene Barefoot Contessa
                                                    Bardene Breezandi
       Ch. Fitzwilliam's Happy Girl
                                                    Eng., Can., Am. Ch. Bardene
                                                      Boy Blue
                                 Ch. Anstamm Dark Venture
                                                    Anstamm Paragon
              Ch. Mar-De's Dark Felicia
                                                    Reanda Kentwelle Kingpin
                                 Reanda Dalblane Moon Dream
                                                    Dalblane Michelle
```

Susan Fitzwilliam's Ch. MarDe's Dark Felicia, by the Stamms' Ch. Bardene Bobby Dazzler, both Lloyd Trophy winners. Happy Girl, bred to her grandfather, Ch. Anstamm Dark Venture, also a Lloyd winner, produced Happy Venture who would rewrite breed history.

Ch. Anstamm Happy
Sonata is shown here
with owner-handler
Miriam Stamm winning
BOB at the 1978 Scottish
Terrier Club of America
Rotating Specialty under
R. Stephen Shaw.
Martin Booth

Ch. Anstamm Heat
Wave, a great-grand-
daughter of Ch.
Anstamm Happy Sonata,
won BOB from the
classes at Montgomery
County in 1988 under
breeder-judge Jim
Reynolds. She won the
1989 Francis G. Lloyd
Memorial Trophy, two
more National Specialties
and a BIS, owner-
handled by Cindy Cooke.

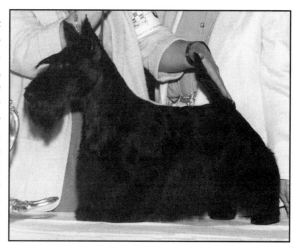

After twice winning the Lloyd Trophy, owner-handled Happy Venture settled down to do what he did best—sire puppies. He sired a total of ninety American champions, breaking not only the record for Scottish Terriers, but for all Terrier breeds, a record he held until 1986. Among his get were three American and two Canadian BIS winners, and numerous Specialty and Group winners. Many of the top winners of recent years, including the great bitches Ch. Braeburn's Close Encounter and Ch. Hughcrest Bottoms Up, are the grandchildren of Happy Venture. Fully one-third of the champions finished in the five years following his death in 1979 were his descendants. His top-winning offspring was Ch. Anstamm Happy Sonata, bred by Mike and Sharon Lowman of Sonata Kennels. Happy Sonata finished by going BOW at three successive Specialties, including the STCA event at Montgomery County in 1976. She went on to a successful specials career, winning nine BIS,forty-one Groups and five Specialty BOBs, including the 1977 STCA Specialty at Montgomery County, retiring in 1978 after winning Anstamm's fifth Lloyd Trophy. Happy Sonata was killed in a tragic accident shortly before her sixth birthday, after producing two litters that resulted in ten champions.

After Tony Stamm's death in 1974, Miriam carried on with the dogs by herself until, in 1978, she acquired her first partner, Cindy Cooke. Four years later, Linda Nolan joined Anstamm. Together, these three women have consistently produced top-winning and producing Scotties. Their top-producing sires in recent years were Ch. Anstamm Venture On (Happy Venture's top-producing son) with thirty-three champions and Ch. Anstamm Summer Lightning with fifty-four champions. In 1988, their Summer Lightning daughter, Anstamm Heat Wave, was BOB from the classes at Montgomery County, owner-handled by Cindy Cooke. Heat Wave went on to win two more national Specialties and the 1989 Lloyd Trophy. Two double Summer Lightning grandchildren have also won Lloyd Trophies for Anstamm: Ch. Anstamm Low Commotion, co-owned by Fred and Patty Brooks, in 1992 and Ch. Anstamm Back To The Future in 1994. Only Relgalf Kennels has won more Lloyd trophies and no other owner-handlers have won the trophy since Betty Munden did it in 1969 with her Ch. Gadiscot Guid Giftie. This kennel has produced over 200 champions through the end of 1994, including many Specialty, Group, and BIS winners.

Sandgreg

Sandgreg, also in Michigan, is another highly successful breeding line based on the Three Bs. John and Barbara DeSaye started in California with Ch. Wee Doc of Rancho Milandy, a grandson of Irene Robertson's great Ch. Glad Mac Rolling Stone. Wee Doc, although not a wheaten himself, was descended on both sides of his pedigree from Heather Asset. Bred to a granddaughter of Mrs. John Gilkey's Ch. Gilkey's Johnny Come Lately, another descendant of Heather Asset through the wheaten, Ch. Bramshire Blazing Sun, Wee Doc sired Ch. Sandgreg's Ball O'Fire, the first of many Sandgreg wheaten champions.

The DeSayes subsequently acquired two bitches from the John Charves, Ch. Charves Dazzler Design, litter sister to the great Ch. Charves Dazzler Dyke, and Ch. Charves Dashing Dawtie. Design, bred to Ch. Bardene Bingo, produced a litter of four champions, including Ch. Sandgreg's Keno Ticket, a Specialty winner in the United States and a BIS winner in Canada. It was Dawtie, however, who would produce two of the breed's most influential sires, Ch. Sandgreg's Headliner and Ch. Sandgreg's Editorial. Headliner was older and had a successful show career, winning the 1979 Scottish Terrier Club of America Rotating Specialty and a number of Groups, all owner-handled. Headliner's younger full brother, Editorial, sacrificed a glamorous show career in order not to compete against Headliner. Instead, Editorial stayed home and became the breed's third leading sire, with sixty-two champions. Editorial's get took honors at Specialties across the country. His top-winning offspring was Ch. Sandgreg's Foxmoor, winner of the Lloyd Trophy in 1987 and 1988. Foxmoor was a BIS winner and won eighteen Specialty BOBs, including three Nationals. He capped his career by winning BOB at Montgomery County in 1989. Sadly, Foxmoor sired only a few litters, but one of

Ch. Anstamm Summer Lightning. *Bernard Kernan*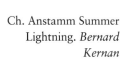

```
                                                      Ch. Anstamm Dark Venture
                                 Ch. Anstamm Happy Venture
                                                      Ch. Fitzwilliam's Happy Girl
              Ch. Anstamm Venture On
                                                      Eng. & Am. Ch. Gaywyn
                                                      Likely Lad
                                 Ch. Anstamm Most Likely
                                                      Anstamm Happy Landings
       Ch. Anstamm Up Front
                                                      Ch. Anstamm Dark Venture
                                 Ch. Anstamm Happy Venture
                                                      Ch. Fitzwilliam's Happy Girl
              Ch. Anstamm Happy Sonata
                                                      Brunnoch Domino
                                 Ch. Reanda Razziella
                                                      Barrow Green Renewal
Ch. Anstamm Summer Lightning
                                                      Ch. Anstamm Dark Venture
                                 Ch. Anstamm Happy Venture
                                                      Ch. Fitzwilliam's Happy Girl
              Ch. Anstamm Venture On
                                                      Eng. & Am. Ch. Gaywyn
                                                      Likely Lad
                                 Ch. Anstamm Most Likely
                                                      Anstamm Happy Landings
       Ch. Sun-Ray's Summer Day
                                                      Ch. Bardene Bobby Dazzler
                                 Ch. Anstamm Dazzler Dynamic
                                                      Ch. Anstamm Dark Paragon
              Fitzwilliams Fancy
                                                      Ch. Lettswynne The Senator's
                                                      Boy
                                 Fitzwilliam's First Lady
                                                      Ch. Fitzwilliam's Happy Girl
```

his seven champion offspring, Ch. Koch's Shadow Fox of Glenlee, is the grandam of Ch. Gaelforce Post Script.

Editorial's top-producing son is Ch. Sandgreg's Second Edition, currently the breed's second top sire, with seventy-two champions. The DeSayes sold Second Edition in 1984, shortly after he was Winners Dog at Montgomery County. When Editorial passed away suddenly in the summer of 1985, the DeSayes were able to buy back the dog who would surpass his famous sire. Second Edition's top-winning offspring is Ch. Brookhill's Morning Edition, twice BIS at Montgomery County.

Editorial's brother, Ch. Sandgreg's Headliner, sired eighteen champions, including the great Ch. Braeburn's Close Encounter, the breed's all-time top-winner; Ch. Braeburn's Main Event, sire of twenty-five champions for Bengt and Cynthia Wallgren; and Ch. Sandgreg's Square Deal, sire of twenty-two champions for owner Irene Robertson.

The boys are not the only top-producers at Sandgreg. Ch. Sandgreg's Sweet Luv is the second top-producing bitch in breed history, with a total of eighteen champions. Ch. Sandgreg's Sweet Charity is the dam of eleven and Charity's daughter, Ch. Sandgreg's Sweet Scarlet, is the dam of eight.

Ch. Sandgreg's Editorial

- Ch. Firebrand's Bookmaker
  - Ch. Carnation Casino
    - Ch. Bardene Bingo
      - Bardene Blue Starlite
      - Bardene Bluecap
    - Ch. Carnation Cynthia
      - Ch. Westpark Derriford Baffie
      - Ch. Carnation Dark Modiste
  - Ch. Firebrand's Dark Velour
    - Ch. Bardene Bingo
      - Bardene Blue Starlite
      - Bardene Bluecap
    - Ch. Firebrand's Mustard
      - Ch. Westpark Rio Grande
      - Ch. Firebrand's Fascinator
- Ch. Charves Dashing Dawtie
  - Ch. Charves Dazzler Dyke
    - Ch. Bardene Bobby Dazzler
      - Ch. Bardene Bingo
      - Bardene Barefoot Contessa
    - Ch. Charves Elsie Marley
      - Ch. Bardene Boy Blue
      - Ch. Balachan Gambit
  - Ch. Charves Maggie Lauder
    - Ch. Gilkey's Johnny Come Lately
      - Ch. Gilkey's Fancy Tammie
      - Apfel's Precious Penny
    - Ch. Balachan Gambit
      - Ch. Balachan Agitator
      - Ch. Glendoune Gwenda

Ch. Sandgreg's Editorial.

Ch. Sandgreg's Sweet
Luv. *Callea*

Editorial, Headliner and Second Edition sired lovely dogs of all colors, but their place in history will rest largely on the fact that their wheaten off-spring were the equal of their black and brindle progeny. For years, wheatens, like blacks, were wrongly thought to have certain undesirable traits some-how linked to coat color. Wheatens were said to have coarse heads, large eyes, bad coats, and numerous other problems. In fact, the only time wheatens were not equal in all respects to blacks and brindles was when breeding stock was

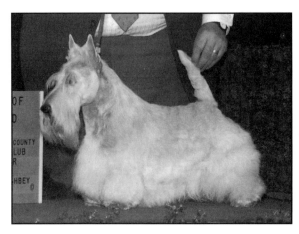

Ch. Sandgreg's Foxmoor.
John Ashbey

selected on the basis of color alone. The DeSayes wisely selected their dogs on overall quality—as a result, the Sandgreg sires produced good dogs of all colors. Still, it was the exciting wheatens who put them on the map. Among these were Ch. Sandgreg's Sweet Charity, multiple Group and Specialty winner and top-producing dam of eleven champions (including Foxmoor); Ch. Wychwyre Liberty, first wheaten Winners Bitch at Montgomery County; and the 1986 Lloyd Trophy winner, Ch. Sandgreg's Sweet Luv. Sweet Luv was the second wheaten Winners Bitch at Montgomery County, the third BIS wheaten in America and the first wheaten Lloyd winner. The DeSayes' success proves Dr. Ewing's maxim that "there was never a good Scottie with a bad color."

Braeburn

Anstamm and Sandgreg provided the foundation for Ron and Helen Girling's Braeburn Scottish Terriers. They purchased their foundation bitch, Anstamm Happy Moment, from Miriam Stamm with an agreement to finish her championship, breed her, and return a puppy to Mrs. Stamm. Happy Moment finished easily, and the Girlings bred her, unsuccessfully, to Ch. Dunbar's Democrat of Sandoone. On her next season, they decided to try a stud nearer home. Mrs. Stamm wanted her bred to Ch. Sandgreg's Editorial but the Girlings preferred Headliner. They agreed to compromise. The Girlings would breed Happy Moment first to Headliner, and to Editorial for her next litter. Miriam would wait for the Editorial litter to take her puppy. Happy Moment produced two dogs and two bitches from the breeding to Headliner.

The Girlings sold one male and brought the others to the DeSayes when the puppies were about twelve weeks old. Headliner's co-owners, Bill and Kathy McGinnis, wanted a puppy from this litter, and Mrs. DeSaye encouraged her friends Evelyn and Frank Morrow to look at the bitches in this litter. The McGinnises arrived first and each picked out a puppy. Bill liked the boy, but Kathy wanted the smaller girl. The Morrows were late, so Bill and Kathy took both puppies. When the Morrows did arrive, only the bigger bitch was left. She did not impress Frank and Evelyn, so they left without her. Being late that day cost them the opportunity to buy Ch. Braeburn's Close Encounter, and they also missed Ch. Braeburn's Topic of Sandgreg, future dam of eight champions.

The McGinnises named the male puppy Braeburn's Main Event, who finished at nine months. His sister, Braeburn's Close Encounter, named "Shannon," finished at a year, in October 1979, and went home to mature.

Shannon began her specials career inauspiciously at the Scottish Terrier Club of Michigan Specialty in September of 1980, where she was left out of the ribbons. Two weeks later, she won her first BIS. By year's end, Shannon, handled by George Ward, had won five Groups and another Best. The McGinnises financed her show career during 1981, but by August 1982, they could not continue. Shannon was pulled from the show ring with thirty-six BIS. For the next few months, Ward searched for a new owner.

In January 1983, with new owners Sonny and Alan Novick, Shannon came out of retirement. Shannon was now five years old, an age when many bitches are disinclined to return to the ring. Not Shannon—she won an amazing ninety-five Groups out of 103 BOBs!

Ch. Braeburn's Close Encounter, the top-winning Scottish Terrier of all-time. *Booth*

Ch. Sandgreg's Second Edition. *Booth*

                                              Ch. Bardene Bingo
                          Ch. Carnation Casino
                                              Ch. Carnation Cynthia
        Ch. Firebrand's Bookmaker
                                              Ch. Bardene Bingo
                          Ch. Firebrand's Dark Velour
                                              Ch. Firebrand's Mustard
Ch. Sandgreg's Editorial
                                              Ch. Bardene Bobby Dazzler
                          Ch. Charves Dazzler Dyke
                                              Ch. Charves Elsie Marley
        Ch. Charves Dashing Dawtie
                                              Ch. Gilkey's Johnny Come
                                              Lately
                          Ch. Charves Maggie Lauder
                                              Ch. Balachan Gambit
Ch. Sandgreg's Second Edition
                                              Ch. Carnation Casino
                          Ch. Firebrand's Bookmaker
                                              Ch. Firebrand's Dark Velour
        Ch. Sandgreg's Headliner
                                              Ch. Charves Dazzler Dyke
                          Ch. Charves Dashing Dawtie
                                              Ch. Charves Maggie Lauder
Ch. Braeburn's Topic Of Sandgreg
                                              Ch. Anstamm Dark Venture
                          Ch. Anstamm Happy Venture
                                              Ch. Fitzwilliam's Happy Girl
        Ch. Anstamm Happy Moment
                                              Ch. Bardene Bobby Dazzler
                          Anstamm Dazzling Deirdre
                                              Ch. Anstamm Bright Promise

Ch. Sandgreg's Headliner, co-owned by William McInnes and Barbara DeSaye (handling), is a multiple Group and Specialty winner and a top sire. He is the sire of the breed's all-time top winner, Ch. Braeburn's Close Encounter.

She won sixty BIS, only eleven fewer than all other Terriers combined that year. By 1984, Shannon was unstoppable. She was the top dog in the country, winning a record 113 Terrier Groups and seventy-two BIS. Amazingly, she won the Terrier Group every single time she won BOB! Shannon made her first trip to Montgomery County in 1984 where, to no one's surprise, she was BIS. The 1984 AKC Centennial Show was billed as a showdown between Shannon and her nearest competitor, the great German Shepherd Dog, Ch. Covy Tucker Hill's Manhattan. The showdown never took place since Shannon was upset in the breed by Betty Cooper's Ch. Perlor Playboy.

The day after Thanksgiving 1984, Alan Novick died, and once again, it appeared that Shannon's career would be ended for financial reasons. Instead, Dan and Amelia Musser, longtime clients of Ward, assumed Shannon's expenses. Without a word of publicity, the Mussers made it possible for Shannon to set a record of 201 Bests in Show before she retired in May 1985.

Understandably, Bill McGinnis wanted to breed Shannon. Ward had other ideas, however, and although Shannon was bred one time, it was late in her season and she did not concieve. While McGinnis was awaiting Shannon's nonexistent litter, her old nemesis, the German Shepherd, Manhattan, was still out winning Bests. As it became more likely that he would break Shannon's BIS record, Ward decided in the summer of 1986, to bring Shannon out again. Skeptics doubted that she could maintain her dominance. After all, she was eight years old then and had been retired for a year. This was no problem for Shannon. Shown nineteen times, she won every Group and thirteen BIS.

Shannon made one final appearance in the show ring at Montgomery County in 1990. Rumors had swept the dog fancy for months before the show but many doubted that the twelve-year-old bitch would really be shown. The day of the show was cold and clear in the morning, but by the time the Veteran Bitch class was called, the sun was beating down on the dogs and their exhibitors. The ring was surrounded by fans eager to see Shannon one last time. She was greeted by thunderous applause, and she responded as she always had, by putting on a show. She was exuberant, playing with her handler, on the edge of being out of control and then settling down just enough to keep him on his toes. In the end, Shannon bowed to the younger Ch. Brookhill's Morning Edition, who went on to win BIS. No one who saw Shannon that day, however, will ever forget the grand old showgirl who never stopped competing.

Terriwall

Still a third prominent kennel is located in Michigan—Bengt and Cynthia Wallgren's Terriwall Scotties. Both Wallgrens had pet Scottish Terriers as children, and, like so many breeders, started their show career with a pet. They purchased their first show dog from the son of Robert McKinven. Shortly after finishing Ch. Ardmore Angus McTavish, they purchased their foundation bitch, Anstamm Bright Promise, a Dark Venture granddaughter out of a Boy Blue daughter. Bright Promise came from a line of producing bitches. Her mother, Ch. Anstamm Ebony, produced five champions, as did her grandmother, Aldon's Angela of Anstamm. Bred to Ch. Bardene Bobby Dazzler, Bright Promise produced seven champions, including Ch. Terriwall Andy

Ch. Braeburn's Main Event, owned by Bengt and Cynthia Wallgren, is Headliner's top-producing son. The sire of twenty-five champions, he is a litter brother of Ch. Braeburn's Close Encounter.

Dazzler, a Group and Specialty BOB winner. From that start, Terriwall has bred more than thirty champions. In addition, they have imported several Bardene dogs, most recently Ch. Bardene Bookmark and Ch. Bardene Be My Guest. The acquisition of Ch. Braeburn's Main Event, a great-grandson of Bright Promise, had a significant impact on the Terriwall breeding program. Main Event was their top-producing sire with twenty-five champions.

Wychwyre

Bill and Sue Martin purchased their first Scottie as a pet through an ad in the newspaper. Their first champion, Sandgreg's Casey at Bat, was a grandson of the DeSayes' Ch. Sandgreg's Keno Ticket. Their second champion was an Editorial daughter, Ch. Sandgreg's Kismet. Kismet is the Arabic word for "fate," and she was aptly named, since Kismet was fated to become not only a top-producing dam of six champions, but the dam of three wheaten bitches who make the color so popular today: Ch. Sandgreg's Sweet Charity, Ch. Wychwyre Liberty and Ch. Sandgreg's Sweet Luv. Liberty was the first wheaten bitch to earn points at a National Specialty and is the dam of ten champions. Her crowning achievement however, was whelping a litter of ten puppies, all surviving. Liberty's son, Ch. Sandgreg's Johnny Come Lately, was a top-producing sire at Sandgreg with thirteen champions to his credit.

Barbary

Because their first try at showing was unsuccessful, Ron and Maurine McConnell went from Afghan Hounds to Scotties. They were determined this time to get a dog that was really good enough to be a champion when they cautiously bought a brindle male puppy, Anstamm Jolly Roger, from Miriam Stamm. During kennel visits Maurine would watch Mrs. Stamm trim, then describe the procedures to Ron. Amazingly enough, he learned quickly. As to the exhibiting, Jolly Roger was a very tough little dog. Maurine let some-one else handle him at a Specialty and burst into tears when he began sparring. She thought he would be excused for misbehaving. When he won his class instead, she began to really understand some of the differences between Terriers and Hounds. Jolly Roger sired four champions out of a daughter of Ch. Amescot's Grand Slam. One of these, Ch. Anstamm Miss Conduct, was the dam of the McConnells' multiple Specialty BOB winner, Ch. Barbary Miss Manners. Miss Conduct's other daughter, Ch. Barbary Bad Medicine, is the dam of Ch. Barbary Somebody Stop Me.

Dunbar

Richard Hensel had been breeding Scottish Terriers in Ohio since the late 1950s. His early champions were fairly closely linebred on Winning Trick, but he was clearly not satisfied with what he was producing. He tried one line and then another until he acquired Eng., Am. Ch. Gosmore Gillson Highland King from Clive and Mabel Pillsbury. They had imported King and his kennelmate, Eng., Am. Ch. Gosmore Eilburn Admaration, in 1969. Both were English BIS winners and continued their show ring successes in America. Admaration, who had been England's Top Dog, all breeds, won the Lloyd Trophy in 1970 (his first full year in the US) and 1971. During those years, Admaration's show record eclipsed that of Highland King. Perhaps that is why Highland King finally went to Hensel. In any event, the acquisition of Highland King was a turning point for the Dunbar Scotties.

At Dunbar, Highland King became a top sire, eventually producing thirty-five champions. Highland King's best known offspring, and the top-winning dog to carry the Dunbar prefix, was Ch. Dunbar's Democrat of Sandoone, bred by Betty Malinka of Sandoone Kennels. Democrat, handled by Bergit Coady, compiled a record unmatched by any male Scottish Terrier, with eighteen BIS, twelve Specialty BOBs (including the 1975 STCA Specialty, where he won from the classes), and fifty-two Groups. Like his father, Democrat was a consistent producer, siring forty-eight champions, including the 1981 and 1982 Lloyd Trophy winner, Ch. Democratic Victory, and the great Ch. Hughcrest Bottoms Up. Hensel passed away suddenly in May 1984, and his dogs were dispersed.

Eng., Am. Ch. Gosmore Gillson Highland King.

Ch. Dunbar's Democrat of Sandoone with handler Bergit Coady.

Hil-Ray

Ray and Hilda Bigelow started with a well-bred pet bitch, and in two generations of careful breeding, they produced their first champion, Hil-Ray's Smoke Signal, by Ch. Gaidoune Great Bear. Their first champion bitch, Gaidoune Gale of Hil-Ray's, went on to produce seven champions. Her son, Ch. Hil-Ray's Anchor Man, sired by Ch. Bardene Bingo, was a top-10 ranked Scottie in the early 1970s. About this time, the Bigelows, in co-ownership with Blanche and Ed Nutter, acquired their top winner of all-time, Ch. Dunbar's Distinction, from Dick Hensel. Distinction, by Happy Venture, was a multiple Specialty, Group and BIS winner, all owner-handled. Although not heavily used at stud, Distinction produced three champion daughters out of the Nutter's Ch. Anstamm King's Tribute: Ch. Reality Stethoscope, Ch. Reality Tassie Lynn, and the Group-winning Ch. Hil-Ray's Reality. These bitches are behind a number of champions in Ohio and the East.

Wayridge

Cass and Wayne Ridgley were Pekingese breeders using the kennel name *Ridge Lei* when Cass's sister in California convinced her to try a Scottie. Charves Kate Dalrymple was a daughter of Ch. Gilkey's Johnny Come Lately and the Charves foundation bitch, Ch. Balachan Gambit. Kate never finished but like so many of the Charves bitches, she was a solid foundation for a long line of champions. Kate was the dam of two champions by Ch. Bardene Bobby Dazzler, but it was her nonchampion daughter, Ridge Lei Dazzling Wendy, bred to Ch. Bardene Bingo, who would produce the first Ridge Lei Group winner, Ch. Ridge Lei Bobby Bingo. Dazzling Wendy was also the dam of the first champion to carry the Ridgleys new kennel name, Ch. Wayridge Beau Bingo. The Ridgleys had decided that Ridge Lei, a suitable name for their Pekingese, sounded too oriental for a kennel composed increasingly of Scots. Dazzling Wendy's top-producing daughter, Ch. Ridge Lei Sassy Girl, produced six champions.

In 1969, the Ridgleys bought Wayridge Warlock from Hilda and Ray Bigelow. Warlock, a son of Ch. Hil-Ray's Smoke Signal, was a Group and Specialty winner and sired nine champions. The last homebred, owner-handled champion for the Ridgleys was Ch. Wayridge Bold Ruler, a grandson of Carol Plott's Ch. Wayridge Becky Nic Bobby.

Lochlaymen

Pauline and Roy Lay put obedience titles on their first two Scotties before becoming interested in breeding and showing in conformation. In 1974, they acquired Wayridge Touch O'Mink from the Ridgleys, becoming the first of many successful Ohio breeders to found a line on a Wayridge bitch. Touch O'Mink, a granddaughter of Warlock, finished at thirteen months and had won her first Group before an emergency C-Section and spaying cut short her specials career. The Lays bought another Wayridge bitch, Wayridge War Maiden, a Warlock daughter, and a dog, Ch. Meade's Touch Of Andy, whose pedigree was strongly linebred on The Three B's. Bred to Touch O'Mink, Touch Of Andy sired the first Lochlaymen champion, Lochlaymen's Storm Warning. Storm Warning went on to a successful specials career. Unfortunately, Storm Warning was a carrier of Von Willebrand's Disease and so was only bred twice, siring five champions out of only eight get.

In the mid 1980s, Judy Hughes placed her Bar-None's Forget-Me-Not with the Lays. Forget-Me-Not already had three champions when she came to live with Roy and Pauline. Bred to Ch. Hughcrest Home-Brew, Forget-Me-Not produced four more champions. The most successful of these was Hughcrest Daiquiri Doll, Best in Sweepstakes and BOB from the classes at the 1986 STCA Specialty at Montgomery. Her younger brother, Hughcrest Kentucky Brew, was Winners Dog and BOW at Montgomery the following year. Daiquiri Doll and Kentucky Brew were handled to these wins by Judy Hughes.

In 1990, Pauline brought some of her old bloodlines back into her breeding when she bought Colemar Irish Rebellion, a descendant of Storm Warning, from Tim and Mary Ann Cole.

Colwick

Dave Luken was only eight years old when he got his first Scottish Terrier puppy from Goldie and John Seagraves. He and his wife, Ginny, bought their

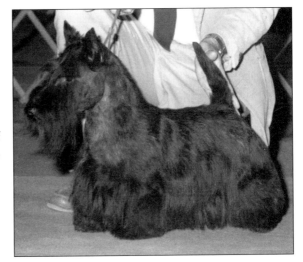

Ch. Charthill Worthy Of
Colwick.

```
                                                    Ch. Anstamm Dark Venture
                                Ch. Anstamm Happy Venture
                                                    Ch. Fitzwilliam's Happy Girl
                   Ch. Anstamm Venture On
                                                    Eng. & Am. Ch. Gaywyn
                                                      Likely Lad
                                Ch. Anstamm Most Likely
                                                    Anstamm Happy Landings
         Ch. Sun-Ray's Summer Sun
                                                    Eng. Ch. Brio Fair'N'Square
                                Ch. Gaywyn Square Deal
                                                    Cass of Kainedale
                   Ch. Sun-Ray's Summer Day
                                                    Ch. Anstamm Dazzler
                                                      Dynamic
                                Fitzwilliam's Fancy
                                                    Fitzwilliam's First Lady
Ch. Charthill Worthy Of Colwick
                                                    Eng. Ch. Brio Fair'N'Square
                                Ch. Gaywyn Square Deal
                                                    Cass of Kainedale
                   Ch. Anstamm Calico Kid
                                                    Ch. Anstamm Dazzler
                                                      Dynamic
                                Fitzwilliam's Fancy
                                                    Fitzwilliam's First Lady
         Ch. Colwick Time After Time
                                                    Ch. Meade's Touch Of Andy
                                Ch. Lochlaymen's Storm Warning
                                                    Ch. Wayridge Touch O'Mink
                   Ch. Colwick First Time Around
                                                    Ch. Wayridge Warlock
                                Ch. Wayridge War Dance
                                                    Camyscot Wee Bonnie Binnie
```

first show bitch, Wayridge War Dance, in 1976 from the Ridgleys. Pauline Lay helped them condition and show War Dance, who finished with four majors. They finished their second champion, Lochlaymen's King of Colwick themselves. Although they bred very few litters, one of their champion bitches, Colwick Time After Time, would have a considerable impact on the breed as the dam of Ch. Charthill Worthy of Colwick.

Charthill

Tom and Charla Hill bought a pet male from Stewart Gettle in 1966, and with his help and inspiration, they developed an interest in showing. In 1981, while living in Dayton, Ohio, the Hills obtained Wayridge Abigail, by Ch. Sandgreg's Headliner, from the Ridgleys. Abigail quickly became their first champion and the dam of six champions. The real foundation for the Hills' very successful breeding program, however, was a male puppy out of Ch. Colwick Time After Time. Time After Time was a daughter of Ch. Anstamm Calico Kid, who was a son of the great producing bitch, Fitzwilliam's Fancy. Her dam was out of the Lukens' Ch. Wayridge War Dance and the Lay's Ch. Lochlaymen's Storm Warning.

"Bosworth," grew up to be a multiple Group and Specialty winner and a prolific sire. He produced forty-one champions, including the BIS winner, Ch. Caevnes Devil's Due, and the 1990 Montgomery County Winners Bitch, Ch. Charthill Tiger Rose. Bosworth's son, Ch. Charthill Seaworthy is following in his sire's footsteps with thirteen champions to date, including the BIS winner, Ch. Thistlepark Seas The Moment. Ch. Charthill Bridget By Briggs, with nine champions to her credit, is the Hills' top-producing bitch. The Hills have bred over forty champions, many who finished with wins at Specialties, and nearly all owner-handled.

Tandem

Tonna Hines' first champion, Tandem's Hellzafire, was sired by Roy and Pauline Lay's Ch. Wayridge Dark Raider out of a homebred bitch. Tonna bought Lochlaymen's Harvest Moon from Roy and Pauline and finished her quickly. Harvest Moon is the dam of two of Tonna's three Sweepstakes winners. The first, Ch. Tandem's Tornado, sired by a son of Ch. Hughcrest Bottoms Up, was Best in Sweeps at the 1988 Atlanta Specialty. The second, Ch. Tandem's Flash of Lightning, was sired by Ch. Anstamm Summer Lightning. In his second litter, Flash of Lightning sired the 1990 Montgomery County Best in Sweeps, Ch. Tandem's Chances Are, co-bred by Ruth Ann Lungociu.

Sandoone

Betty Malinka lived near the sand dunes on the southern shore of Lake Michigan, which gave her kennel its famous name: Sandoone. She began her

Ch. Charthill Tiger Rose is shown here with breeder-owner-handler, Charla Hill.
Sue Baines

breeding program with some of the best from nearby breeders in Indiana. Her first champion, Frangan Blue Chip Of Sandoone, was one of three champions in a litter bred by Frances Gannon. Ms. Malinka added bitches from Hosea Bayor's Fran-Jean kennel and Mary German's Cantie line. Ms. Malinka hired Bergit Zakschewski, a very talented young kennel girl who was working for Elizabeth Meyer in England. Today this girl is better known as Bergit Coady, one of the top terrier handlers in the United States.

With Mrs. Coady's help, Ms. Malinka begin to acquire a number of stud dogs. She imported Ch. Reanda Rocksand and Ch. Reanda Rosko from England. She bought the Bingo son, Ch. Sandgreg's Poker Chip, and the Specialty and Group-winning Ch. Sandoone Rob Roy of Mil-Bran. Rob Roy was by Ch. Gillsie Prince William, a son of Eng. Ch. Kennelgarth Viking. Prince William was purchased for Milarie Bliss by Bergit Coady, who handled him to his championship. Although his show career was undistinguished by any Specialty or Group wins, Prince William proved to be an outstanding sire, eventually producing twenty-three champions. Rob Roy was one of his top-winning sons and he in turn sired Ms. Malinka's Lloyd Trophy winner, Ch. Sandoone Royal Barclay, top Scottish Terrier in 1975. Royal Barclay's record was soon eclipsed, however, by the young Sandoone-bred dog owned by Dick Hensel, Ch. Dunbar's Democrat of Sandoone. In addition to breeding dozens of outstanding champions during more than twenty-five years as a breeder, Betty Malinka was the heart and soul of the Scottish Terrier Club of Chicago until her death in 1978.

Prairyhill

A great Sandoone bitch was the foundation for Prairyhill, another successful Midwestern kennel of the 1970s. In 1970, Louise Lemke and her daughter, Karen, were looking for a dog to show in 4-H obedience competition. They decided to get a Scottie because no one else they knew had one and because they thought it was a "cute" breed. They purchased Sandoone Prairyhill Rebecca with money saved by Karen (and some contributed by Karen's grandmother). Ms. Malinka advised them to contact Mrs. Coady for help with the grooming. That was the beginning of a good friendship. Rebecca was bred to Ch. Gillsie Prince William and whelped the first two of nine Prairyhill champions they would produce together. Mrs. Coady taught Karen to groom and encouraged her to show Rebecca herself. Rebecca went on to finish her championship quickly, but these honors did not cause Karen to forget her original goal—a 4-H trophy for the highest scoring registered dog. It was to be Rebecca's only failure—she did earn her CD, but without enthusiasm. The highlight of her obedience career came when she captured and killed a mouse in front of the judge's table. Rebecca was 1975's top-producing terrier dam.

Ruff-Me-Tuff

Jake and Nancy McClosky were also beneficiaries of Betty Malinka's Sandoone heritage. Their first champion, Sandoone Ruff-Me-Tuff Toffee, was a daughter of Betty's English import, Ch. Reanda Rocksand. Bred to Betty's Ch. Reanda Rosko, Toffee produced the McClosky's first champion, Ruff-Me-Tuff Trump Suit. Their own imported bitch, Ch. Stedplane Suki, was a daughter of Eng. Ch. Reanda Ringold, and she produced four champions, including the first Ruff-Me-Tuff Group and Specialty winner, Ch. Ruff-Me-Tuff Roustabout. Roustabout's show career as a top-ranked Scottish Terrier spanned four years between 1973 and 1976. Bred back to Ch. Ruff-Me-Tuff Run Amuk, another Suki offspring by Eng., Am. Ch. Gosmore Gillson Highland King, Roustabout sired Jake and Nancy's top-winning Ch. Ruff-Me-Tuff Rabble Rouser, the 1979 and 1980 Lloyd Trophy winner, owned by Bill and Judy Shanholtz. The McCloskeys were also the breeders of Nancy Becker's Ch. Anstamm Go For It!, a multiple Group and Specialty winner. Their last import was Ch. Reanda Royal Sovereign, a successful sire of nine champions.

Bear-Bee

Debbie Kinsey Mims's Bear-Bee line was also based on imported bitches: her first champion, Reanda Relcia, another Reanda Ringold daughter, and Bonnie of Argyll, a granddaughter of Eng. Ch. Kennelgarth Great Scot. Relcia, like so many Reanda bitches, was an outstanding producer. Her first champion son, Bear-Bee Bo Jangles, by Ch. Ruff-Me-Tuff Roustabout, was Winners Dog at the 1974 STCA Rotating Specialty and went on to a successful specials career. Still another Relcia son, Ch. Reanda Bear Bee King, by Highland King, was the number three Scottish Terrier in 1977. King's sister, Ch. Dunbar's Bear Bee Doll, tied for the top-producing Scottie bitch of 1977 and was behind many top-winning Texas dogs of the early 1980s. Although Relcia was Mrs. Mims's top-producing bitch, Bonnie of Argyll was the dam of Debbie's all-time top-winning dog, Ch. Bear Bee's Bit of Dunbar, a BIS winner ranked in the top ten during 1976 and 1977.

Camydnas

Allen Jack Cartwright started his breeding program about the same time as Mrs. Malinka, using very similar lines. His early Camydnas (Sandymac spelled backwards) champions combined Fran-Jean, Frangan and Blanart bloodlines. He later introduced crosses to Anstamm and Gilkey. He bred over twenty champions and provided foundation stock for a number of Midwestern breeders.

Mac Cal

Ruth Ann and David Krause began with Camydnas stock. They fell in love with someone else's pet Scottie named Laddie, described by Mrs. Krause as "an eccentric Scottie who excelled in character though he lacked in conformation." After listening to Laddie's owners describe their dog's wonderful character and exploits, the Krauses decided that their lives would not be complete without a Scottie of their own. They purchased their first two champion Scots from a couple who were disbanding their kennel. The bitch, Ch. Camydnas Calamity Jane, was a double granddaughter of Allen Cartwright's top-producing Ch. Camydnas Island Queen. The dog, Ch. Camydnas MacGregor, was a son of Ch. Camydnas Anstamm Blue Dart, a Boy Blue son. The Krauses then purchased Hughcrest Happy-Go-Lucky, a Happy Venture son, who finished quickly and sired the first homebred Mac-Cal champion, Lady Fortune O' Mac Cal. The Krauses's next champion, Sandgreg's Warrior of Mac Cal, like so many of Editorial's offspring, carried the wheaten gene. He passed this on to his nonchampion daughter, Mac Cal's

Ch. Jabberwok Bristol Stomp is shown here with his breeder-owner-handler Merle Taylor, after winning BOB at the 1982 STC of Greater Dayton Specialty under breeder-judge Elizabeth Cooper. *Alverson*

Mi Tee Dina Mite, and she produced the Krauses's first wheaten champion, Jacob the Best, co-bred with Helen and Herb Malzacher. Over the past ten years, the Krauses have greatly curtailed their breeding program but have still managed to produce over a dozen champions, many of whom have finished with points at Specialties.

Dana

Nancy Fingerhut was a successful Miniature Schnauzer breeder when she took a Scottie in the ring for Miriam Stamm and decided that "basic black" suited her. At Nancy's request, Miriam found her a black bitch, Anstamm Happy Days, a granddaughter of the Lemkes' Ch. Sandoone Prairyhill Rebecca, CD, by Ch. Happy Venture. Happy Days had a "producer's pedigree," as did Nancy's next bitch, Ch. Hughcrest Hot Fudge Sunday, out of Fitzwilliam's Fancy, also by Happy Venture. Both bitches lived up to their promise, with Happy Days producing three champions in her first litter, including Ch. Dana's Constant Comment, making Happy Days the top-producing bitch for 1979. Hot Fudge Sunday produced six champions, including Ch. Dana's Typesetter, multiple Group winner and top-10 ranked Scottish Terrier during 1983 and 1984; Ch. Hughcrest Hellzapoppin', Dee Carter's 1980 Montgomery

Ch. Jabberwok Here Comes The Sun, the top-winning son of Ch. Jabberwok Bristol Stomp, was BOB at Montgomery County in 1983 under breeder-judge T. Howard Snethen. He was handled by Merle Taylor. *William Gilbert*

County winner; and Ch. Dana's Amber Edition, dam of nine champions. Nancy's third bitch was also beautifully bred. Ch. Sandgreg's Barbie Doll was a daughter of Ch. Braeburn's Main Event, brother to Close Encounter, out of Sandgreg's Special Edition, an Editorial sister. Barbie Doll produced four champions, including the Group-placing Ch. Dana's Dynamite Doll. Hot Fudge Sunday's top-producing son was Ch. Dana's Sunday Edition, who carried the wheaten gene. Since he was not heavily campaigned or promoted as a stud dog, few breeders used him. When his last litter, out of Ch. Hycourt's Blush With Pride, produced three lovely champion bitches, he was suddenly in demand but, sadly, was too old to begin an active career as a sire. His daughter, Ch. Dana's Gold Coin, was the dam of five champions. As Mrs. Fingerhut's judging career gathered momentum, she chose to focus on this area, and is no longer breeding or actively exhibiting.

Jabberwok

Also in Illinois, Merle and Carolyn Taylor have combined owner-handling their Scottish Terriers with professionally handling dogs of all breeds. The Taylors started showing Scotties in 1972 with a dog purchased from Thelma Miller. Thelma had been campaigning her Bingo grandson, Ch. Rinklestone Bryndle Bryar, that year. The Taylor's first champion, Rinklestone Black Rhapsody, was Bryndle Bryar's littermate. They bought Neidfyre Bright Star, a daughter of Ch. Seagraves Rogue's Image out of Gail Gaines' Ch. Neidfyre Almanie Whistle. Bright Star never finished but produced four champions by Bryndle Bryar. One of those, Ch. Jabberwok Bristol Stomp, attracted much favorable attention as a puppy and would become the Taylors' first multiple Group and Specialty winner. Bristol Stomp sired eighteen champions. His top-winning son was Ch. Jabberwok Here Comes the Sun, an all-breed BIS-winner, and BOB winner at Montgomery County in 1983.

In 1986, the Taylors campaigned another Bristol Stomp son, Ch. Rosha's Bristol Cream, bred by Rob and Shauna Pratt out of a daughter of Ch. Barberry Knowe Spitfire. Bristol Cream was also a Specialty and Group winner. His daughter, Ch. Starbelle Diamond Lil, was a BIS, Group, and Specialty winner in 1992.

Ch. Jabberwok Bristol Stomp, sired his last litter in 1987. Upon hearing of Bristol Stomp's death, the breeders of that litter, Kathi Brown and Gerry Poudrier, gave the pick puppy to Merle and Carolyn. Ch. Blueberry's Born To Boogie lived up to his early promise, finishing as a puppy and winning three sweepstakes, including that of the 1988 Rotating Specialty. Although not campaigned heavily, Berry was a Group and Specialty winner and ranked in the top ten during 1988 and 1989.

Firebrand

In 1958, Robert Houde finished the first of seven Firebrand champions produced by his bitch, Ch. Garthright's Dark Sorcery, and sired by Ch. Westpark Derrieford Baffie. In 1962, John Sheehan became Houde's partner at Firebrand. Today it is John, and later his friend, Muriel Lee, who are associated with the Firebrand name. Dark Sorcery was an outstanding producer, and through her granddaughter, Ch. Firebrand's Mustard, her family would produce most of the top-winning and producing Firebrand Scotties. Mustard was the dam of Ch. Firebrand's Viking Rex, sire of seven champions, and grandam of Ch. Viking's Camy Ann, dam of six champions. Through her daughter, Ch. Firebrand's Dark Velour, Mustard was also the grandam of Ch. Firebrand's Bookmaker, John's top-winner. Bookmaker, a BIS, Group, and Specialty winner, was ranked in the top ten during 1972 and 1973. Retired to stud, Bookmaker embarked on an equally successful career as a sire. He produced twenty-seven champions, including the Sandgreg brothers, Chs. Editorial and Headliner, and the Group-winning Ch. Firebrand's Omenmaker, whose specials career was cut short by his early death.

Bookmaker is behind all the top-winning Firebrand Scots including the BIS winners, Ch. Firebrand's Foolish Fun, Ch. Firebrand's Top Gallantry and Ch. Firebrand s Station Master, and the Group winners Ch. Firebrand's Paisley Monarch, Ch. Firebrand's Sunday Scherzo, and Ch. Firebrand's Winter Promise. Sheehan also owned Ch. Scotsmuir Sandpiper, the last Bingo son to stand at stud and the sire of fifteen champions. Top Gallantry proved to be a successful brood bitch, producing four champions sired by Janet Bartholomew's Ch. Hillview's Friar Tuck.

THE HEART OF AMERICA

The breeders in the central states are few in number and spread out over great distances. In many cases, these breeders have had to drive farther, ship more extensively, and use the services of professional handlers in order to get their dogs to the shows. In addition, many of these true Scottie fanciers live in states with unsavory reputations for housing puppy mills. Despite these obstacles, good breeders manage to thrive.

Hillview

Janet Bartholomew thought she was paying a lot of money for a dog when she paid a local breeder sixty dollars for her first Scottie. She undoubtedly revised that opinion over the next few years as she acquired several well-bred bitches and began to breed her first champions. Touzie Tyke's Twiggy, whose pedigree was primarily Firebrand breeding, was the dam of Janet's first Hillview champion, Hillview Nikki, sired by Ch. Hillside Bear Politician, a son of Ch. Gaidoune Great Bear. Janet's second bitch, Scots Delight Theme Song, was tightly linebred on Great Bear. Theme Song was bred to Ch. Dunbar's Democrat of Sandoone and produced Janet's first champion bitch, Hillview's Sara Lynn. Janet's third champion was Sandoone Miss Patches, litter sister to Ch. Dunbar's Democrat of Sandoone. Miss Patches and her son, Ch. Hillview Tippecanoe, sired by Ch. Dunbar's Royal Flush, finished within weeks of one another. Miss Patches nonchampion daughter, Hillview Anastasia, was the dam of Janet's first homebred Group winner, Ch. Hillview's Friar Tuck. Ch. Hillview Tracy of Dabob, a daughter of Ch. Reanda King's Ransom, is the dam of the 1985 Montgomery County Winners Dog, Dabob's Highland Chief.

Fitzwilliams'

Susan and Ed Fitzwilliams were only active breeders for about seven years, but they had an enormous influence on the breed. Their first bitch, Ch. Mar-De's Dark Felicia, won the 1967 Lloyd Trophy and then went on to produce six champions, one of which was Ch. Fitzwilliam's Happy Girl, the dam of Ch. Anstamm Happy Venture. Their first champion dog was the multiple Specialty-winning Bobby Dazzler son, Ch. Anstamm Dazzler Dynamic, winner of the Stud Dog trophy in 1973 and sire of the 1973 Montgomery County BIS winner, Ch. Schwer's Dynamic Happy Boy. The Fitzwilliams also owned the Group-winning specials, Ch. Lettswynne the Senator's Boy, a Bobby Dazzler son, and Ch. Brentnut Bravo, a Boy Blue son out of Dark Venture's litter sister. Dazzler Dynamic's daughter, Fitzwilliam's Fancy, is a modern-day Annie Laurie. She produced eleven champions, four by Happy Venture and seven by Ch. Gaywyn Square Deal. She had over 100 champion descendants including some of the breed's top producers.

Schwer

Wilfred and Mary Schwer bought their foundation bitch, Ch. Fitzwilliam's Happy Girl, from the Fitzwilliams and bred her first to Dazzler Dynamic.

The Schwers' first homebred champion, Schwer's Dynamic Happy Boy, achieved the goal of all terrier breeders—BIS at Montgomery County in 1973. The Schwers then bred Happy Girl to the 1964 Lloyd winner, Ch. Anstamm Dark Venture, and again produced a very special puppy, Ch. Anstamm Happy Venture. The Schwers' success is an example of the influence so many small breeders have had on the Scottish Terrier.

Sandissy

Barry and Marilyn Meador began showing in 1964 and soon finished their first champion, Zelwyn's Dainty Lyadee, a daughter of Ch. Cantie Captivator out of a daughter of Eng., Am. Ch. Wyrebury Wrangler. Dainty Lyadee produced their first homebred champion, Sandissy's Pettina Dee Lynn, by the Wrangler son, Ch. Lynbrier of Zelwyn. Pettina Dee Lynn was a multiple Group winner, and ranked in the top ten Scottish Terriers during 1970 and 1971. Her four champions included Ch. Sandissy's Amazing Grace, by the Bingo son, Ch. Carnation Casino. Grace, like her mother, was a Group and Specialty winner.

Topper

Lee Hastings has successfully bred all of his Topper champions out of just three bitches. The first, MacGeorge's Fancy Frolic, was a granddaughter of the Kirks' English import, Ch. Viewpark Vindicator. Bred to the BIS-winning Ch. Balachan Night Hawk, Fancy Frolic produced Lee's first champion, Topper's Thunderhawk. Lee's second bitch, Ch. Balachan Noelle, produced two champions, sired by Thunderhawk, before being sold to Sandi Hach Lewis. Lee then imported Ch. Viewpark Heatherbelle and bred her twice to Ch. Dunbar's Democrat of Sandoone. Each litter produced four champions. One, Ch. Topper's Highland Rider, had a successful career, handled and conditioned by his owners, Mel and Josephine Musson.

Tardun

In October 1987, J.P. Dodgson died in England. Several of his Tiddlymount Scottish Terriers were brought to the United States by Harry Sebel. Theresa Duncan acquired a dog, Ch. Tiddlymount Imprint, and a bitch, Ch. Tiddlymount Phamie. Imprint, Mrs. Duncan's first champion, was by England's top-winning Scottish Terrier dog, Ch. Mayson Monopoly. Her second was another British import, Ch. Basie Of Lomondview. Basie produced five champions, including Jeanice Ronden's Ch. Tardun Teatime At Haslemere, Winners Bitch at Montgomery County, 1991. Basie's son, Ch. Tardun Talisman, sired Ch. Tardun Treasure Too, owner-handled to Winners Bitch, Montgomery County, 1993. Mrs. Duncan has bred seventeen champions in just over seven years.

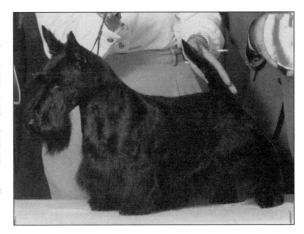

Ch. Anstamm Low
Commotion, #1 Scottish
Terrier in 1992, and
winner of the 1992
Francis G. Lloyd
Memorial Trophy,
owned by Fred and
Patty Brooks and
Anstamm Kennels.
Beth Tobias

Brookwood

Fred and Patty Brooks were friends of Chris and Judy Hughes, who encouraged them to try Scotties. In the spring of 1978, The Hughes offered them a littermate to Ch. Hughcrest Bottoms Up. Their choice, Kenwood's Toast Of Brookwood, was also their first champion. Toast of Brookwood finished easily, but the Brooks could not get her bred. Their disappointment, plus family obligations, kept them out of the ring until 1988. They returned with a small, black, stylish bitch named Hughcrest Southern Comfort. She was a Specialty BOB winner and a champion before her first birthday. Unlike her predecessor, she was also a good producer, having five champions in two litters, including the multiple Group-winning Ch. Brookwood Toasts Hughcrest. The Brooks co-owned the 1992 Lloyd Trophy winner, Ch. Anstamm Low Commotion and her Group-winning son, Ch. Anstamm Brookwood Joint Venture by Ch. Amescott's Lotta Talk.

TEXAS—A GREAT STATE FOR SCOTTIES

St. Lea

Julia J. Smith had her first homebred champion, Lea's Count Courtney, in 1964. Count Courtney, a Group winner, was by L.H Frost's Ch. Frosthaven Sunfire. Julia's second homebred champion was another Group-winner, Lea's Silver Sentinel, by Ch. Carnation Silver Note, out of a Ch. Glad-Mac's Rolling Stone granddaughter. He was then bred to a Group-placing Bingo granddaughter, Ch. Gaidoune Go Between, to produce her third champion, Lea's Hi Go Silver. At this time, Julia teamed up with Peggy Kahl, whose Ch. Scots Delight Audacious, bred to Bingo, was the dam of St. Lea's Domino, the first champion to carry their combined kennel name.

Ellscot

Louise Ellsworth spent her most active years as a breeder in Florida where her program was strongly influenced by Bruce Webb's Middlemount Scots. On retirement, she moved to Texas. Louise always had an interest in the more unusual colors, first wheatens and later, some unusual shades of brindle. Her first champion, Ell-Scot-T's Van Guard, was a brindle son of Ch. Blanart Bondsman out of a granddaughter of Ch. Bramshire Blazing Sun. Van Guard's unfinished daughter, Ellscot Sugar and Spice, was behind three Ellscot champions who could almost be described as *silver wheatens:* Ch. Ellscot Winner's Tips; her son, Ch. Ellscot's Roughten Ralph; and their daughter, Ch. Ellscot Silver Sparkle.

Dunwoodie

Bill and Shirley Justus began showing Scotties in the 1950s, starting with a pet bitch who did not finish. In the mid 1960s, they purchased Gaidoune Scots Delight, a granddaughter of Ch. Edgerstoune Troubadour and Ch. The Laird of Scots Guard. Bred to Ch. Gaidoune Grin and Bear It, Scots Delight produced their first homebred champion, Gaistoune Dockie Plaid. Dockie Plaid also produced one champion, Gaistoune Heather Honey. Their next champion was Kinsmon's Kount Kadence, purchased from Ed and Alice Watkins and sired by Ch. Gaistoune Linebacker out of Heather Honey. When they acquired Dunwoodie of Dunbar from Dick Hensel, however, Bill and Shirley began to establish their own line. Dunwoodie, who would give her name to all their subsequent champions, was by Ch. Anstamm Happy Venture out of Ch. Dunbar's Bear-Bee Doll. She was the dam of four champions. The Justuses also imported Ch. Reanda Rosie May, and added Ch. Anstamm Sudden Impact, tightly linebred on Ch. Anstamm Summer Lightning, to their breeding program. Now retired, they have somewhat curtailed breeding and exhibiting as both are judging actively.

Whiskybae

Dick and Carla LaCoe bought their first pet Scottie in 1960 while Dick was with the Air Force. They began exhibiting in 1970 and soon finished their first champion, Milady Molly Merry'O. Shortly thereafter, they bought Barberry Knowe Fashion Fare, a granddaughter of the two great rivals, Ch. Bardene Bingo and Ch. Carmichael's Fanfare. Fashion Fare made her mark in the whelping box, producing four champions. In the meantime, Molly Merry'O was bred to the Bingo son, Ch. St. Lea's Domino. Their daughter, Whiskybae Walkaway, bred to another Bingo son, Ch. Meeder's Discord, produced Ch. Whiskybae Ginger Bear, the foundation bitch behind the Amescot and Whiskybae Yanky Scots of New England. Dick and Carla LaCoe's top-producer is Ch. Dunbar's Victoria, a daughter of Ch. Dunbar's Democrat of Sandoone. Victoria is the dam of four champions, three by Ch. Perlor Playboy.

Scotsbairn

Jan and Jim Beaman began showing Scotties in 1971 in Alaska, where Tom was stationed with the Air Force. Their first two champions, Beaman's Wee Bairn and Beaman's Wee Lord Jamie, were locally bred, but their first Group-winning special, Ch. Dunbar's Royal Resolution, was a Highland King son bred by Linda Nolan, out of her Reanda Reflection. After settling in Texas, they bred a Royal Resolution daughter to Dick Hensel's Ch. Dunbar's Royal Flush and produced their first BIS and Specialty winner, Ch. Scotsbairn's Gambler's Dream, top-10 ranked during 1979 and 1980. Their second BIS winner was Ch. Scotsbairn's Baron Dhu.

Ruffton

Rick and Debbie Fowler's first champion, Dunbar's Southern Dancer, was a litter sister to Ch. Dunwoodie of Dunbar. She produced five champions. One of the three in her first litter, by Ch. Dunbar's Democrat of Sandoone, was Ch. Ruffton's Dynamo. Dynamo had a successful specials career with both Group and Specialty BOB wins and was in the top ten for 1980 and 1981. The Fowler's next special, Ch. Scotsbairn's Baron Dhu, was co-bred with Tom and Jan Beaman. He was by Ch. Reanda King's Ransom ex Ruffton's Compliments of Sadie, a sister to Dynamo. Baron Dhu was a multiple Specialty BOB, Group and BIS winner, and ranked in the top ten in 1983 and 1984.

Laurenleigh

Harry Sebel and Anne Moller, then husband and wife, started showing in the early 1970s. Their first champion bitch, Gadiscot Gypsy Flirtation, was a daughter of Dorothy Morris's Ch. Scot's Delight Rough Rider. Bred to Ch. Firebrand's Bookmaker, Gypsy Flirtation produced three champions in her only litter, tying for top brood bitch of 1975. Her daughter, Ch. Laurenlee's Happy Hooker, dam of six champions, was in the top ten for two years and, in 1977, won the STCA trophy for top-producing bitch. Beginning in the early 1980s, Sebel imported a number of Scots, bred by J.P. Dodgson. The most successful being Ch. Tiddlymount Freeman—a multiple BIS, Group and Specialty winner.

Claudon

Claudia and Don Leffler started showing and breeding with Charves' Scotties. Their first champion was the Group-winning daughter of Ch. Charves Dazzler Dyke, Ch. Charves Dashing Dainity. They then purchased Dainity's younger full brother, Charves Dashing Dino, and finished his championship. Dainity and Dino were full brother and sister to the DeSayes' foundation bitch, Ch. Charves Dashing Dawtie. Mrs. Leffler gradually doubled up on her Charves foundation by using Sandgreg studs (particularly Editorial) and by the addition of two Sandgreg bitches to her breeding program: Ch. Sandgreg's Luv Story, a black daughter of Ch. Sandgreg's Sweet Luv, and a wheaten, Ch. Sandgreg's Stars And Stripes.

Justscott

Texas in the 1980s saw an explosion of interest in the Scottish Terrier. New breeders and exhibitors appeared spontaneously all over the state. One sign of this growth is that in 1990, for the first time in history, a Lloyd Memorial Trophy winner, Ch. Justscott Reanda Just Rite, was bred and owned in Texas. His breeders, Jim and Susan Justice, had finished their foundation bitch, Ch. Rigadoon's Just In Time, and her son from her first litter, Ch. Justscott's Judge Roy Bean. They had intended to breed her to Bergit Coady's Ch. Reanda King's Ransom, but he died before they could. On Bergit's advice, they bred Just In Time to Ch. Reanda Dennis The Menace, a son of King's Ransom out of the German-bred bitch, Ch. Downtown Jolly. Bergit chose a male puppy from that litter and took him home to grow up.

Caevnes

Bob and Jane Phelan had bred Rottweilers, but as Bob's retirement approached, they decided to change breeds. They bought their first Scottish Terrier show dog, Whiskybae Yanky Stunt Man, in 1984, shortly after he won the Sweepstakes at Montgomery County. Stunt Man, handled by Judi Hartell, won nine Groups in 1986, ending as number two Scottish Terrier dog for that year. Stunt Man was forced into early retirement after a leg injury, but he sired four champions before his accidental drowning.

The Phelans then bought Ch. Stonecroft's Victory Design, a Ch. Democratic Victory daughter from Phyllis Dabbs. She produced three champions in her first litter, by Ch. Kennelgarth Romeo. During the same time, the Phelans co-owned a Stunt Man daughter, Ch. Piper's Scotch Robyn, with Mary Neck. Bred to Ch. Charthill Worthy Of Colwick, Scotch Robyn produced two champions.

In the spring of 1989, Bergit's stud puppy, Justscott's Reanda Just Rite was Reserve Winners Dog at the STCA Rotating Specialty under Swiss breeder-judge Elsbeth Clerc. The Phelans purchased him shortly thereafter. In October, 1989, Just Rite was Winners Dog at Montgomery County, handled by Bergit. He was campaigned during 1990 to three Specialty BOBs, ten Groups and one all-breed BIS. Just Rite sired six champions before he was sold to Japan. His non-champion daughter, Caevnes Amy March Of Alcott, out of Ch. Caevnes Aldie Castle, is the dam of Ch. Caevnes Devil's Due. Devil's Due and his brother, Ch. Caevnes Ghost Rider, were the sensations of Montgomery County weekend in 1992. Devil's Due is now a Specialty and BIS winner.

Triscot

Renee Stolz thought she was just buying a family pet when she bought Triscot's Cagney Go Man Go from Clifford and Mildred Blake. The Blakes encouraged her to show her young son of Ch. Whiskybae Yanky Stunt Man, so she sent him out with handler Michael Kemp. "Cagney" was not away from home very long, finishing his championship at age eleven months.

By now, Mrs. Stolz was thinking she would like a Scottie to show herself. The Blakes referred her to the Phelans and Mrs. Stolz bought Caevnes Abbey of Driburgh, the litter sister to Aldie Castle. Once a week, Mrs. Stolz took grooming lessons from Jan Merritt. Mrs. Stolz was a good student, and she and Abbey made a good team. So good, in fact, that in October 1988, they won the 6-9 Sweepstakes division at their very first Montgomery County under Gail Gaines. Abbey finished owner-handled soon afterward and produced seven champions.

Hycourt

Allene Haldy bought her first Scottie puppy in 1973 from a breeder she found in the Yellow Pages. Like many newcomers, Allene believed her Maggie "had" to have a litter, so Maggie did. Allene kept Maggie's wheaten son, Hycourt McKuen's Sonnet, and began to train him for obedience. McKuen was one of those exceptional Scotties who loved everything about obedience training. He earned his CDX at just fifteen months and was also one of the first Scottie High in Trial at an all-breed show.

Allene now wanted a wheaten Scottie to show in conformation. At that time, show-quality wheatens were hard to find. Finally, she bought Plain-Scot Vamp Of Savannah from Mrs. Loomis Giles. Vamp was Allene's first champion and also the first Scottie to earn a "T T" title from the American Temperament Testing Society. Allene's top-producing bitches have been Ch. Glad-Mac's Cracklin' Rosie, a wheaten daughter of Ch. Sandgreg's Mr. Hot Shot, with three champions, and Rosie's daughter, Ch. Hycourt's Blush With Pride, by Ch. Sandgreg's Square Deal. Blush With Pride is the dam of a remarkable eleven champions, many being Group winners.

Owyn

Carole and Ray Owen were living in Kansas City when Ray's mother sent them a Scottie puppy. After attending the 1967 Heart of America Specialty they thought they might like to show their bitch. She was by Ch. Ell-Scot-T's Van Guard and heavily linebred on Blanart. Despite her qualifications, the Owens decided that dog showing was beyond their financial means at that time.

In 1982, the Owens bought another Scottie bitch, which they originally planned to train for obedience competition. When Carole decided to show Lucky in conformation, she turned to her Scottish Terrier Club of America handbooks for help. Using Anne Gilkey's articles on stripping as a guide, Carole began grooming Lucky for her debut. The judge that day was Mrs. Heywood Hartley. As Carole left the ring, Mrs. Hartley told her gently that her bitch should not be shown. Carole was disappointed but decided to take Mrs. Hartley's advice, a decision she has never regretted. Lucky's story had a happy ending, though. She won the STCA Award for High Scoring Companion Dog in 1984.

Meanwhile, Carole and Ray located their first show bitch. They bought Passmore's Fascination, a Ch. Glenby Gallant Lad daughter, in co-ownership with Jeannie Passmore. Fascination finished owner-handled and conditioned by Carole and produced one champion daughter in her first litter, Am., Can., Mex., Int. Ch. Owyn Twin Sisters Passmore. Fascination's second litter was by Carole and Ray's Am., Can., Mex., Int. Ch. Passmore's Gringo Gold, a wheaten son of Ch. Passmore's Rowdy Rruff. This litter produced three champions.

Carole has been very active in Scottish Terrier rescue programs and has written extensively on this subject and others for the Scottish Terrier Club of America magazine, *The Bagpiper*.

Belfyre

At about the same time Carole and Ray got their first Scottie puppy, Mike O'Neal gave his wife, Polly, a Scottish Terrier puppy for her birthday. Two children and many years later, Mike decided to get Polly another Scottie. She wanted a black bitch, but her husband and son fell in love with a six-month-old brindle male at a local dog show. Mrs. O'Neal's "present," Piper's Scotch Rascal, finished his championship the following month, handled by Judi Hartell and Patsy Wade. By then, Mrs. O'Neal had developed an interest in showing and grooming. She made up her mind that her next "present" would be chosen by her. Ms. Hartell advised Mrs. O'Neal to come to Montgomery County to choose a foundation bitch. She also told Mrs. O'Neal to watch the dogs without a catalogue and write down the numbers of the dogs she liked. By day's end, Mrs. O'Neal had decided to buy an Anstamm bitch.

The following spring, the O'Neals selected Anstamm Maid In America, sired by the import Ch. Make My Day Of Mayson. Maid In America had already won the 1986 California Sweepstakes and had gone BOW at the 1986 Chicago Specialty. Handled by Judi Hartell and Patsy Wade, Maid In America finished with back-to-back five-point majors at the 1987 California Specialty and Beverly Hills shows. She was campaigned for the second half of 1987, winning two Groups and ending 1987 as number one Scottish Terrier bitch.

In 1988, while waiting for Maid In America's puppies to grow up, the O'Neals finished two more champions, including their first owner-handled champion, Anstamm Sheer Energy. In 1989, Mrs. O'Neal handled and conditioned their first homebred champion, Bellefire Maid Of Tejas, who finished by going Winners Bitch at the 1989 Houston Specialty under breeder-judge Fred Stephens. Maid In America's other daughter, Anstamm Got It Maid, was Winners Bitch at two National Specialties and finished with a third five-point win at the 1990 Northern Ohio Specialty.

Haslemere

Jeanice Ronden was introduced to Scotties and the show ring when she and her husband Elio were living in England. They purchased Kencroft Pashia, a son of Betty Penn-Bull's Ch. Kennelgarth Romeo. Pashia made his debut in 1986 at the Scottish Terrier Club of England championship show. Jeanice showed him in England for a year, winning many firsts and one Best Puppy in Breed. In 1987, the Rondens moved to Spain where Pashia won a C.A.C.I.B. toward his International and Spanish championship.

When the Rondens returned to the United States in late 1987, they sent Pashia to Bergit Coady who quickly finished him. In 1989, the Rondens purchased Hycourt's Roxy Rose O'Haslemere, and this time, Mrs. Ronden handled her own dog very successfully. Roxy Rose won two majors from the puppy class enroute to her championship. Her first outing as a special netted her a BOS at the 1990 Dallas Specialty and she won her first Group at only fourteen months. Mrs. Ronden next purchased Tardun Teatime At Haslemere, bred by Theresa Duncan. Teatime, conditioned and handled by Mrs. Ronden, was Winners Bitch from the 9-12 Puppy class at Devon and Montgomery County in 1991. She went on to win several Specialty BOBs and Groups Is before retiring.

Blackmount

Leonor Gurrola and her children, Felicia and Gerard, finished the last St. Lea champion, St. Lea's Heavy Cruiser, in 1986, and then bought a St. Lea-bred bitch. Three years earlier, Gerard had caught a glimpse of a male Scot, and his image captured his imagination. When their bitch was old enough to breed, the Gurrola's sent her to that dog, Ch. Glenby Gallant Lad. For novice Scottie breeders, the Gurrolas luckily hit on a good combination, producing three champions in their first litter. A bitch from this breeding, Ch. Blackmount Dream Weaver, also produced three champions in her first litter, by Ch. Glenby Royal Ruler.

Other Texas fanciers include Marshall and Daphne Branzell (Scotswind), Steve and Angela Eisert (Impact), Joseph and Betty Martin (Jo-Bet's), Eldon and JoAnn Meyer (Bluethistle), Mary Neck (Piper's Scotch), Barbara Pierce (Castlebar), Colleen Privitt and Connie Smith (Lanshire), Jana Trent (Mad For Plaid) and Donna Winslow (Springbok).

THE WEST

The far West, with the exception of the coast, is sparsely populated and exhibitors must travel long distances to shows. This situation seems to have had the most impact in the Southwest where few breeders have persisted more than ten years.

Capre

Carol Preuss's Capre Scottish Terriers won well throughout the Southwest in the 1970s. Carol's first champion, Capre's Corbeau of Gartland, was by Ch. Anstamm Dazzler Dynamic and was the dam of Carol's Group-winning bitch, Ch. Capre's Desert Piper. Corbeau's sister, Gartland's Brad's Bonnie, bred to a son of Ch. Firebrand's Bookmaker, produced Carol's top-winning dog, Ch. Capre's Blackjack of Gartland. Blackjack, a multiple Group and Specialty winner, took the now-defunct Phoenix Club's Specialty in 1975 and 1976.

Wixom

Francis LaFortune once had the distinction of being the only STCA member in Nevada. Her first champion, Wixom's Sassy Shana O'Shanter, was by Ch. Capre's Blackjack of Gartland. Although Shana was only able to have one litter, by Ch. Barraglen's Beachcomber, she produced two male champions: Wixom's Bear Essentials and Wixom's Warrior, BOW at the STCA 1982 Rotating Specialty. The LaFortunes' second bitch, Democratic Playgirl, a sister to Ch. Democratic Victory, also produced two male champions, sired by Ch. Reanda King's Ransom. One, Ch. Theodore Rough Rider of Wixom, was the first of Tom Hossfeld and Jane Nuñez's Rough Rider Scots. It was Francie's unfinished bitch, Wixom's Tribute To Tuff, who produced, at long last, a homebred champion bitch. Wixom's Topaz, sired by Ch. Wixom's Warrior, won a Group enroute to finishing, handled by Francie's good friend, Barbara Gentry Casey.

Simonsez and Roughrider

After Carol Preuss stopped breeding, the late E. Louise Simon, Barbara Gentry Casey and Thomas Hossfeld and Janie Nuñez comprised nearly the entire Scottish Terrier fancy in Arizona. Louise's 1985 Lloyd winner, multiple Specialty, Group, and BIS winner, Ch. Simonsez Charlie The Charmer, was a top-producing sire during the late 1980s. His sixteen champion offspring include a BIS winner, several Group winners and several that won at specialties. Thomas Hossfeld and Janie Nuñez's first champion, Theodore's Rough Rider Of Wixom, won multiple Groups and sired Roughrider's Pepper Korn, a California Sweepstakes winner.

Ch. Simonsez Charlie
The Charmer.
Missy Yuhl

Casi's

Barbara Gentry Casey started with a male show puppy from Francie LaFortune. In 1982, Mrs. Casey bought her foundation bitch, Rosha's Sterling Silver, from Rob and Shauna Pratt. Sterling Silver, by Ch. Jabberwok Bristol Stomp, finished with style, going Winners Bitch, BOW and BOS at the 1983 California Specialty from the 9-12 Puppy Bitch class. Sterling Silver's son, Baggpiper's Top Gun, by Charlie The Charmer, started his show career by going Winners Dog at the same show four years later. This time, Barbara was grooming and handling by herself.

Colorado is the one exceptional western state in which the popularity of the Scottish Terrier has grown rapidly. In 1976, when the STCA held the Rotating Specialty in Denver, fewer than one-third of the entries were Colorado-owned, and even fewer were Colorado-bred. Today the state can boast of a number of fine Scots bred by a growing number of fanciers. In the late 1960s, however, Weeknowe Walsing and Mountview were among the few well-known Colorado prefixes.

Weeknowe Walsing

Annabel and George Gilbert started with a Barberry Knowe-bred bitch, Ch. Georgeanne's Walsing Fanfare, a granddaughter of Ch. Walsing Wild Winter. In two litters sired by Ch. Barberry Knowe Wintry Knight, Walsing Fanfare produced five champions. Her grandson, Ch. Weeknowe Walsing Bandboy, was the sire of two champions, including Ch. Weeknowe Walsing Lady Stuart, who finished in 1983, shortly after her ninth birthday. The Weeknowe prefix reappeared in 1994 when Graceann and Richard Stewart adopted the name as a tribute to the Gilberts.

Mountview

Ray Bay began his breeding program with two English imports: Ch. Sterncrest's Miss Margaret, who combined Westpark, Wyrebury, and Penvale lines and Ch. Kennelgarth the Red Boy, by Eng. Ch. Kennelgarth Viking ex the Bingo daughter, Eng. Ch. Gillsie Principal Girl. Miss Margaret's daughter, Ch. Mountview's Top O' The Morn, by Eng. Ch. Penvale Plutocrat, produced Ray's top-winning dog, Ch. Mountview's Stop the World, a Group winner and the sire of six champions. Because he was a professional handler, Ray's breeding program was limited. Still, his line provided the foundation stock for many of this region's breeders.

Clanronald

Ron and Lois Giese's first champion, Heathcliff II, was by a double Red Boy grandson out of a sister to Stop the World. The first Clanronald champion, Clanronald's Bobbie Girl, was sired by Heathcliff II out of a bitch carrying Crescent Hill, Balachan and Reanda bloodlines. Bred to Stop the World, Bobbie Girl produced Ch. Clanronald's Watch My Smoke, a BIS and Specialty BOB winner, who was ranked in the top ten between 1976 and 1978. Bobbie Girl eventually produced seven champions for the Gieses. Their Ch. Gregorach King of the Isles, an imported grandson of Kennelgarth Viking, sired seven champions.

Gladwatch

Clanronald bloodlines provided the foundation for Nancy Reese's Gladwatch Scotties. Nancy begged the Gieses for eighteen months to sell her a puppy. She was sixth in line when they had a litter in July 1977. Ron offered Nancy the "middle-sized dog left!" Nancy was thrilled with her black-brindle boy. While he was sweet-tempered at home, he had one odd habit—he would not sleep at night! This puppy liked to stay up late to watch television, so he was named Clanronald Niteowl Gladwatch. Nancy's first Specialty win came in 1985. Her homebred bitch, Gladwatch Royal Blush, was Winners Bitch and BOW at the Heart of America Specialty. Royal Blush finished in November 1985. Finishing was a good thing, because she presented Nancy with a litter of four the following month. Two from this litter finished. In her next litter, Royal Blush was bred to Sonya Neve's Ch. XXIV Kt Dunbar Gold. All four of these puppies finished and one, Ch. Gladwatch Almost Autumn, became a Group winner. To date, Royal Blush is the dam of seven champions.

Besscott

Betty Cooper's first homebred champion, Besscott's Brocade, was out of a Bingo daughter by Stop the World. In 1976, Betty was handling Scotties for William and Margaret Conley when she imported the brother and sister, Perlor

Ch. Perlor Playboy, with his owner-handler Elizabeth Cooper, winning BOB at the 1984 STCA Rotating Specialty under breeder-judge Fred Stephens.
Fox & Cook

```
                                                        Eng. Ch. Gaywyn Emperor
                                  Eng. Ch. Gaywyn Joel
                                                        Gaywyn Busybody
              Eng. Ch. Gaywyn Landmark
                                                        Eng. Am. Ch. Gosmore Gillson
                                                           Highland King
                                  Eng. Ch. Gaywyn Lisa
                                                        Eng. Ch. Gaywyn Bonetta
        Int. Ch. Woodmansey Woden
                                                        Eng. Ch. Gaywyn Kingson
                                  Eng. Ch. Woodmansey Gosmore Royal King
                                                        Gosmore Eilburn Royal Lady
              Woodmansey Wendy
                                                        Eng. Ch. Gillson Grandiloquence
                                  Coldstream Jenny
                                                        Coldstream Ginty
Champion Perlor Playboy
                                                        Toryglen Top Of The Pops
                                  Toryglen Twa Brigs
                                                        Toryglen Timmingo
              Toryglen Time To Shine
                                                        Toryglen Tower Bridge
                                  Toryglen Tilly Girl
                                                        Toryglen Telstar
        Perlor Principale
                                                        Eng. Am. Ch. Gosmore
                                                           Eilburn Admaration
                                  Eng. Ch. Gillson Grandiloquence
                                                        Eng. Ch. Gillsie Highland Lass
              Eng. Ch. Prix Noire of Perlor
                                                        Bobby Barthea
                                  Christina Of Dunsville
                                                        Margaret of Dunsville
```

Perfect Match, and Perlor Perfect Harmony, by Eng. Ch. Gaywyn Landmark. These were the first of many successful Perlor Scots imported by Betty. Perfect Harmony finished with Group placements, and her brother was a Group winner. Betty's next import was the bitch, Perlor Flower of Scotland. Bred to Perfect Match, Flower produced three champions. In 1982, Betty imported Perlor Playboy. He finished in three consecutive shows and went on to a very successful career as a special, winning multiple Groups and Specialty Bests. He was top-ten-ranked during 1982 and 1983, and he finished 1984 as the number one Scottish Terrier dog. He closed his career with BOB at the prestigious AKC Centennial Show under Dr. Kirk in November 1984. Playboy was a very influential sire, producing forty-one champions. His progeny include numerous top-ten-winners, including the 1992 Montgomery County BOB, Ch. Hopscotch Heads We Win (a daughter), and the 1992 Montgomery Sweepstakes winner, Ch. Alchemy's Tincture of Angel (a double great-granddaughter). Mrs. Cooper's most recent import is the multiple Specialty winner, Ch. Balgownie Bulletin, co-owned by Helen Prince and Andrea Duncan.

Scotties in this region were heavily influenced by Ch. Perlor Playboy. Jeanne-Marie Heyder-Hunt has bred over a dozen Hyscot champions, crossing Bardene lines from Boy Blue and Bobby Dazzler with Perlor from Playboy and her imported champions, Perlor Pawnee and Perlor Picquant. In Wyoming, Larae Shafer's Ch. Dana's Amber Edition produced nine champions, eight by Playboy. Amber Edition, bred by Nancy Fingerhut, was a daughter of Ch. Hughcrest Hot Fudge Sunday, dam of seven champions, and a granddaughter of Fitzwilliam's Fancy, dam of eleven champions.

Kenjo

Ken and JoAnn Glaser bought their first Scottie bitch, Glaser's Lady MacTavish, and began showing in 1966. Although she never finished, she was well-bred and produced the Glaser's first champion bitch, Kenjo Sho Go Bo Peep, by Ch. Bardene Bobby Dazzler. In 1970, the Glasers acquired Ch. Wayridge Wistful Wise Guy from the Ridgleys. Wise Guy was a dark brindle son of Ch. Bardene Boy Blue, and bred back to a Boy Blue great-granddaughter, sired the Glaser's first wheaten champion, Kenjo Gold Braid Commander. Commander was BOW at the 1973 STC of Greater Washington D.C., spring Specialty, making him one of the few wheatens with Specialty points at that time. Commander was also the Glasers' top-producing sire with five champions. His son, Ch. Kenjo Gold Strike Commander, sired three champions, including the Glaser's first Group winner, Ch. Kenjo Gold Rush Commander. Gold Rush Commander's wheaten son, Am., Can. Ch. Kenjo Touch O' Gold Commander is a two-time Canadian BIS winner. The Glasers' top-producing bitches have included Kenjo Venturing Star, Ch. Kenjo Roughcastle Rainbow, and Ch. Kenjo Maggie of Anstamm, each the dam of four champions. Frequent transfers enabled the Glasers to influence breeders in different parts of the country. Many of the Scots bred by Betty Lou

Ch. Kenjo Gold Braid Commander with breeder-owner-handler, Kennan Glaser, in a win under breeder-judge, John Hillman. *John Ashbey*

Breese (Hiwood) and Helen Krisko (Kriscot) trace back to Kenjo stock. After settling in Colorado, the Glasers retired from breeding and showing.

Faith Erlacher's Roughcastle Scotties and Bob Harley's Tinker Scotties were both heavily influenced by Kenjo breeding. Ms. Erlacher's Ch. Kenjo Roughcastle Rainbow, a daughter of Bardene By Gosh out of a wheaten Kenjo bitch, was the dam of five champions, including the Glaser's Group winner, Ch. Kenjo Gold Rush Commander, and one of Bob Harley's first champion bitches, Ch. Roughcastle Kenjo Tinker Toy. Bob Harley has owned over twenty-five champions, and most of his homebreds combine Kenjo and Sandgreg. He has also introduced a number of English imports, and more recently three Danish imports: Ch. Danskot's Valentino, his son, Ch. Danskot's Oskar De La Renta, and his daughter, Ch. Danskot's Devil In Disguise.

McCree

Sonya Neve began with Dunbar's Emerald Exodus purchased from Dick Hensel. After finishing her championship in 1986, Emerald Exodus was bred to Charlie The Charmer. With help from Ray Bay, Sonya finished two from this litter: Dark Pearl Of Dunbar, and XXIV Kt Dunbar Gold, a Group, Specialty and BIS winner. Mrs. Neve included Dick Hensel's Dunbar prefix in the names of her first champions to honor the memory of the man who gave her her start.

Mystigael

In 1975, Pat Gruda (then Pat Brown) finished her first champion, Mystique Paladin's Quest, by Ch. Medrick's Monopoly. Seven years later, when her Glad Mac's Globetrotter was BOB from the classes at the San Francisco Specialty, Pat was married to Tony Gruda, a Schipperke fancier. Globetrotter, by Ch. Sandgreg's Square Deal, was one of many winners the Grudas have owned and bred. Their top-producing sire has been Ch. Sandgreg's Desert Fox, litter brother to Ch. Sandgreg's Foxmoor. To date, he is the sire of eight champions, five from the Grudas' top-producing bitch, Ch. Glad-Mac's Gingham Girl. One of these five is Ch. Mystigael Good As Gold, a Group Winner ranked in the top-ten in 1989 and the sire of six champions. A more recent Group winner is Ch. Mystigael Imminent Thunder, out of a sister to Good As Gold.

Roylaine

In the late 1960s, Elaine and Roy Lee began their breeding program in Utah with a pair of imports. The bitch was Aberscot Aristocrat, a Bardene Blue Steptoe granddaughter, and the dog, Callum of Lakelynn, a Bardene Bo Jest son. Shortly thereafter, they imported Tiddlymount Tam O'Shanter, whose pedigree included Niddbank, Bardene and Dalblane. Aristocrat finished her championship first, followed closely by Tam O'Shanter. The Lees imported two more English bitches, Rockland's Adulation and Lakelynn Pirouette, both of which finished their American championships. Callum sired two champions, Roylaine Robin of Royley, and the Group-placing Roylaine Little Corker.

Donarry

The Lee's top-winning dog, by Tam O'Shanter ex Aristocrat, was Ch. Donarry's Wee Doc'N'Doris, the first champion for Harry and Donna Erskine. Doc'N'Doris was a top-ten ranked special in 1978 and 1979 and sired five Donarry champions. Doc'N'Doris's litter sister, Donarry's Brigadoon, produced three champions by Ch. Perlor Perfect Match. Two of them, Ch. Donarry's Wee Cooper of Fife and Ch. Donarry's Dark Star of Lomond, were Group winners.

Glenby

Bertha Russell was a very close friend of Christine Stephens's parents. So when the grown and married Christine wanted a Scottie, Bertha told her to wait until the youngest Stephens child was five years old. When that day came, Bertha sent Christine and her husband, Fred, to Lena Kardos, who sold them a black bitch who was, she told them, "too small to show." Greyridge Wicked Witch, as she was named, was a daughter of Ch. Mar-De's Martin Reanda out of a bitch who combined Barberry Knowe and Bardene bloodlines.

Ch. Glenby Gallant Lad.

```
                                                            Eng. Ch. Kennelgarth Viking
                                        Eng. Ch. Brio Cabin Boy
                                                            Kennelgarth Gleam
                    Eng. Ch. Brio Fair'N'Square
                                                            E.C. Am. Ch. Bardene Bingo
                                        Eng. Ch. Brio Call Me Madam
                                                            Eng. Ch. Gaywyn Viscountess
        Eng. Am. Ch. Gaywyn Likely Lad
                                                            E.C. Am. Ch. Bardene Bingo
                                        Eng. Ch. Gaywyn Emperor
                                                            Eng. Ch. Gaywyn Viscountess
                    Eng. Ch. Gaywyn Leila
                                                            Eng. Am. Ch. Gosmore Gillson
                                                            Highland King
                                        Eng. Ch. Gaywyn Lisa
                                                            Eng. Ch. Gaywyn Bonetta
Am., Can. Ch. Glenby Gallant Lad
                                                            Champion Gilkey's Johnny
                                                            Come Lately
                                        Castlecrag Little John
                                                            Charves Gillie Callum
                    Lockton of Leys
                                                            Charves Golden Rod of Ban
                                        Loch Moy's Sand Storm
                                                            Loch Moy Silver Bridget
        Champion Theda Theda
                                                            Champion Carnation Casino
                                        Am. Can. Ch. Firebrand's Bookmaker
                                                            Champion Firebrand's Dark
                                                            Velour
                    Heritage Farm's Stewardess
                                                            Dalblane Maestro Superb
                                        Champion Gillsie Dream Girl
                                                            Gillsie Marian
```

Ch. Glenby Royal Ruler.
Missy Yuhl

Ch. Glenby Royal Viking.
Callea

The Stephens were introduced to the fancy by winning the Terrier Group at a fun match, and they were hooked. Mrs. Stephens regularly made the 200-mile round trip to Bertha's for grooming lessons while Wicked Witch grew up. After her first litter, Wicked Witch proved the experts wrong by finishing handily. In that litter, by her half-brother, Merryscot's Mr. Marty, Wicked Witch produced two champions. With Bertha's consent, the Stephens gave them the Glenby name. These two bitches, Ch. Glenby Gay Contessa and Ch. Glenby Merry Marchioness, are behind the more than seventy Glenby champions. Merry Marchioness was bred to a Happy Venture son and their daughter, Ch. Glenby's Leading Lady, was the first of many Glenby Scots to become top winners and good producers. Leading Lady was a multiple Group winner and the dam of five champions. Her daughter, Ch. Glenby's Special Blend, was the Stephens' top-producing bitch with nine champions, all by Ch. Glenby Gallant Lad.

Gallant Lad, by Roger and Nancy Abbott's English import, Ch. Gaywyn Likely Lad, was seventeen months old when the Stephens acquired him. He soon blossomed into a first-class show dog and provided his owners with many exciting wins—three BIS, thirty Group Is, and seven Specialty Bests—and he sired thirty-four champions. In 1986, the Stephens's English import, Glenecker Galivanter, was Reserve Winners Dog at Montgomery County under judge Susan Gaskell. Two years later, Galivanter's son, Glenby Royal Ruler, won the award his father just missed—Winners Dog at Montgomery County. Royal Ruler was only lightly campaigned but still managed to win a number of Groups and the 1989 California Specialty, and he sired eighteen champions. Royal Ruler's grandson, Ch. Glenby's Royal Viking has almost caught up to his illustrious grandsire with fourteen champions of his own to date. This highly successful kennel has produced over seventy champions in just over twenty years, including Specialty and Group winners.

Patcay

When Robert and Carol Mohney put their Blueberry-bred bitches to Ch. Glenby Royal Ruler, they made one of those lucky strikes that sometimes happens to new breeders. Ch. Blueberry's Centerfold produced two champions and Patcay's Mistress of Mischief produced one. That one, Ch. Patcay's Looks Are Everything, produced four champions by Ch. Glenby Royal Viking.

Barraglen

Ann Bower was another Oregon breeder who grew up with Scotties. In the late 1960s, she and her husband, Ross, bought a pet Scottie with "show potential." Like so many first dogs, Laird did not manifest that potential when he grew up, but by then, the "bug" had bitten and the Bowers decided to get a bitch they could show and breed. From Betty Malinka, they bought the Bingo granddaughter, Stand's Fire Witch, and from the Heywood Hartleys, came Woodhart Whimsical. Although Whimsical did not finish, she was the dam of the Bowers' first homebred champion, Barraglen Ballad, by Ch. Gosmore Eilburn Admaration. Fire Witch finished and, in 1976, her daughter, Ch. Barraglen Bewitched, by Merryscott's Mr. Marty, was the first Barraglen Scot to be ranked in the top ten. Bewitched was the dam of four champions, two by Democrat and two by Ch. Barraglen Beachcomber, a great-grandson of Fire Witch. Beachcomber's litter brother, Ch. Barraglen Brindle Bacardi, finished by going Winners Dog at Montgomery County in 1981. Beachcomber went on to sire six champions.

Passmore

In 1966, Elaine Young was dispersing some of her dogs to concentrate on judging. Jeannie Passmore bought Young's Rowdy Red of Passmore, a grandson of Ch. Silver Eve's Anastasia. Rowdy Red finished his championship and earned his UD degree in under ten months, winning five High in Trial awards. In 1967, Jeannie purchased the Group-winning, Ch. Young's Cat Ballou, a granddaughter of Irene Robertson's Rolling Stone. Cat Ballou was bred to Ch. Marlorain Heather Jack, a double grandson of Ch. Marlorain Dark Seal. Cat Ballou's daughter, Ch. Passmore's Sassy Bonnie Lass, produced five champions by three different sires. Her top-winning son was Jeannie's first home-bred champion, Passmore's I'm Rowdy Two, by Rowdy Red. Rowdy Two was a Group winner in the United States and a BIS winner in Canada. Over the next decade, Mrs. Passmore introduced Sandgreg breeding into her line, breeding to Irene Robertson's Ch. Sandgreg's Square Deal and to a half-brother of Square Deal named Ch. Sandgreg's Investigator. A daughter of Investigator, Ch. Passmore's American Beauty, has the distinction of being one of the only three American champion Scottish Terriers to be exported to Australia. Mrs. Passmore has produced over twenty champions and provided foundation stock for several newer breeders, including Carole and Ray Owen in Texas and Jorge and Patricia Torrejon in Canada.

Sunrise

Sandy and Tom Lehrack were living in California when they bought their foundation bitch from Barbara and Brum Dunham. The Dunhams had bred their Highland King daughter, Ch. Anstamm King's Treasure, to Ch. Gaywyn Likely Lad and sold the Lehracks a promising puppy from this litter. The Lehracks named their puppy Sorcery and finished her in 1981. They have based their breeding program largely on Ch. Gaywyn Likely Lad, his son, Ch. Glenby Gallant Lad, and a series of imported dogs carrying lines to Gaywyn. From the Stephens, Tom and Sandy acquired a brother and sister pair, Ch. Glenby's Sunrise Conspiracy and Ch. Glenby's Sunrise Scoundrel. Their top-producing sire is Ch. Kentwella Solo Of Gaywyn, with five champions. Recently, in co-ownership with Jeffrey and Mori Scheer, the Lehracks imported a multititled dog from Finland: Danish, Finnish, Swedish, European, International, Canadian and American Ch. Raijaj Tom Dick and Harry.

Hisum

Florence Hicks is another Northwestern breeder who has emphasized Gaywyn lines in her breeding. She had a pet shop Scottie that she considered "perfect" until she saw some of Elaine Young's dogs. Mrs. Hicks's first champion was Braemar Kilts-A-Swinging, out of two imported Gaywyn Scots. Kilts's daughter, bred to Ch. Gaywyn Likely Lad, produced Mrs. Hicks's second champion, Hisum Black Magic Lucky Lad. Mrs. Hicks later imported Ch. Gaywyn Alvira, a daughter of England's all-time top-winning male Scottish Terrier, Eng. Ch. Mayson Monopoly. Lucky Lad and Alvira were the parents of the first Hisum Group winner, Ch. Hisum Black Magic the Admiral.

The Gaywyn-bred imports of the Lehracks and Mrs. Hicks have provided breeding stock for other breeders in the Northwest like Richard and Margaret Vinciguerra (Winwar), Jeffrey and Mori Scheer (J Branigan) and Ted and Julie Bare.

McVan

Vandra Huber's first Scottie was not purebred, but she had purebred Scottie character. She kept Ms. Huber company for ten years before succumbing to the then new parvovirus. At that time, Ms. Huber was a graduate student in Indiana and bought her first purebred Scot from an area breeder with the intention of showing. Upon graduation, Ms. Huber went to work at Cornell University. She wanted to breed her bitch, Spunky, but a breeder of her acquaintance, Ginger Middleton, told her that Spunky was not suitable for breeding. By then, Ms. Huber had made up her mind she wanted a wheaten, so she decided to wait for one from Ginger.

Ms. Huber waited for two years. When Maggie McMuffin V finally arrived, Ms. Huber's first problem was grooming. Ginger lived three hours away, so Ms. Huber took her wheaten puppy to a local groomer. Although instructed to strip Maggie for show, the groomer clipped the puppy's coat. By the time the coat grew back, Ms. Huber had moved to Utah. She decided that Maggie needed the professional touch and sent her to Maripi Wooldridge. Maggie finished easily in 1986 and retired to the whelping box where she continued to excel. In four litters, she produced eleven champions, by three different dogs. Her top-winning offspring to date is Ch. McVan's Sandman, by Ch. Sandgreg's Second Edition.

Sandman started his show career by going Reserve Winners Dog at Montgomery County in 1987 from the 6-9 Puppy Dog class and finished the following spring. Campaigned heavily in 1989 by Maripi, he won sixty-four BOBs, one Specialty BOB, five Group Is and one all-breed BIS. Sandman is also a Specialty winner in Canada and a Group winner in Canada and Puerto Rico. His half-sister, Ch. McVan's Ebony Rose, by Ch. Glenecker Galivanter, was also a Group and BIS winner.

In 1992, Ms. Huber bought a puppy bitch from Camille Partridge. The puppy was sired by Mrs. Partridge's Ch. Glad-Mac's Taliesin The Bard out of Ch. Glenlee's Sable Fox. The puppy was named Gaelforce Post Script, but she came to be well known by her call name, Peggy Sue. Peggy Sue had a remarkable career, winning five successive national Specialty Bests and twice placing in the Group at Montgomery County. She won the Lloyd Trophy in 1993, and would have repeated that win in 1994 but for the fact that her new co-owner, Dr. Joe Kinnarney, was not a member of the STCA, thereby making her ineligible. She was a multiple BIS winner and capped her all-breed career by winning BIS at Westminster in 1995, the seventh Scot to do so.

Ch. Gaelforce Post Script after winning the Terrier Group under judge R. Stephen Shaw at the 1995 Westminster Kennel Club show enroute to Best in Show. Handled by Maripi Wooldridge, Peggy Sue was the seventh Scot in history to make this highly coveted win. *John Ashbey*

There is a post script to the story of Peggy Sue's dam. In 1995, the American Kennel Club created the new title of Earth Dog for terriers and other dogs bred to dig in the earth after their prey. Ch. Glenlee's Sable Fox was the first dog of any breed to earn this title.

SCOTTISH TERRIERS—CALIFORNIA STYLE

California is the home of two Specialty clubs, the Scottish Terrier Club of California, which claims to be the oldest regional club, and the San Francisco Bay Scottish Terrier Club. California has always been the home of many outstanding breeders, but the Scottish Terrier fancy in California is heavily influenced by professional handlers. This is not only because of their successes in the show ring. The number of experienced breeders in California has dwindled while the size of the fancy in general has increased. Handlers like the late Lena Kardos, Bergit Coady and Mark George have filled the niche usually occupied by old-time breeders by offering guidance on breeding as well as on exhibiting. Stud dogs promoted by these handlers have been extraordinarily successful in California. The widespread use of Boy Blue, Dark Venture and Bobby Dazzler on the West Coast was directly attributable to Lena Kardos. In recent years, virtually all of the top-producing California sires have been dogs owned by clients of Mrs. Coady or Mr. George.

Lena Kardos

Lena Kardos was originally a social worker from Kentucky, but she was already a well-established terrier handler when, upon the death of Jake Terhune, Ch. Bardene Boy Blue came under her care. Together they started with a BIS and went on to amass a record that included many BIS wins. Mrs. Kardos's next star was the Boy Blue son, Ch. Anstamm Dark Venture, a Specialty and Group winner who went on to win the 1964 Lloyd Trophy. The following year, the Stamms imported Bardene Bobby Dazzler, a Bingo son, and, teamed with Mrs. Kardos, he achieved a record of Group and Specialty wins that led to another Lloyd Trophy win in 1966. In 1967, Mrs. Kardos again handled the Lloyd Trophy-winning Scottish Terrier, this time a daughter of Ch. Anstamm Dark Venture, Ch. Mar-De's Dark Felicia. In 1971, Mrs. Kardos showed another Bardene dog, imported by Wesley Slease, Ch. Bardene Blue McBain, a double Bingo grandson. During these years, Mrs. Kardos guided numerous breeders and exhibitors, and was in large measure responsible for the widespread use of Boy Blue, Dark Venture and Bobby Dazzler on the West Coast. For years, long after she retired from handling, Mrs. Kardos offered weekly training classes for would-be Scottie exhibitors, where she taught them the finer points of handling and grooming.

In 1977, a rare *Terrier Type* foldout introduced Eng. Ch. Gaywyn Likely Lad to America. Likely Lad brought with him from England an impressive show record: twenty-seven Challenge Certificates, two STC of England Specialty BOBs, and an all-breed BIS at Paignton in 1975. His pedigree was equally impressive combining Bingo, Highland King and Kennelgarth Viking. Lena had purchased Likely Lad for her clients, Roger and Nancy Abbott.

Lena Kardos with Ch. Bardene Bobby Dazzler.

Sporting a new American trim, Likely Lad finished with two Specialty majors and went on to win multiple Specialty BOBs and Groups. An outstanding sire, he produced thirty champions.

Bergit Coady

The second influential California handler began her career in her teens when she emigrated from Germany to England, where she worked at Elizabeth Meyer's famous Reanda kennels. In the mid 1960s, Betty Malinka convinced the young kennel girl to emigrate again, this time to her Sandoone Kennels near Chicago. For several years, Ms. Coady worked for Betty, conditioning and handling her dogs. Shortly after her marriage to Clay Coady, Ms. Coady moved to California where she and her former husband have proved themselves to be among the country's most successful terrier handlers. Ms. Coady's first big winner upon her move to California was Dick Hensel's Sandoone-bred Ch. Dunbar's Democrat of Sandoone. Shortly after Democrat's retirement in 1977, Ms. Coady began to show a young son of Democrat out of Ch. Prairyhill's Promenader, Ch. Democratic Victory, bred by Barbara and Robert Willis. Victory was a multiple BIS, Group and Specialty winner, going BOB at Montgomery County in 1980 and 1981, and winning the Lloyd Trophy in 1981 and 1982.

Ms. Coady also handled the 1985 Lloyd winner, Ch. Simonsez Charlie the Charmer. Charlie, bred by Louise Simon, was by Eng., Ital. and Am. Ch.

Enchanter of Eilburn, and a great-grandson of Eng. and Am. Ch. Gosmore Eilburn Admaration. Charlie and his brother, Ch. Simonsez Bodacious Kirley, were Louise's first homebred champions. Charlie, a Specialty, Group and BIS winner, was the top-ranked Scottish Terrier dog in 1985 and the sire of Ray and Hilda Bigelow's Group-winning, Ch. Dunbar's Braw Blackie. In 1988, Ms. Coady handled Margaret Plumb's English import, Ch. Kennelgarth Romeo, a multiple Specialty winner, and as this book goes to press (1996), Ms. Coady is successfully campaigning Robert and Jane Phelan's Ch. Caevnes Devil's Due.

Mark George

The third influential California handler learned his skills from Bob and Mildred Charves as a boy. Mark George was just starting to make his mark as a handler when he scored his biggest coup—convincing John and Barbara DeSaye to part with one of their very best bitches. John and Barbara DeSaye took a big risk in 1985 when they sold co-ownership in Ch. Sandgreg's Sweet Luv to James and Elizabeth Boso, breeders and exhibitors of West Highland White Terriers. When they became interested in Scotties, their handler, Mark George, referred them to the DeSayes. George had handled Sweet Luv to Winners Bitch at Montgomery County in 1984, the second wheaten to do so. George rightly thought she would make a good specials bitch. In April 1985, Sweet Luv became the second BIS wheaten Scot and in 1986, she won six Specialties and five Group Is and made breed history as the first wheaten to win the Lloyd Trophy.

While campaigning Sweet Luv, George had been readying a young wheaten dog named Sandgreg's Foxmoor. Foxmoor was by Ch. Sandgreg's

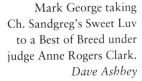

Mark George taking Ch. Sandgreg's Sweet Luv to a Best of Breed under judge Anne Rogers Clark.
Dave Ashbey

Eng., Am. Ch. Gosmore Eilburn Admaration.

Editorial out of Sweet Luv's big sister, Ch. Sandgreg's Sweet Charity. Mark George surprised everyone by showing Foxmoor at the 1986 STCA Rotating Specialty instead of Sweet Luv. This striking young wheaten justified George's faith in him when he went BOB, another first for wheatens. The Bosos bought Foxmoor shortly afterward, but he had to take a back seat in 1986 to his aunt "Luvie." Despite a very limited campaign during 1986, Foxmoor won three Groups, one all-breed BIS, and was BOS at Montgomery County.

The Bosos had three specials out with Mark George in 1986. In addition to Sweet Luv and Foxmoor, the Bosos had also purchased Ch. Balgair's Redoubts' Take A Bow. The Bosos purchased this smart little brindle bitch shortly after her impressive debut at the 1986 Atlanta Specialty, where she won BOB from the 9-12 Puppy class. Take A Bow won four Specialty BOBs in 1986, also handled by Mark George.

Over the next two years, Foxmoor won thirteen more Specialties, and eleven more Groups. He won the STCA Rotating Specialty in 1988 and the 1988 and 1989 Lloyd Trophies before going into semiretirement. In 1989, Foxmoor crowned his career with BOB at Montgomery County, another first for a wheaten Scottish Terrier. He is also the sire of seven champions.

Ch. Kennelgarth Romeo.
Missy Yuhl

				Eng. Ch. Kennelgarth Viking
			Eng. Ch. Kennelgarth Knight Errant	
				Bardene Bingotessa
		Eng. Ch. Kennelgarth Edrick		
				Eng. Ch. Kennelgarth King of Scots
			Kennelgarth Queen of Diamonds	
				Eng. Ch. Kennelgarth Black Diamond
	Kennelgarth Nelson			
				Eng. Ch. Gaywyn Joel
			Eng. Ch. Gaywyn Landmark	
				Eng. Ch. Gaywyn Lisa
		Kennelgarth Nell Gwyn		
				Eng. Ch. Gillson Grandiloquence
			Gillson Enterprise	
				Gillson Serene
Eng. Am. Ch. Kennelgarth Romeo				
				Eng. Ch. Kennelgarth Viking
			Eng. Ch. Kennelgarth Knight Errant	
				Bardene Bingotessa
		Eng. Ch. Kennelgarth Edrick		
				Eng. Ch. Kennelgarth King of Scots
			Kennelgarth Queen of Diamonds	
				Eng. Ch. Kennelgarth Black Diamond
	Eng. Ch. Kennelgarth Caprice			
				Eng. Ch. Kennelgarth Viking
			Eng. Ch. Kennelgarth King of Scots	
				Eng. Ch. Gaywyn Teasel
		Kennelgarth Daisybell		
				Kennelgarth Conspirator
			Eng. Ch. Kennelgarth Deborah	
				Kennelgarth Delilah

Clive and Mabel Pillsbury

Clive and Mable Pillsbury bred on a very small scale, but they imported some of the top-winning Scotties on the West Coast during the early 1970s. Eng. Ch. Gosmore Gillson Highland King was first, followed by Eng. Ch. Gosmore Eilburn Admaration. Admaration was a big winner in England, holding the record for more all-breed BIS in a single year than ever won by any other dog, and he continued his winning ways in the United States, where he was the Lloyd Trophy winner in 1970 and 1971. In 1972, the Pillsburys imported Viewpark Vanna, a multiple Group winner who was BOB at Westminster in 1973, the same year her sister, Eng. Ch. Viewpark Anna, England's Top Dog that year, was BOB at Crufts. The Pillsburys' last champion was the English import, Viewpark Vintner.

Medrick

In the twenty years between Medora Messenger's first Medrick champion, Medrick's Masterpiece, and her last one, Medrick's Merrymaker, Ms. Messenger provided assistance and breeding stock to many of today's California breeders. Ch. Medrick's Merry Minx, a Ch. Relgalf Rebel Leader granddaughter, co-owned with Ann Wooldridge, was Ms. Wooldridge's first champion. Medora's Medrick's Maxine was the dam of three champions.

Ms. Wooldridge also co-owned Ch. Sandgreg's Double or Nothing with Irene Robertson. He was by Keno Ticket, who finished with a Group win from the classes. In 1979, Ms. Wooldridge imported the first of many Scarista dogs that would ultimately come to these shores. Ann co-owned Aristocrat of Scarista with Harry Warren. Aristocrat finished handily and sired five champions. In 1983, Ann imported Scarista Gloriana for Sanford Rosenfeld.

McArthur's

Betty and Ken McArthur had already finished two champions when they began looking for a foundation bitch. They found her in the Midwest, a daughter of Nancy Fingerhut's Ch. Anstamm Happy Days. Dana's Constant Comment was an elegant black who seldom went unnoticed at Specialties. She was BOW at the 1978 San Francisco Specialty and BOS from the classes at the 1979 STCA Rotating Specialty. She was also BOS at the San Francisco Specialty in 1979 and 1981. In two litters by Ch. Aristocrat of Scarista, Constant Comment has produced three champions. The McArthurs then imported Scarista's Uptown Girl, a sister to Ch. Scarista s Rocky. Uptown Girl finished easily but produced no champions for them. They were more successful with Sally Rand, co-owned with her breeder Sanford Rosenfeld. Sally Rand, a daughter of Ch. Scarista Gloriana and Ch. Glenby Gallant Lad, had a successful show career. She won three Sweepstakes and was BOS at five Specialties, including the 1988 STCA Rotating. She then produced three champions from two litters.

Kellscot

Lynn Kelley Huffaker had remarkable success in a very short time with a breeding program based on two McArthur Scotties. Mrs. Huffaker's first champion was McArthur's Constant Challenge, out of Constant Comment. Constant Challenge was BOW at the 1984 STCA Rotating Specialty. Mrs. Huffaker's first two homebred champions were by Constant Challenge out of his half-sister, McArthur's CC of Maranscot. Kellscot Pacesetter was the first to finish and did so in style. She earned one major by going BOW at the 1987 San Francisco fall specialty, and a month later, was Winners Bitch at Montgomery County, owner-handled and conditioned by Lynn. Pacesetter was bred to Eng., Can., Am. Ch. Scarista's Rocky and produced two champions. One, Kellscot's Rockslide, won two Sweepstakes and was Reserve Winners Bitch in 1989 at Montgomery County. The second, Rockslide's brother, Kellscot's Bedrock, was Winners Dog at the 1990 STCA Rotating Specialty.

Charves

Mildred and Bob Charves had great success with their combination of Balachan, Gilkey, and Bardene bloodlines. They finished their first champion in 1953 and by 1965, they finished nearly thirty champions and provided foundation stock for many successful breeders. Their Charves Dazzler Dyke, a Bobby Dazzler son out of a Boy Blue-Balachan Gambit daughter, was a multiple Specialty winner in the early 1970s. Bred back to Ch. Charves Maggie Lauder, by Ch. Gilkey's Johnny Come Lately ex Gambit, Dazzler Dyke sired eight champions in two litters, including the Lefflers' Group-winning Ch. Charves Dashing Dainity and the Desayes' foundation bitch, Ch. Charves Dashing Dawtie. Maggie Lauder was the last of the Charves's great producing bitches. Her sister, Ch. Charves Silver Tassie, had five champions and her half-sister, Ch. Charves Elsie Marley, by Boy Blue, had three.

Meeder

Marge Meeder's foundation bitch, Ch. Wee Kelbie of Argus, was by Ch. Charves Rory O'More, a brother to Maggie Lauder. Wee Kelbie was the dam of four champions, three by Ch. Bardene Bingo and one by Ch. Charves Dazzler Delegate. The Bingo son, Ch. Meeder's Discord, owned by the Charves, was BOB at the 1972 California Specialty and was ranked in the top ten for 1972.

Moorscott

Betty Pengra began her breeding program in the late 1960s with two Charves bitches, Charves Honeybee, and Moorscott Dazzler Debutante, sister to Ch. Charves Dazzler Dyke. Breeding to Bingo and the Bingo son, Ch. Meeder's Impresario, Betty bred half a dozen champions. Two were the foundation for William and Peggy Burge's J-Mar Scots. The Burge's first champion, Burge's Unsinkable Molly, was sired by Ch. Moorscott Masterpiece, a Bingo-Dazzler Debutante son. Unsinkable Molly produced two champions sired by Marge Meeder's Bingo sons, Ch. Meeder's Cadence and Ch. Meeder's Impresario. The Burges also owned Ch. Moorscot Mystic Moment, sired by Impresario.

Castlecrag

Barbara and Brum Dunham's Castlecrag Scottish Terriers were bred along similar lines to the Charves dogs. The Dunhams started with a Charves bitch, Charves Gillie Callum, a daughter of Ch. Balachan Advocator out of Ch. Balachan Gambit. Their first homebred champion, Charves Highland Wander'r, a Boy Blue son, finished in 1968. Over the next twelve years, the Dunhams bred to Bardene-sired dogs to achieve their successes. In the late 1970s, they acquired the Highland King daughter, Ch. Anstamm King's Treasure, who produced two champions by Likely Lad.

Merrilland

Martha Merrill started showing in the late 1960s with a double Winning Trick granddaughter, Ch. Merrilland Drambuie. Shortly thereafter, Martha imported Niddbank Wise Guy from England, a dog linebred to Bardene Blue Steptoe. Mrs. Merrill's Ch. Anstamm Dazzler Dynamic daughter, Ch. Merrilland Burma Star, was bred to Admaration to produce Martha's multititled Merrilland Too Shoos, the only Scottish Terrier to hold both conformation and obedience titles in America, Canada and Mexico.

Cederbrae

Harvey and Louise Cederstrom were the lucky co-owners of Connie Swatsley's BIS winner, Ch. Revran Reprise. From a Reprise daughter, Ch. Revran Cantata, the Cederstroms bred over a half dozen Cederbrae champions. Cantata was bred to Ch. Marlorain Alfie of Anstamm to produce the Cederstroms' top-winning Scottie, Ch. Lady Chips of Cederstrom, owned by Joyce Gast. Lady Chips started her career with a Specialty win, going BOW at the 1974 California Specialty. She returned in 1984 to win BOS at the 1984 STCA Rotating Specialty.

Seaforth

Jerry Roszman and Donn La Vigne's Seaforth prefix has appeared on over twenty champions, beginning with their first homebred champion, Seaforth's Kelly MacHamish. Kelly was by Sueannette and Elsie Wood's Ch. Schwer's Dynamic Happy Fellow, brother to Dynamic Happy Boy. From this start, the Seaforth Scotties have demonstrated their consistent type and temperament in the show ring and the whelping box. Jerry and Donn were fortunate to have several top producing bitches, including Dunbar's Sable of Sandbark, dam of six champions, and Kenjo's Venturing Star and Ch. Hilcar's Royal Lady, each the dam of three champions. Sable, a daughter of Ch. Dunbar's Special Agent, was the dam of Ch. Seaforth's FDR, Best in Sweepstakes at the 1978 STCA Specialty at Montgomery County. Jerry and Donn's top-winning bitch, Ch. Dunbar's Royal Achievement, by Highland King, started her show career by going Winners Bitch and BOS over specials at the 1977 San Francisco Specialty, and finished by going BOW that fall at Montgomery County. She then went on to a successful career that included Group wins.

Ravenscraig

Margaret Plumb's imported Ch. Kennelgarth Romeo, the sire of thirty-three champions, owes much of his success at stud to Al and Jeannie Jennings's bitch, Ch. Ravenscraig Rhapsody. Al and Jeannie fell in love with a park ranger's Scottie and bought their first from a backyard breeder. Al was dissatisfied with the local groomer, so he bought Dr. Kirk's book and set out to do the job himself. Between what Al taught himself by grooming and what they learned from the book, the Jennings soon concluded that Angus was not exactly the dog described by the Standard. At the STC of California puppy match, they were referred to Lena Kardos. Through Lena, they bought their first show bitch, Shadowfax Empennage, bred by D. Gayle Christensen and sired by Gayle's BIS winner, Ch. Sudden Kaos of Shadowfax, a brother to Ch. Glenby Gallant Lad.

Empennage was tightly linebred on Ch. Gaywyn Likely Lad so, after she finished, she was bred to her cousin, Ch. Glenby's Sunrise Scoundrel. Empennage's daughter, Ch. Ravenscraig Rhapsody, was the Jennings' first homebred champion. Together Rhapsody and Romeo have produced eleven champions. The Jennings also imported Ch. Pendlehill Viceroy, who was BOB at the 1995 STC of California Specialty.

R-Starr

Robin Starr's first champion, a male, was by Tim and Patricia Bennett's Ch. Boulder Legend Landslide, by Gallant Lad. Her foundation bitch was

Ch. Glenby's Royal Lady, by Ch. Glenby's Royal Ruler and the BIS-winning English import, Ch. Lady Morag of Wyndham. Royal Lady's son, Ch. R-Starr's Tug O War, was Best in Sweepstakes at Montgomery County in 1993.

Stonecroft

It was nearly thirty years between Phyllis Dabbs's purchase of her first pet Scottie and the purchase in 1983 of her first show Scottie, Stonecroft's Highland Ransom, from breeder Kay Hevle. Shortly afterward, Phyllis purchased Dunbar's Miss Della from Bergit Coady. Both bitches were linebred on Ch. Dunbar's Democrat of Sandoone and Bergit's English import, Ch. Reanda King's Ransom. Bergit finished both bitches within a month of each other in the fall of 1984.

Although their pedigrees were very similar, only Miss Della was a good producer. In her first litter, by Ch. Charmar's Enchanter, Miss Della produced three champions, including Ch. Stonecroft's Gaelic Warrior, Winners Dog at Montgomery County, 1986. Miss Della and Enchanter produced two more champions in her second litter. She produced two more champions by Charlie The Charmer and her eighth by Ch. Jusctott's Reanda Just Rite.

Top Brass

Marilyn Garfield founded her Top Brass Scotties with a Charlie the Charmer daughter, Ch. Bairnsdale's Golden Girl, and a granddaughter of Phyllis Dabbs's top-producing Ch. Dunbar's Miss Della, CD, Ch. Caevnes Dark Star of Top Brass. Her third bitch, Ch. Top Brass Jacglen's FoxyLady, introduced Mystigael breeding into the line. In her first five years of breeding, Marilyn Garfield has already bred four champions.

Koch's

With Mark George's help, Fred and Ann Koch have based their successful breeding program on a top-producing mother and daughter team. Their foundation bitch was Ch. Glad-Mac's Georgette, a black daughter of Ch. Sandgreg's Square Deal out of a Happy Venture daughter. Georgette's first two champions were Ch. Koch's Olympic Flame and her brother Ch. Koch's Olympic Entry, by Ch. Sandgreg's Editorial. Georgette is also the dam of three champions by Ch. Sandgreg's Foxmoor. Their son, Ch. Koch's Rambo of Aberglen, has won two Specialties. Olympic Flame finished with three five-point majors, handled by Mark George, before retiring to the whelping box. She produced five champions from two litters and all finished in 1989, making her the top brood bitch for that year. Olympic Flame is also the dam of Int. Ch. Koch's Forty-Niner, owned by Finnish breeder Raija Jarvinen.

Glenlee

Tom and Linda Lee have also relied on Mark George's advice and handling skills with much success. Their first champion was Merrilland Gypsy Moth, a showy wheaten bitch bred by Martha Merrill, by Ch. Sandgreg's Desert Fox. Handled by Mark, Gypsy Moth finished with four Specialty majors. The Lees' second champion was Koch's Shadow Fox of Glenlee, a black daughter of Ch. Sandgreg's Foxmoor.

Jacglen

Jacki and Glen Herron are among the many newcomers introduced to the fancy by Martha Merrill. They had a pet shop Scottie and Mrs. Merrill taught Mrs. Herron how to trim him. The Herrons later bought a show puppy from Mrs. Merrill but he developed prostate problems before he could finish and had to be neutered. Their second "first" show dog was Dunedin's Lady Elizabeth, a daughter of Gaywyn Telford bred by Margaret Lockette. Lena Kardos showed and conditioned Lady Elizabeth until the 1984 Beverly Hills show. Mrs. Kardos was unable to make it to the Scottie ring so a nervous Jacki made her handling debut. She and Lady Elizabeth did well enough for Reserve Winners Bitch and a new owner-handler was born. Lady Elizabeth ultimately finished, but never had any puppies. The Herrons finally got a bitch who would show and reproduce when they bought Ch. Jacglen's Lindsay O'Mystigael from Tony and Pat Gruda. Lindsay has produced three champions from two litters.

SCOTS OFF THE MAINLAND

Alaska and Hawaii have obstacles to breeding and exhibiting purebred dogs that are unique to each state. Both states have only a few shows each year. Neither is contiguous to the mainland states. Alaska has a very small population relative to its size, while Hawaii has a 4-month rabies quarantine for dogs. This quarantine makes it virtually impossible for Hawaiian dogs to compete on the mainland and very difficult for Hawaiian breeders to avail themselves of the services of mainland stud dogs.

Alaska

In Alaska, Gayle Christensen's Ch. Sudden Kaos Of Shadowfax, was the first Scottish Terrier BIS winner. Sally Johnson's first two champions, Wychwyre Sorceress and Aberglen Northwest Passage, have been her best producers with two champions each. Northwest Passage's son, Ch. Heather Isles Black Ice, is a multiple Group and BIS winner. Sara Cebulski co-owns three champion Scotties with Mrs. Johnson. Doreen Cross and her daughter, Rebecca, started their breeding program with Ch. Anstamm Flash Flood, the first champion son of Ch. Anstamm Summer Lightning, and a bitch from Phyllis Dabbs, Stonecroft Black Watch, CDX. These two have produced two champions at this writing.

Hawaii

As long as Hawaii maintains its quarantine regulations, the purebred dog fancy there will always have an uphill struggle. In 1975, Joy and Charles Denman and Nancy Scarci imported Noonsun Merry Monarch from England. Merry Monarch finished in four shows with four majors and, at that time, he was one of the very few Scottish Terriers to finish his championship entirely within the state. Unfortunately, Merry Monarch did not live long enough to make his mark on the breed in Hawaii and his owners apparently lost interest in breeding or showing. In 1977, Ann Wildrick began importing a number of quality Scottish Terriers. She was plagued by bad luck and none of her bitches ever produced a champion. Jim and Ruth Terna's first champion, Sonata Happy Hula Girl, was a full sister to Ch. Sonata Serenade and Ch. Anstamm Happy Sonata. Hula Girl was bred to John Sheehan's Bingo son, Ch. Scotsmuir Sandpiper, before leaving the mainland and produced three champions in this litter. The first, Ch. Alohascott Polynesian Piper, finished in 28 days in Hawaii, a state record for all breeds at the time. He had multiple Group placements as a special and his sister, Ch. Alohascott Moonlight Lady, was a Group winner. Hula Girl was bred a second time to Lena Kardos's Likely Lad son, Ch. Sodark Tally Ho, and produced her fourth champion, Alohascott Dark Mirage. Sadly, however, the Ternas, too, have stopped breeding or showing their dogs. Today, Dorinne Higuchi and Florence Kaaloha represent nearly the entire Scottish Terrier fancy in Hawaii. They have bred six champions, including Alohalani Luck O'The Irish and his son, Alohalani Marvalous Marvin. Each dog won four Groups and Luck O'The Irish won one all-breed BIS. This record is particularly impressive because Hawaii only has five all-breed clubs. Florence and Dorine's top-producing bitch is Ch. Seaforth's Lady Maurine, the mother of five champions.

IN SUMMARY

No history of a breed can be complete, particularly as the story approaches its present. No one can predict which dog or bitch will leave a mark on the breed and which will fade into obscurity. The breed's next great sire may be in the first litter of a novice breeder. Also, it is nearly impossible to predict what problems breeders may face in the future. The number of bad mouths has declined while bad fronts seem to be everywhere. There is something rather existential in this hobby in that breeders never really reach their goal and must take pleasure in the constant attempt. It is, in part, that constant striving for perfection, the anticipation of the great one to come, that keeps the fancy going forward. Most of all, however, Scottie breeders are united by the fact that at some point in each of their lives, a funny, sober, loving, exasperating, independent and utterly unique little dog changed each of them forever. Whatever their differences, they will always be united by that fact, and by their responsibility for the welfare of the Scottish Terrier, who has made their lives so special.

Chapter 6

Description of the Scottish Terrier

The extreme variations in size, shape, color, coat and temperament seen among modern purebred dogs demonstrate that early breeders were primarily guided by the well-worn adage *form follows function*. To fully understand the structure and temperament of the Scottish Terrier, one must first understand what he was bred to do. This Scottish Terrier "job description," written in 1934 by Dr. William Bruette, describes the grim life's work of early earth dogs:

> There the cairns in which the despoilers of the flocks take refuge are mountains of tumbled rock sometimes a quarter of a mile in circumference. The terrier that enters these labyrinths of granite leaves hope of human aid behind. He must wind his way through miles of clefts and crevices, the walls of which will not yield to tooth or claw. The battle is his alone. He must, unaided, drive his prey into the open or fight the battle underground without hope of help from human hands. It is well that his hide be tough and clothed with a cushion of bristling hair, his muscles strong and his frame elastic; for, as he follows his prey among the crevices, there is always the danger of the narrow cleft through which he crushes with shoulders and ribs only to feel the deadly grip of relentless rock. He can no longer go forward; he cannot pull back. His voice is lost in the winding caverns that is [sic] destined for his tomb. His only hope is that hunger and thirst will reduce his sturdy frame and set him free before he is too weak to win his way to the open. It can be truly said that there is not a cairn in all the hills of Scotland that has not its tale to tell of these canine tragedies.

143

The harsh life of early Scottish Terriers took its toll on dogs who could not do the task for which they were bred. Dogs too large to easily dig into the den of a wild animal and those too insubstantial to fight their way out again were quickly eliminated from the huntsman's breeding stock. When the breed came to the attention of the show fancy at the end of the nineteenth century, the qualities that served the working Scottie were preserved in the written Standard of the breed. The Standard has been revised over the years, but the purpose of these revisions was only to make the language more precise and not to change the dog.

That is not to say that the Scottish Terrier has *not* changed over the past hundred years. For the most part, the changes have been made to improve the breed without changing its general appearance: a small but substantial, low-to-ground and active terrier, with a long head in proportion to its size, a rough coat, short legs, prick ears, and an undocked carrot-shaped tail carried vertically or with a slight curve forward.

There is no question that today's Scottish Terrier is often larger (though rarely as tall as twelve inches), and nearly always heavier than his forebears. The first written Standard called for a dog ranging from nine to twelve inches in height at the withers and weighing from fifteen to twenty pounds. Specimens over twenty pounds were to be discouraged. In England, size crept upward with each revision of the Standard except the most recent. In 1933, the English Standard, while making no height recommendation, called for a dog "of a size to get to ground," weighing from seventeen to twenty-one pounds. Seventeen years later, the Kennel Club again upped the weight range to a range of nineteen to twenty-three pounds. In addition, it added a height-at-shoulder measurement of ten to eleven inches. The membership of the Scottish Terrier Club of England was outraged. In its final attempt to stave off this change, it published a plea in the 1949 *Yearbook* which said, in part:

It is a mistake to tamper too much with fundamental things, and the Standard of a breed is fundamental. The Standards of our British breeds were drawn up by wise men, and aided and abetted by succeeding generations of breeders, the Scottish terrier became a power in the land, not only in the British Isles but in many parts of the world to which his popularity had carried him. He is world renowned, so why tamper with the basic rules laid down? If the weight were raised now, to suit those who wish to cross the T's and dot the I's, mark my words, in five years there will be bigger— but I much doubt better—Scottish terriers. Then it will be "up she goes again" and the grand little Diehard will no longer be a handy-sized terrier, but an awkward misfit, who will no longer be eligible to enter the category of low-legged Terriers, and may be dangerously near getting pushed into the long-legged section!! The Scot must retain his size in order to maintain type, and pray let us keep Scottish Terrier type as our main consideration.

It is interesting to note that American fanciers have been more conservative than the British regarding size and weight. The first American Standard, of course, adopted the same height and weight recommendations of the then-current Scottish and English Standards. The first revision to the American Standard in 1925 set the height at about ten inches at the shoulder. This Standard came under some criticism from British and American breeders because it set the weight at eighteen to twenty pounds for dogs and bitches, rather than setting a separate range for each sex. The most significant point about this Standard is that it narrowed the range of size allowed for the breed. This was as much due to the fact that breeders were beginning to produce a more consistent type as it was to a desire to keep the Scottish Terrier fairly small.

In 1947, the American breed Standard was revised by a committee consisting of Edwin Megargee, Theodore Bennett, John Kemps and Maurice Pollack. Height at shoulder remained the same, but weight crept up slightly: eighteen to twenty pounds for bitches and nineteen to twenty-two pounds for dogs. The committee that prepared the 1993 revision, consisting of Barbara DeSaye, Evelyn Kirk, Neatha Robinson, Jerry Roszman, Miriam Stamm, and Christine Stephens, left size and weight untouched.

For the first time, however, the Standard included a measurement of body length: "about 11 inches from withers to set-on of tail." This number was not selected without considerable research. The first Scottish and English breed Standards described the body as "of moderate length, not so long as a Skye's . . . " This picture of Eng. Ch. Ems Cosmetic (whelped in 1903 and universally agreed to be one of the finest Scottish Terriers of her day) gives some idea of what was considered "moderate length" by the drafters of that Standard.

Eng. Ch. Ems Cosmetic

Eng. Am. Ch. Rookery
Repeater of Hitofa

The 1925 American Standard described the body as "moderately short and well ribbed up . . . " while the 1933 English Standard described the back as "proportionally short and very muscular." A photograph of Eng., Am. Ch. Rookery Repeater of Hitofa, considered an outstanding specimen of the breed in the early 1930s, shows a dog that does not look exceptionally short-backed to modern eyes.

In 1952, Seth Malby, John McLay and Johnny Murphy formed a committee to draw up a guide, the stated purpose of which was "to fix more precisely some of the more or less indefinite points of the official Standard of our breed." The Scottish Terrier Club of America included these measurements and ratios in 1980 when it adopted a *Clarification and Amplification of the 1947 American Standard:*

CORRECT DIMENSIONS For dog (inches)			CORRECT DIMENSIONS For bitch (inches)
Length of Head	L	$8^1/_4$	8
Length of Skull	.5 L	$4^1/_8$	4
Length of Muzzle	.5 L	$4^1/_8$	4
Width of Skull	.455 L	$3^3/_4$	$3^5/_8$
Length of Neck	.727 L	6	$5^7/_8$
Clearance-Floor to Brisket	.455 L	$3^3/_4$	$3^5/_8$

Distance inside Elbows	.455 L	3³/₄	3⁵/₈
Length of Tail	.788 L	6¹/₂	6¹/₄
Height at Withers	1.21 L	10	9³/₄
Length of Back	1.33 L	11	10⁵/₈
L = Length of Head			

In 1959, Edwin Megargee, a well-known breeder, judge and artist wrote an article called "The Ideal Scottish Terrier," which appeared in the 1959 *Handbook* of the STCA. In the article, he wrote the following on the matter of body length:

Bodies are more often too long than too short, but they can be too short. When this occurs, and is accompanied by the immense head advocated by a few extremists, the effect is weird and monstrous. A nice balance between body and head is what is desired. While no hard and fast rule as to the proportion can be laid down, I like to see one and three-quarters to two head lengths from the point of the shoulder to the rear end, as the desirable body length.

Anyone who doubts that Scotties have grown significantly shorter in back over the past one hundred years need only look at these measurements of Ch. Dundee, one of the two founding sires of the breed, and the celebrated bitch of Captain Mackie, Ch. Glengogo, taken by D. J. Thompson Gray:

	DUNDEE	GLENGOGO
Occiput to eye	5 inches	4¹/₂ inches
Inner corner of eye to nose	3	3
Shoulder to root of tail	15	16
Height	10	10

The following three pictures illustrate the problem that breeders encounter when trying to convey the correct mental picture of the Scottish Terrier. Figure 1 is a drawing that was originally created to illustrate an article on the ideal Scottish Terrier. The dog is very pleasing to the eye, but the proportions are incorrect. Assume that this "ideal" dog is eleven inches from withers to set-on of tail. By its proportions then this dog would be seventeen inches tall with an eleven-inch back, an eleven-inch neck, and an eleven-inch head!

Figure 2 is Megargee's drawing used to illustrate his ideal Scottish Terrier. Megargee, having the advantage of an artist's eye combined with a breeder's knowledge, has drawn a perfectly balanced dog of correct proportions. Grooming styles have changed so drastically that it is difficult for the untrained eye to see that, with a modern trim, the dog in Figure 2 would look almost identical to the dog in Figure 3.

The head is extremely important in establishing breed type and is the reason so much space was allotted to it in the new Standard. More than any other component of the Standard, the head distinguishes the Scottish Terrier from his closest terrier cousins, the Cairn and the West Highland White Terriers. The new Standard describes in considerable detail the elements that make up the head:

Figure 1.

Figure 2.

Figure 3.

Viewed from the side, head must be long in proportion to the size of the dog. For a dog with an eleven-inch topline, a head of about eight inches from occiput to tip of nose is correct. Longer-bodied dogs must have longer heads to be in proper balance. The slightly-domed skull and the muzzle should form two parallel planes of equal length. When the planes are not parallel, expression will be wrong. The most common fault of this type is where the skull falls away at the occiput, creating a down-faced look. Even more unpleasant, but seen less frequently, is the "dish face," where the muzzle rises upward toward the nose.

The two parallel planes of the head are separated by a slight but distinct stop between the eyes. Breeding for excessive length of head often results in the gradual flattening of the stop. This must be avoided as the stop is an important characteristic of the Scottie head. In profile, the stop causes a slight but distinct drop from the level of the topline of the skull to the level of the topline of the foreface. It also allows the eyes to be set deeply under the brow where they are less susceptible to injury.

Looking at the dog head-on, the width of the skull should be slightly narrower than the length of the skull. If the dog has an 8¼-inch head, the ideal skull should be just slightly over four inches long and about three and a half inches wide. The Scottie's jaw muscles lie along the cheeks and attach to the skull. It is the length of the muscles that gives the jaws their power, not breadth of the skull or prominence of the cheek. The inner corner of the eye should mark the location of the stop and the longitudinal center of the head from nose to occiput. The muzzle should be well filled in front of and beneath the eyes and taper just slightly toward the nose. The muzzle must have plenty of depth from top to bottom; enough, as the Standard says, "to fill an average man's hand."

It is important here to look at the evolution of the language describing the Scottie mouth. The first Scottish, English and American Standards said, "The jaws should be perfectly level and the teeth square." It was a fault for the muzzle to be "either under or over hung." In 1925, the drafters of the revised Standard amended the "Faults" section to read, "Jaw over or undershot." The 1947 Standard gave a more detailed description of correct teeth: "The teeth should be evenly placed, having a scissors or level bite, with the former being preferable." Overshot and undershot jaws were listed under "Penalties." It was not until the 1993 Standard became effective that the size of the teeth was included: "The teeth should be large and evenly spaced, having either a scissor or level bite, the former preferred. The jaw should be square, level and powerful. Undershot or overshot bites should be penalized."

Notice how the original Standard called for a level *jaw*, while today's Standard allows for a level *bite*. In a letter to Fayette Ewing in 1932, A.G. Cowley, the famous "Wizard of Albourne," wrote that the level bite had "sneaked" into the American Standard as a result of misunderstanding. According to Cowley, the early breeders wanted a powerful, square scissors bite where the incisors formed a straight line perpendicular to the outside line of the jaw. They never intended to allow a level bite, that is, a bite where the incisors meet tip to tip rather than the scissors bite in which the uppers overlap the lowers. If Cowley was correct, this mistake was an unfortunate one. Veterinary dental specialists consider the level bite to be the most damaging symmetrical bite. Not only is there is a constant erosion of the cutting edge of the front teeth, but the continual trauma of the incisors coming together creates inflammation of the supporting tissues surrounding the roots of the teeth. This inflammation can lead to periodontal disease. The fact that no British Standard has ever approved a level *bite* gives credence to Cowley's assertion.

In any event, a Scottie's teeth are an important part of his arsenal. They should be strikingly large for the size of the dog—it has been said that the Scottie has the largest teeth of all terriers, except the Airedale. As heads lengthen, there is a tendency for the arch of the jaw to become increasingly narrow, causing the teeth to become crowded. Breeders must guard against this tendency. In the 1930s, dog writers were always bemoaning the fact that Scotties had more bad mouths than the other terrier breeds. Certainly today's breeders and judges seem much more fastidious about penalizing crowded mouths or crooked teeth than their predecessors and the number of bad mouths seems to be declining. Unfortunately, since the art of cosmetic dentistry is not a new one and has only benefitted by advances in technology, one can never be certain if the improvements are genetic or environmental!

The Standard calls for the nose to be of good size and black, "regardless of coat color." This language is used because some, not all, wheaten Scots have brownish-pink or pink noses. In some cases, the nose is lighter in winter months and darker in the summer. The cause of so-called *winter nose* is uncertain, but since many wheatens have black noses all year round, winter noses need not be tolerated in the breed.

Another important characteristic of the nose is its projection over the mouth. As fashion gradually encouraged the breeding of fuller face whiskers, this attribute of the Scottish Terrier became less obvious to the casual observer. The Scottie is not to have a blunt muzzle like a West Highland White.

Correct eyes should be dark, almond-shaped, set wide apart and deeply set under the brow and should carry a keen, penetrating look. It would seem unnecessary to define "almond-shaped," but no one has done it better than Dorothy Caspersz in her book, *The Scottish Terrier:*

> To give the correct expression, the curve of the upper eyelid should be accentuated, especially at a point a little nearer the haw than the center of the lid, while the lower lid is a flat curve. The outer point of the eye is slightly higher than the haw so that at the broadest part, the eye appears to be slightly oblique.

This dog has perfect almond-shaped eyes, giving correct Scottish Terrier expression. The ears are somewhat too large and the outer edge of the ear extends too far out from the side of the skull.

Of course, all eyeballs are round, so the almond shape is really created by correct placement of the eye in the skull. Another key element in determining correct expression is the distance between the eyes. Small eyes set too closely together give an unpleasant, "piggy" expression. The inner corner of the eyes should be between one and two inches apart, depending on the length of the head. Above all, the eyes must be deeply set in under the brow. This is more than an aesthetic requirement. When struggling with a prey, the bony skull protects the Scottie's deep-set eye.

Eye color, on the other hand, *is* purely aesthetic. Until 1925 in the United States and 1933 in England, the Standard allowed for dark brown or hazel eyes. Dark eyes came to be preferred and, eventually, required by the Standards. In evaluating the importance of eye color, William McCandlish cautioned the fancy in his 1909 edition of *The Scottish Terrier:*

> If the exhibition of dogs is to escape the charge of being a fancier's hobby or business, and not for an improvement in the appearance of the breed from a workman's and companionable point of view, criticisms such as [preferring dark brown eye color to hazel eye color] must be regarded as ridiculous by judges and the general body of breeders and exhibitors. The placement of the eye is of greater importance in attaining correct expression than either colour or shape, as is exemplified by the fact that individual Terriers whose eyes were light in shading and too round have possessed the desired expression, but no dog, however correct the eye in itself was, has ever looked right if the eye placement was wrong.

You do not have to examine a Scottie closely to determine if the eyes are placed correctly. When a dog with correctly placed eyes is standing at attention and looking forward, the topline of the skull is not horizontal but rather forms a right angle with the topline of the neck. In other words, the dog looks outward or downward but not upward.

The size, shape, placement and use of the ears also have important bearing on the Scottish Terrier's expression, but they also are perfectly designed for a working terrier. Watch a Scottie out in the rain and you will notice that he can fold the two edges of his ear together and then bend them back, forming a double fold. This keeps out not only rain, but dirt as well, useful to a dog who digs for a living. Such ears also present a minimal target for injury when the dog is locked in combat with his quarry.

Viewed from the front, the ears should be erect and what is usually described as V-shaped, although Λ-shaped would be more accurate. The outer edge of the ear, however, should extend straight upward, perpendicular to the topline of the skull. The lobe should extend outward as little as possible. Ideally, it should be possible to place a hand flat against a Scottie's cheek and run straight up the outer edge of the ear.

From the side, the ears should be placed well back on the skull, the base extending slightly behind the occiput. The front edge of the ear should form an angle just slightly greater than 90 degrees with the topline of the skull. Ears set too far forward on the skull, too wide apart or too close together detract from the desired expression and impression of sharpness. Ears can be too small, making it impossible for the dog to fold them tightly when necessary, but more common faults include ears too wide at the base, ears with rounded tips and ears set too low on the skull. Other less common faults include ears placed too high on the skull, ears too tall and ears set so close together that the inner edge becomes the perpendicular edge.

Scottie ears are mobile and expressive. Most will fold their ears back slightly when moving and nearly all will do likewise when spoken to in a playful manner. The ears should immediately stand stiffly erect, however, when something attracts the dog's attention. The hair on the back of the ears should be short and soft in texture.

After back length, length of neck is probably the part of the Standard most debated by breeders. There are always breeders and judges who push for longer necks on Scottish Terriers, notwithstanding the Standard which calls for a "moderately short, strong, thick, and muscular" neck. Breeds that require long necks were nearly always bred for one of two purposes: to gaze into the distance to find prey or to chase down a fleeing animal. A Scottie needs a "moderately short," strong neck for fighting in close quarters and dragging an unwilling enemy from its den. The Malby committee determined that a "moderately short" neck would measure approximately six inches, measured from the occiput to the withers.

A moderately short neck does not have to look "stuffy." Two factors give style to the correct Scottie neck. First, the neck must taper slightly from the shoulders up to the head, creating a very slight arch to the back line of the neck. A neck whose circumference is the same from top to bottom is referred to as a "ewe neck." Straight shoulders often accompany long, thin ewe necks, creating a "stove pipe" effect where the nearly vertical neck line meets the horizontal topline. Second, the neck must be set into well laid-back shoulders. In a correctly made Scottish Terrier, the angle formed by the back line of the neck and the topline of the skull is a right angle, but the apex of that angle leans slightly forward from the dog.

The Scottish Terrier front is designed for the same five functions as all other dogs, plus one extra. The front must support weight, absorb concussion, propel on turns, offset lateral displacement, maintain the level of the center of gravity, and *dig!* Good forequarters have always been difficult to achieve and maintain in this breed. It is easy to see why good fronts are so rare. For one thing, the forequarters are made up of a number of parts, each of which must be in correct proportion to the other and placed correctly in relation to the other. For another, we are asking Nature to do something "unnatural," that is, make short legs out of heavy bones and attach them to a ten-inch high dog.

The forequarters comprise the two shoulder blades (scapulae), the upper arms (humeri) and the front legs consisting of the foreleg, pastern and toes (radius and ulna, metacarpals and phalanges). The region where the tops of the scapulae come together is called the withers. The forechest between the front legs is also called the brisket.

A good front starts with shoulders. In the ideal Scottie, the scapula and the upper arm should approximate a right angle, the scapula should be well laid-back, and the upper arm must be just slightly shorter than the scapula. In a well laid-back shoulder, the top of the scapula points farther back toward the tail. It has long been an article of faith that the correct degree of layback was 45 degrees back from vertical, measured up the scapula ridge. Rachel Page Elliot's in-depth studies of canine movement indicate that 30 degrees is a more correct measurement. In any event, good layback is *very* important for two reasons—first, the head of the upper arm has a knob that prevents the complete straightening of the joint with the scapula. A straight line, drawn while the dog is standing, down the center of the scapula marks the limit of forward reach. Thus, the farther back the shoulder, the farther forward the dog can reach with the front leg. A dog with poor layback walks with a mincing, inefficient gait. Secondly, straight shoulders make the back longer and the neck shorter—not as pleasing to the eye. Finally, if the scapulae are set too far apart at the withers, there will be a muscular buildup under the blades, often referred to as "loaded" shoulders.

Good angulation and layback are still not enough. If the upper arm is too short, the front legs can still be too far forward. The upper arm must be long enough so that the front leg is set down behind the dog's forechest. In profile a Scottie should show a good handful of chest (not just hair) extending in front of the legs. The elbow joint should be well behind the front line of the chest and above the bottom line of the brisket. This placement allows the dog to rest his weight on the chest while freeing the legs for digging. Viewed from the front, the elbow must not protrude to the side, nor should it be tucked under the body. When the dog is moving, the elbow should move smoothly against the ribs. The brisket should be wide and deep. From the front, the chest should appear to be slung between the two legs rather than set on top of them.

The forelegs must be big and muscular. When the leg is grasped, the bone should feel round, not flat. The feet should be big with firm, arched toes and strong, black nails. Nails should be kept reasonably short, but a digging breed need not have its nails cut nearly to the quick as is done with many other show dogs. The Standard allows for a *slight* toeing out, although this has been a point of controversy for many years. Older Scottie breeders argued that long-legged terrier breeders-turned-judges were responsible for the development of a straight-legged Scottish Terrier. Most modern experts on canine structure agree with the old-time breeders who insisted that a very slight outward bend of pastern was necessary to keep the shoulder and front leg assembly in balance.

The shape of the body is largely determined by the ribs. A Scottie should be big-ribbed for its size. As the ribs move outward from the spine, they should form a broad back, then flatten to form the deep body. This shape enables the dog to maneuver in tight, underground spaces. It is also important that the ribs be carried well back, extending beyond the halfway point of the body. Shortness of back is obtained not at the expense of good ribs, but by a short, muscular loin. The importance of the correct loin is often overlooked. William McCandlish wrote:

> The loin should be short, very broad and muscular. . . . A little extra length of loin is not, in my opinion, much of a fault provided it is very muscular, but a short, thin loin is particularly obnoxious for a dog so made is sailing under false pretences. He is complying with the letter of the law, but breaking it in effect, more especially obnoxious because there are so many people about who know a Scottish Terrier ought to have a short back, but who could neither tell you what the object is, nor even what constitutes a short back. They judge only by the eye, and have no knowledge of anatomy. A dog whose ribs extend well back, and who has a slightly long but very muscular loin, might measure more from neck to stern than a dog too short in barrel and with a longish, weak loin, and in all probability the ordinary dog show judge would commend the latter dog for his short back over the dog that complied much closer with the real requirements, merely because the term "short back" is readily acquired by the novice as a recognized virtue; and so many people, even among those who have kept the breed for years, never acquire a greater knowledge than is to be obtained from stereotyped phrases. If the loin is broad and muscular, a little extra length is a very minor fault.

The topline was not addressed in the English Standard until 1933 when the following language was adopted: "In general, the topline of the body should be straight." Strangely, the subject was not addressed by any American Standard until 1993. Apparently the fancy shared the opinion of Dorothy Caspersz who wrote: "If the two ends of the dog are properly constructed there is seldom any need to worry about the middle-piece, for the correctly placed humerus and stifle in a Scottish Terrier are the keynotes to correct type." The Standard now says the topline of the back should be firm and level. Any student of canine anatomy knows that the spine of every dog actually curves downward slightly at the withers and just slightly upward over the loin (that curve may be more pronounced in some breeds). In a properly constructed Scottie, however, those slight spinal curves are virtually imperceptible, whether the dog is standing

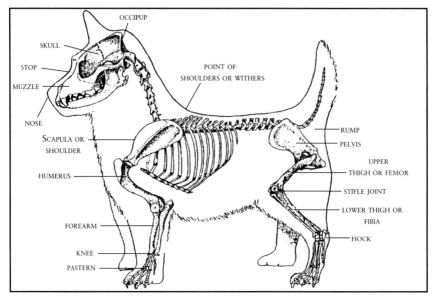

Skeletal structure of the Scottish Terrier.

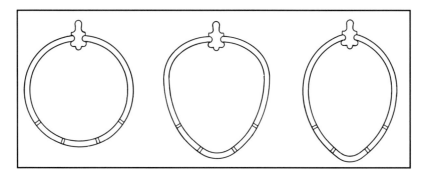

Rib structure. A round rib without depth (left), improper on a Scot. A heart-shaped rib (center), well-sprung and with good depth. A poorly sprung rib (right), which will not provide sufficient lung capacity.

The shoulder with sufficient layback (left) provides correct overhang and blends the neck into the back to shorten the latter. The straighter or more upright shoulder (right) reduces the degree of overhang and lengthens the back.

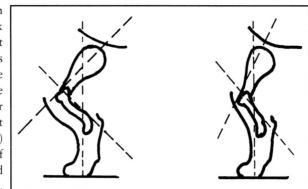

or moving. There should be no dip at or just behind the shoulders or any roaching over the loin.

It has been said that the Scottish Terrier should have the front end of a duchess and the backside of a cook. The broad, powerful rear starts with a well-bent stifle. The upper thigh (femur) should slope sharply forward from the pelvis, meeting the lower thigh (tibia and fibula) in a 90 degree angle at the stifle. The lower thigh slants backward to the hock (tarsus and metatarsus). Viewed from behind, the hocks should be perfectly straight. Viewed from the side, the dog should stand so that a line drawn from just behind the root of the dog's tail would *just* touch the back line of the hocks. This statement would seem to be contradicted by the exaggerated stance seen in many show photos, but all of the writers on the breed are in agreement.

In 1909, McCandlish wrote:

The hocks ought not to be placed so that they stand clear of a line drawn perpendicularly from the body at the back, for if the hocks are not placed just under the body there is always loss of power. Nor should they be placed too much under the body, another sign of weakness.

Caspersz in 1937 wrote:

Looked at from the side, an imaginary vertical line drawn down from behind the root of the dog's tail would just, and only just, touch the hocks. If the hocks are not this much under the body there is loss of power, but to be either too much under or too far away behind are both signs of weakness.

In 1940, Morgan Steinmetz wrote an article entitled "Movement in Scottish Terriers." The article appeared in *Dog News* magazine and was reprinted there again in April, 1952. Steinmetz wrote:

The more nearly correct is the dog in his hind quarters, the greater will be his drive. Straight-stifled dogs, and those with the hocks extending beyond the end of the body, lack this drive. They patter along with dainty steps, and give the impression that the body is carrying the hind legs, instead of the hind legs propelling the body.

The hocks from the side view should also be absolutely vertical and short in relation to the length of the thigh. A perfect Scottie rear is heavily muscled and should extend as far behind the tail as the chest extends beyond the front legs. In the words of Dorothy Caspersz, "A thin-looking thigh ought to be regarded as an abomination by all Scottish Terrier breeders."

The tail is a more important part of the Scottish Terrier's anatomy than it might seem at first glance. The Standard calls for a tail with a thick base, tapering gradually to a point, carried erect, and covered with short, hard hair. Grasping and pulling by the tail was often a huntsman's only method of retrieving his Scottie from an underground den so the tail needed to be thick and sturdy. Moreover, several of the thigh muscles are attached to the fused vertebrae in front of the tail so a dog with a high tail set has longer muscles (and is therefore quicker in action).

Tail carriage is one of the most obvious means by which the Scottish Terrier proclaims his character. For that reason, there are four references to tail carriage in the 1993 American Standard. Under "General Appearance," the Standard says an erect tail is a salient feature of the breed. The "Tail" section specifically requires the tail to be carried erect, either vertical or with a slight curve forward. The metaphor used to describe Scottie temperament is "heads up, tails up attitude." Finally, failure to show with the tail up is specifically listed as a fault under "Penalties." Despite the fact that the tail is only allotted five points in the new STCA Standard (up from 2½ in the 1947 Standard), an otherwise perfect Scottish Terrier who lacks that jaunty, devil-may-care tail carriage is, and should be, doomed to failure as a show dog.

There are three muscles in the tail, two which activate the top side and one the bottom. If a Scottie has a "gay" tail, that is, a tail carried too far forward over the back, then the muscle on the bottom lacks sufficient tension to balance the muscles on the top. Unfortunately, this can be easily remedied by nicking the top muscles with a knife. This clandestine practice has, apparently, been going on as long as Scotties have been show dogs. Since the corrective measures are not discernable, even to a veterinarian, many breeders have unwittingly used stud dogs with defective tails. Accordingly, gay tails continue to appear in virtually every family in the breed. Tail fixing, like all other artificial means of altering the dogs, should be eschewed by all reputable breeders. While a gay tail must be discouraged as a fault, it is more in keeping with correct temperament than is a "one o'clock tail"; that is, a tail carried backward from vertical.

The tail should be covered with the same double coat as on the dog's body. One feature that crops up frequently in black or dark brindle Scottie puppies is a ring of white hairs around the tail. This is of no concern as these hairs eventually disappear, leaving the tail the same color as the jacket. Puppies are also born occasionally with kinks in their tails. There is no consensus among breeders or veterinarians as to the inheritability of this feature. Generally, most breeders will not discard such a puppy from their breeding program unless the kink is so severe as to affect tail carriage.

The Scottish Terrier is a double-coated dog. In its natural state, the undercoat is soft, short and very dense. The outer coat is straight and harsh to the touch. It is interesting that the first Scottish and English Standards neglected to point out that the Scottie is a double-coated dog. All that was said on the subject of coat was, "The coat should be rather short (about 2 in.), intensely hard and wiry in texture, and very dense all over the body." Perhaps the drafters were unable to conceive of a Scottish Terrier who would lack a dense undercoat, since such a one would be unlikely to survive long in the cold, damp climate of his native Highlands. In any event, this omission was remedied in the 1933 English Standard which said: "The dog has two coats; the undercoat short, dense and soft; the outercoat harsh, dense and wiry; the two making a weather-resisting covering for the dog."

Throughout the revisions to both English and American Standards, the basic requirements for a correct Scottish Terrier coat have remained *very* consistent. Notwithstanding, a review of photographs of leading Scotties over the past century shows a rather dramatic change in the appearance of the coats. The most evident change occurred sometime around the 1920s when face and leg furnishings became more profuse. For show dogs, this added hair served two purposes. First, it gave the dog a more glamorous appearance, thereby increasing the breed's popularity with the general public. Second, it enabled artful trimmers to disguise defects in their show dogs. Dorothy Caspersz and other conservative fanciers argued the benefits of the original coat: that the dog required almost no trimming to maintain his appearance, and the correct coat repelled both water and dirt.

It is impossible today to say with certainty whether modern coats are really softer than the turn-of-the-century coats, but the fad of the 1930s for whiskers and furnishings has become a fact in the 1990s, as has trimming. The 1993 STCA Standard is the first to address the issue of trimming: "The coat should be trimmed and blended into the furnishings to give a distinct Scottish Terrier outline. The dog should be presented with sufficient coat so that the texture and density may be determined. The longer coat on the beard, legs and lower body may be slightly softer than the body coat but should not be or appear fluffy."

A properly presented Scottish Terrier coat is trimmed by pulling out the hairs. This is accomplished either by finger and thumb, called "plucking," or with the use of a specially designed grooming tool, called "stripping." The jacket should look clean and shiny and lie flat and tight around the muscular body. When examined closely, the outer coat of the jacket should be long enough so that the crisp texture of the hair can be felt. When the hair is parted, the soft undercoat should be easily seen. Ideally, one should not be able to see the skin on a correctly coated Scottish Terrier, but most groomers today remove much of the undercoat.

The craze for profuse furnishings peaked in the early 1950s when so much leg hair was exhibited that Scotties nearly lost their tailored, workmanlike appearance. Exhibitors have, to a large extent, returned to sanity in this regard. The furnishings should never be fluffy or matted, nor should they be so long as to drag the ground. All four legs and some "daylight" should be plainly visible under the dog. This is accomplished by stripping the furnishings. If done correctly, the texture of the furnishings will also be harsh, although, because the hair is longer, it will feel somewhat softer than the hair of the dog's jacket. Unfortunately, too many exhibitors today shape the leg furnishings with scissors and thinning shears and then restore the texture by adding mousse or hair spray.

The first Scottish and English Standards tried to give a comprehensive list of all of the colors in which the Scottish Terrier may adorn itself: steel or iron gray, black-brindle, brown-brindle, gray-brindle, black, sandy or wheaten. While some writers have insisted that these colors were listed in order of preference, there is no evidence to support this. The huntsman had little interest in the color of his dogs—the gamest terriers had the most opportunities to reproduce themselves and did so. In the first revision of the English Standard, and in all subsequent English Standards, the list of colors was reduced to the following: black, wheaten and brindle of any color. The 1993 American Standard adopted this succinct list of colors but added language allowing for sprinklings of white or silver hair which may appear in black or dark brindle coats, and for a small amount of white hairs on the chin and chest.

When the Scottie became a show dog, two factors began to influence color in the breed. One was the public fancy. Most early breeders supported themselves, in whole or in part, by the sale of their puppies. If the public wanted black puppies, these breeders had little choice but to produce black puppies. Another important influence on color in the 1930s was the fact that English Chs. Albourne Admiration and Heather Necessity were black. These highly successful stud dogs passed on their color along with their numerous other virtues.

The remnants of that particular controversy still exist today with partisans on each side arguing that *their* dogs' color was *the original* color. This notion is preposterous since it is impossible to single out the "original" Scottish Terrier. Volume I of the Stud Book of the Scottish Terrier Club (Scotland) was published in 1895 and contains 531 registrations, including many pillars of the breed. While the many shades of brindle are the most common colors represented, there were also blacks and wheatens. In fact, the range of colors listed in that Stud Book include some rarely seen today, such as red, gray and what seems to have been black and tan.

The writings of Dorothy Caspersz and Dr. Fayette Ewing are often cited in support of antiblack sentiment. In fact, both were adamant that all colors were equally beautiful. While Caspersz had a personal preference for brindles, she argued vigorously that there was no special merit in color as long as white was discouraged. Ewing developed an interest in wheatens and imported the first wheaten to achieve an American championship. He did not *prefer* the color, but had a strong interest in ensuring its survival.

McCandlish and the other early writers made no comment on any relationship between coat color and coat texture. By the 1930s, however, when black had become so wildly popular, breed experts decried the relative softness of black coats when compared to brindles. (Wheatens being sufficiently rare seemed to be regularly omitted from these discussions.) There is no denying that many breeders, in their haste to meet the demands of a fickle public for black puppies, must have ignored the importance of coat texture. Today, however, good (and bad) coats come in all colors. All the evidence points to the fact that color is not genetically linked to coat texture or density.

Thanks to the work of Rachel Page Elliott, we now know that, regardless of breed, all canine movement has some commonality. Among these is a tendency to single track as the dog moves faster. The angle of inclination begins with the shoulders and hips. This angle may vary depending on the structure of the breed, but the natural laws of balance always apply.

As a long-legged terrier moves forward at moderate speed, his feet will be roughly the same distance apart as his elbows. His feet will incline inward only as he accelerates. Because of the Scottie's broad, deep chest and short legs, the laws of balance require that he reach inward almost as soon as he starts moving forward. At moderate speed where a Fox Terrier's elbows will be the same distance apart as his feet, the Scottie's feet will be closer together than his elbows. This is the source of the so-called Scottie "roll." It is not really a "rolling" motion, but rather refers to the slight motion caused in the front as the dog shifts its weight from side to side during the trot.

In profile, the action shows flexion of the front pastern occurring as the forefoot leaves the ground, just slightly in advance of the hind foot to avoid interference. At full extension, the scapula, leg, pastern and foot form a continuous straight line, which is maintained by the leg, pastern and foot through the full arc of the downward swing. Contact with the ground is almost equally divided between toes and heel pad. In traveling, the object of the front leg is to reach as far forward as possible. At full extension, there is little height between foot and ground; therefore, any tendency towards a hackney gait or an exaggerated high-stepping gait is incorrect.

Rear movement is what drives a Scottie forward. The hind leg swinging forward contacts the ground at approximately mid-length of the body, the foot strongly pushing back, effectively thrusting the body forward. As the leg moves beyond the line of the body, the foot is quickly lifted. Viewed from behind, the rear legs should move in line with the front legs. The hocks should turn neither inward nor outward and should be the same distance apart as the feet. The pads of the dog's rear feet should be visible as he moves away from the observer.

Viewed from the side, a Scottie should have ample reach in front and drive behind. Moving at a trot, a well-made Scottie in show condition should have almost no perceptible "bounce" in his topline. He should be able to move as quickly as eight miles per hour in a free, easy, ground-covering trot.

The most important language in the American Standard are these words: "The principal objective must be symmetry and balance without exaggeration." McCandlish wrote almost one hundred years ago:

> Whether it be the question of size or any other desired feature, it does the breed no good to take up a hard and fast position. The Scottish Terrier, owing to his sturdy build and short stature, must above all things be proportionate, and breeders should also take proportionate view of the various merits and defects. If proportion is kept ever to the forefront, the breed will avoid those exaggerations of fancy points which are the curse of dog exhibiting. Let the first thing aimed at in breeding be a dog that is palpably an active, intelligent creature, capable of doing a good day's work over rough country, and in all sorts of weather, and not as a conglomeration of a number of points. If this be done, we need have no fear of the future of the sturdy little Hielander.

People are often drawn to the Scottish Terrier because of his unique appearance. They give their heart to the breed because of his character. A classic tale of the impact of Scottie character on the unsuspecting was told almost one hundred years ago to Williams Haynes by Campbell Covil, a fellow enthusiast. According to Mr. Covil, a friend of his wife's came for a visit. Her initial response to the Scottish Terriers in the house was, "Take those ugly little brutes away." She left for home a week later having paid the princely sum of fifty dollars for a Scottie puppy and thought it a bargain.

What do people find in this little dog to inspire such devotion? His courage is legendary. His nickname, the Diehard, too often described the fate of early Scotties. Every tod hunter had stories of the gameness of his dogs. Over and over, tales are recounted of two Scotties fighting to the death underground under the mistaken assumption they were fighting a fox; of a Scottie bitch, after losing a foreleg in a fight with an otter, still managing to drag him from his lair; how a retired Scottie, sleeping in the bedroom of his master's child, by itself killed a fox who thought to outrun the hunter's pack by taking a shortcut through the house. Whether the stories are true or not, they capture the essence of Scottish Terrier character. No one who has ever lived with Scotties would doubt them.

The Scottie's courage sometimes works to his disadvantage. Scotties are incredibly stoic about pain, which can cause the inattentive owner to overlook serious illness. A Scottie bitch who was notoriously intolerant of the presence of other dogs was taken to the veterinarian to be put down because she was dying of kidney disease. Her illness was advanced and she lay quietly in her owner's arms, head resting on the owner's shoulder while she awaited the veterinarian. Just at that moment, a friend, carrying her own Scottie, came into the room to commiserate with the grieving owner. At that moment, the dying Scottie raised her head, fixed the other Scottie with a look of withering contempt and began to growl her disapproval.

Another manifestation of the Scottie's courage is his unflinching willingness to take life as it comes. He will walk all day with a busy owner, or sleep contentedly on the bed of an invalid. Like all true aristocrats, he is at home in the meanest dwelling or the grandest palace.

The Scottish Terrier is affectionate and devoted to those he knows and loves but can, and often will, completely ignore those who are strangers to him. His love, however, does not make him the foolish slave of his owner. He will do his owner's bidding in most things because it pleases him to do those things. When ordered to do something distasteful, he may completely ignore the command. Of course, you may bend him to your will by virtue of superior physical strength, but you will not break his spirit that way. On the subject of Scottie obedience, Dorothy Caspersz wrote:

> Other breeds may be more clever, more readily taught tricks, but there is no breed possessing in the same degree that sympathy with and understanding of man which go to make him a personality in every house in which he finds a home. . . . Yes, much can be learnt from one's dog, and if that dog is a Scottish Terrier he will teach unconsciously, and, by a disapproving look here or an appreciative glance there, will assert strength of character and independence of thought, so that before very long all the human beings in his immediate circle are his humble slaves without knowing it.

Terriers have a reputation for barking, which is, after all, part of their arsenal of weapons for inspiring fear in their prey. Scotties, however, rarely bark without reason. William McCandlish writes:

> The philosophic Scottish Terrier, like the typical Scottish kelt, is not given to much gossip or an adeptness in the art of small talk. When he does speak it is after due deliberation as to its necessity, and plainly expresses a desire or an opinion. He soon learns what he can obtain by means of his speech, and he is not slow to take advantage of his gift. In consequence he reserves it for times when he requires it, and is not perpetually barking at trifles. This is only one of his characteristics which makes human the only word to adequately describe his nature.

Nearly any person with a talent for straightforward, narrative writing can write a decent description of the physical characteristics of the Scottish Terrier. A writer needs a talent for poetry to talk about the character of the breed. People who are blunt, plainspoken and otherwise not given to fancies tend to be attracted to the Scottish Terrier and then find themselves grasping for metaphors to describe the breed that has stolen their hearts. Listen to some of the words that have been written to describe Scottie character:

Hard as a diamond-tipped drill, thoroughly game to the utter extremity, bright as polished brass, true and lovable, Scottie with his odd little ways, is just the ideal dog . . . Williams Haynes, *The Scottish Terrier*, 1915

As a guard it is impossible to better him. He gives his warning, and if it passes unheeded, he shows very definitely that he is there and in charge. He is self-centred, deep-natured with a soul both for laughter and tragedy . . . There is nothing frothy or shallow in the nature of a Scottie. He never forgets—his heart may break with grief, but he will not yowl about it. He is absolutely honourable, incapable of a mean or petty action, large hearted and loving, with the soul and mind of an honest gentleman. Dorothy Gabriel, *The Scottish Terrier*, 1934

A gentleman! That is perhaps the whole story. The Scottie is a gentleman. He is reserved, dignified, honorable, patient, tolerant and courageous. He doesn't annoy you or force himself upon you. He meets life as he finds it, with an instinctive philosophy, a stoical intrepidity and a mellow understanding. He is calm and firm, and he minds his own business—and minds it well. He is a Spartan and can suffer pain without whimpering . . . He will attack a lion or a tiger if his rights are invaded, and though he may die in the struggle he never shows the white feather or runs away. He is the most admirable of all sports—forthright, brave and uncomplaining . . . He is one of the few dogs with whom human beings can actually argue. Scotties have their own ideas about things—they work out their problems and arrive at very definite conclusions—and they will go to the mat with you on any issue. If you are right they will, in the end, give in; but if you are wrong from their canine point of view (which, incidentally, is a highly sensible one), they can be as stubborn as only a Scotchman can be . . . One of the most delightful qualities of a Scottie is his aloofness. He has a sense of bashfulness, and despite his vigorous nature, he is highly sensitive. Like all wellbred people he hates to be stared at. If you look straight at him in a critical way he will turn his head and attempt to act indifferently . . . It is these qualities—gentleness and gameness, intelligence and modesty, courage and reserve—that have endeared him to every one that knows him, and have brought about his great popularity. S. S. Van Dine, Introduction to the Third Edition of *The Book of the Scottish Terrier* by Fayette C. Ewing.

This character ought to be stamped on his appearance. His face should express human understanding, the eyes should twinkle from under heavy eyebrows, with a keen, alert, inquiring look, yet containing in their depths something of the continual presence and depth of human tragedy. He is a Celt, and in all Celts there is an underlying sense of sorrow. But this tragic outlook on life is not the predominating characteristic. Its existence is almost concealed, but that it does exist gives to those who know him a feeling of security in that, whatever may befall, he will attune himself to the changes and chances of his human companion. In ordinary life he is self-contained, at times, perhaps, a little self-centred, and he has this much of the canniness, supposed to be Scotch, that however much he grieves when he sees boxes and bags in his master's bedroom, knowing this means absence from home, yet when departure has taken place he will stroll unaffectedly into the kitchen or to the stable and domineer in his own particular fashion over the domestic or outdoor servants, and enjoy the change from ordinary conditions. To the lover of Scottish Terrier character, the tales of dogs grieving for an absent master or mistress fall on unsympathetic ears, and temptation arises to inquire why a dog is kept which cannot enjoy the pleasures available to it, but must pine for what it cannot get, and in thus pining cause discomfort to a tenderhearted owner. A dog loves nonetheless because it can put up with other people in the absence of those it loves best. William McCandlish, *The Scottish Terrier, 1909*

With all his many merits, the Scottie has other traits which can be provoking. Chief of these is his stubbornness; he will hurry only slowly and the more the owner tries to hustle him the less cooperative he may become— he has four-wheel brakes and is quite prepared to use them. Anger will not help for he will collapse completely, shocked and hurt. Instant obedience and slavish subservience are not in his nature and are a betrayal of his inheritance. He is a king, a laird, a chief and will meet you as a friend and equal, but not as a servant or a menial. Betty Penn-Bull, *The Kennelgarth Book of the Scottish Terrier*, 1983

One final anecdote sums up much of the good that is found in the Scottish Terrier contrasted with some of mankind's less admirable qualities. This story was told by James Steele Mackenzie, first Secretary of the Scottish Terrier Club of America, to Dr. Fayette Ewing and appears in Dr. Ewing's *The Book Of The Scottish Terrier*, 1949 Revised Edition:

The tinker, sound in drunken slumber, lay across the pavement that skirts the palatial pile of St. John's [cathedral]. The terrier was vigorously protesting all unwarranted attempts to interrupt the slumber of his liege lord; defying even the majesty of the Law in the person of the policeman who, urged to desperation by the gibes and jeers of the "haflins" was making ready to make an end of the game little canine with his baton when the process was interrupted by an intimation from the big, burly, moleskin-clad carter, a fancier himself: "Het the wee beastie an'l caw th' helmet o'er the lugs."—an ultimatum calculated to strike terror into a much stouter man than the "bobbie." The tinker, aroused by the altercation, slowly staggered to his feet; the terrier, emboldened by the activity of his master, renewed his noisy demonstration with increased vigour, receiving two vicious kicks for his pains from the ungrateful master, that sent the dog howling into the background. This display of brutality toward the faithful dog proved too much for the burly carter who advanced slowly and deliberately towards the tinker and administered two sounding slugs upon his ear. A rough and tumble fight ensued from which the valiant carter emerged the victor, but so badly bitten that he had to go to a hospital to have his wounds cared for.

Scottie fanciers are the first to admit that their breed is not for everyone. Eyes accustomed to more traditionally beautiful dogs like Afghans and Collies may find the Scottie's rough hair unappealing; his short legs too stunted; his blocky body too thick; his long head too big. Those who seek a more malleable companion will find his independent nature provoking. If, however, you can appreciate a dog whose every feature makes him perfect for his particular work, you will begin to appreciate his appearance. And then, if you can imagine him in his native land, with a crisp wind blowing around him, his eyes sparkling and his tail wagging gaily as he bounds across the rocky terrain, hurrying forward and then back to urge his slower master on, willing to meet whatever comes on his own terms, then you will see the splendid Scottish Terrier as he really is.

Chapter 7

A Scottish Terrier in Your Home

There are certain aspects of successfully raising a puppy that are common to all dogs. All require good quality food to eat, clean water to drink, sufficient exercise, a comfortable place to sleep, quality veterinary care and loving companionship. In addition to these, Scottish Terriers have certain special requirements every new and prospective owner should know about.

If you bought your puppy from a reputable breeder, you were probably told that Scottish Terriers are not for everyone. Raising a Scottie puppy is a challenge. Each seems to know that he is descended from a race of warriors. He is proud, tough and willing to resist rather than bow his head to anyone. Your Scottie will love you but he will not blindly obey you because of that love. Some essentials, such as house training, he will learn easily, in part, because he *wants* to eliminate away from his living quarters. "Come," however, is a command that he will carefully consider before obeying. If the call is "Come" because dinner is ready, he will come bounding to the door. If the call is "Come" for a grooming session, he will have a sense of your intent and will have a long list of squirrels to chase, sticks to chew, holes to dig, and other projects that take priority over your need for his compliance.

Scottie puppies begin to exert their will at birth. Although they cannot see or hear, they are born with the urge to push and fight to get their way. Any breeder can describe struggling with a one-pound puppy whose eyes are still sealed shut, merely in an effort to cut his nails. The first growl is usually heard between eleven and fifteen days of age. Even before they can walk, Scottie puppies start to squabble among themselves.

Young Scotties are loving and good-natured, but like their elders, they are stubborn and strong-willed. A good breeder will have taken some of the rough edges off your puppy before you brought him home. Your puppy should be used to handling by people and to grooming. Depending on his age, he may also be lead-trained. He should also have had some experience riding in a car. Once the puppy is in your home, however, you can undo all the breeder's hard work if you are not as determined and as smart as your puppy.

PREPARING FOR THE NEW PUPPY

Before you bring your puppy home, you should prepare in a couple of ways. First, your yard must be fenced with *real* fencing. Electronic fences may work for some dogs but your Scottie will only need to see one squirrel outside the perimeter to forget a low-level electric shock. Once he has broken out, he will never forget that escape is possible. Scotties have a high tolerance for pain and it would take a strong enough jolt to hurt him before he would believe that any barrier he could not see should be taken seriously.

Second, your yard should contain no toxic plants or bulbs and no bodies of water deeper than six inches. Your Scottie will dig—some dig more and some dig less, but they ALL dig—and he will, especially in the spring, eat dirt, sticks and bulbs if he finds them. Ponds, real or man-made, and swimming pools present serious danger to a Scottie. If a bug or a mouse should find its way into your pond or pool, you can bet that your Scottie will notice something flailing around in the water. He will pounce before he thinks and quickly find himself in serious trouble. You do not have to be a physics expert to understand that Scotties are poorly designed for swimming. The Scottie's short legs cannot displace enough water to hold up his heavy body and his big head for more than a few minutes. Do not think that you can train your Scottie to find the steps or ladder in the pool. Surprise and fear may cause him to panic and forget those lessons when he most needs them. *NEVER leave your Scottie unattended around a pool or pond, even for a minute!*

Third, purchase a crate for your new puppy. One of the sturdiest, most readily available, easiest to clean and economical is the #200 Vari-Kennel, a brand of airline shipping crate. You can find one at a pet supply store or at the nearest air freight office. The crate will serve as a bed for the new puppy for naps during the day or through the night, a safe place where he can be fed or rest when he is home alone, a puppy seat for him when traveling in the car, and, after he is grown, a den where he can escape for some peace and quiet.

You must establish the rules for your puppy as soon as he comes to your house, however, you must set rules that are appropriate for the puppy's age. Contrary to some currently popular notions, it is easier for an older puppy to adjust to a new home than a younger puppy, assuming your puppy came from the home of a reputable breeder. A puppy of over twelve weeks, for example, is able to housebreak faster than a younger puppy. He is also less likely to cry during his first night away from the home he was born in.

HOUSE TRAINING

The key to successfully house training a puppy is consistency. All dogs, even Scotties, like routine and if you establish a routine for your puppy, he will

Only child.

learn it quickly. The puppy should be taken outside first thing in the morning, after each meal, after each nap and just before retiring for the night. The puppy will also need to go out every two or three hours at first, until he gets the idea. After that, the puppy will be able to wait longer between trips outside.

Do not give the puppy complete run of the house when you are away as he may get into mischief. If you must leave the puppy unattended briefly, put him in his crate. Most normal dogs will not eliminate in a confined space, particularly if they are accustomed to sleeping in a crate. If the breeder raised

Unwatched puppies can get into all sorts of mischief.

your puppy on newspaper, the puppy will be used to eliminating on paper. If you have to leave your puppy alone for more than a few hours, confine him to a small area and put some newspapers on the floor so that he may use them if he needs to relieve himself. You may wish to purchase a 3' x 3' puppy pen for this purpose. It is the canine equivalent of a playpen for your puppy and, when the dog is older, you can use it when traveling as a place for your dog to exercise and relieve himself.

Scotties want to please, so a stern reprimand is all that is necessary to correct your dog if he makes a mistake. You must, however, catch him in the act if the correction is to have any effect. Never strike your puppy with your hand, with a rolled-up newspaper or with any other object. When the puppy does what you want, praise him lavishly for his exemplary behavior. While house training, it is important to keep your puppy confined to an area where you can watch him carefully, rushing him outdoors as needed.

When you first bring your puppy home, the best place for him to sleep at night is in the crate. Place the crate in the bedroom of a family member. This is the room in the house that smells the most like the family and sleeping in the bedroom quickens the bonding between you and the newest family member. Just before bedtime, exercise your puppy outdoors and then put him to bed in the crate. Be sure you have lined the crate with a sleeping rug. If the puppy is restless or unhappy, place a toy in the crate with him. Puppies do not usually soil their beds so, as soon as you get up in the morning, take the puppy outside before he can make a mistake. When you feel the puppy has caught on to the idea, you can start leaving the crate door open so the puppy can come and go at will.

It takes a skilled photo-
grapher to capture the
expression on black or
dark brindle puppies.
Pets by Paulette

LEAD TRAINING

Most serious breeders do not put collars on their young puppies. You can
expect that your puppy will probably be unhappy about wearing his first
collar. The initial reaction is usually to scratch furiously at the offending
neckwear. Some puppies, however, will sulk, sitting quietly in a corner or
under a piece of furniture, hoping that you will be seized with pangs of guilt
and remove the strange object of torment. Be warned, as Scotties, even young
ones, can hold out for a long time. Your puppy will eventually accept the
collar; you just need to be patient.

Once the puppy accepts the collar, you can start to lead train him. Take
the puppy out in the yard and attach the leash to the collar. Let the puppy
walk you at first. Occasionally the puppy will move too quickly and he will
feel a tug as the leash tightens. Let him get used to this feeling once or twice
and then end the session. Slowly teach the puppy to follow you while he is
wearing the leash. Make a game of it and praise him as he walks along beside
you. If he balks, give him a gentle tug with the leash while calling him. Give
lots of praise and petting when he decides to come. Some Scottie puppies resist
lead training very strongly. If your puppy is such a one, be firm. Jerk him
with the leash, not too hard, but enough to move him toward you. Praise
him when he gets to you, then move away and start over. Do not let him win
this little war or you will be carrying him around when he weighs over twenty
pounds!

If you have an older dog who is already lead-trained, you can accelerate
the training process by walking the two together. The puppy will see how
the older dog reacts and modify his behavior accordingly. Regular walking is
the best exercise for your Scottie, even if he has a large yard to roam in
during the day. The improved muscle tone and lung capacity are not the

only benefits of daily walks. Encountering novel sights and smells not only stimulates your dog's intelligence, it also builds his self-confidence. A dog that has seen, heard and smelled a garbage truck clattering down the road is not likely to be unsettled by much!

FEEDING

You should have received feeding instructions for your puppy from the breeder. Generally speaking, your puppy will thrive on a diet of any good quality brand-name dog food. It is better for a dog's dental health to feed a dry kibble rather than canned food, but this is one time when brand names *do* make a difference. Many generic foods have been found to be lacking in essential nutrients. Semi-moist foods should also be avoided as they are loaded with sugar, chemical preservatives and food dyes.

If your puppy is a finicky eater, do not add any flavor enhancers to the food to make him eat. If you wish to add a small amount of canned food to his meal, mix no more than a tablespoon of meat with some warm water and pour it over the dry food. If the puppy hasn't finished in within twenty minutes, pick up the bowl and throw the food away. Remember, no healthy dog ever voluntarily starved himself to death. Your dog will always eat enough to survive and usually a lot more.

It is fine for your puppy to be a little pudgy, but as your Scottie matures, he will live longer if you keep him a little on the lean side. If your adult dog is overweight, you can take those pounds off safely by placing him on a brand-name diet food and increasing his exercise. Replace dog cookies with raw carrots or green beans for treats.

Dog food manufacturers spend millions of research dollars annually looking for a precisely balanced diet for your dog. Do not undo all of their hard work by oversupplementing with vitamins or human food. If your dog is eating a healthy diet of quality dog food, a single daily multivitamin will more than meet any extra nutritional needs. Above all, never give your dog bones (they can splinter or chip, causing internal injury), chocolate (it is poisonous to dogs), raw eggs (salmonella is also dangerous to dogs and the raw egg white can interfere with the absorbtion of certain vitamins) or salty or highly seasoned foods (these can upset your dog's stomach).

GROOMING

Your Scottie will require regular grooming to maintain his characteristic appearance. If you plan to show your puppy, his coat will have to be stripped or plucked; that is, the coat and furnishings will need to be shaped by pulling out hairs in a specific pattern. Show trimming is a skill that takes considerable practice. If you bought your puppy as a show dog, the breeder will either teach you to trim, trim the puppy herself or give you the name of

A healthy litter of Scottie puppies.

someone else who can teach you. Pet grooming is much simpler. The coat and head are clipped, usually with electric clippers and the rest of the furnishings are shaped with scissors and thinning shears. Both types of grooming require certain minimal equipment: a grooming table with an arm and collar, Oster A-5 clippers and blades, thinning shears, scissors, nail clippers, and, for show trimming, stripping knives. The Scottish Terrier Club of America has published a guide to grooming the Scottie, written by Merle Taylor, that is very helpful in learning show trimming. The STCA and the regional Scottish Terrier Clubs periodically offer grooming seminars where you may get some hands-on experience.

In addition to regular grooming and trimming, brush and comb your Scot's furnishings weekly, using a pin brush and a metal comb. Pay particular attention to whiskers, chest, skirts, legs and underside, for this is where mats are especially likely to form and accumulate. Use a soft bristle brush or grooming glove to polish the top coat. Weekly brushing will keep your dog cleaner and reduce shedding.

Whether you trim your dog yourself or take him to a professional groomer, you can save yourself and your Scottie a lot of trouble by teaching him three things: to become accustomed to the sound and vibration of clippers, to get used to a hair dryer and to allow his nails to be cut. Long before your puppy needs trimming, accustom him to the sound of an electric clipper, if you have one, or an electric razor if you do not. Turn the device on and run it near the puppy, making him stand quietly until the sound no longer bothers him. Give him a treat and lots of praise for good behavior. After he is used to the sound of the clipper (or razor), hold it next to his body so he can feel the vibrations. Gradually move it towards his head until he will allow you to hold the clipper or razor next to his cheek. Accustom him to the hair dryer in a similar fashion. First turn the dryer on low and let the puppy get used to the sound. Make him stand while you blow air gently on his legs and sides. Gradually, he will learn to accept both the strange noise and the blowing air. The key to success is making the puppy feel safe as he confronts these strange new devices.

Nail cutting is always a problem for Scottish Terrier owners. Scotties have thick, strong nails and their black color makes it difficult to locate the blood supply, or quick. Start training your puppy to allow you to handle his feet as soon as you bring him home. If you are uncomfortable cutting your puppy's nails, go to a hardware store and get a coarse metal file. You may have to ask a machinist to cut it down to a size that fits in your hand. Lay the puppy on his back and grasp his leg in your hand. Put one finger behind the nail you intend to file. Move the file away from you and file on a downward angle. As you move around the edges of the nail, you will expose the quick without cutting it. The more often you do this to your puppy while he is young, the easier it will be for you or your groomer to keep the nails short when your Scottie is grown. Do not be surprised if your sweet loving puppy turns into a little beast the first time you do his nails. Be firm while your puppy is small or you will be fighting this same battle every time he needs his nails cut as long as he lives. If your puppy tries to bite you, grasp his muzzle firmly, stare right into his eyes and tell him, *No!*, in your most convincing Marine Corps Drill Instructor voice.

TEETH

Your puppy will start losing his first teeth at about three-and-a-half to four months. Watch them carefully. The upper and lower incisors (front teeth) will probably come out on their own as the permanent teeth come in. If not, the baby teeth may need to be pulled. You can probably do this yourself with forceps or tweezers. The four canines (the fangs) are a different matter. The new ones quite often erupt without displacing the baby teeth. If this happens and the adult teeth reach a quarter inch, the baby canines should be pulled immediately. Dental hygiene is a sadly neglected aspect of canine health. A study conducted by Upjohn indicated that by keeping his teeth clean, you can extend your dog's life by 25 percent. Your veterinarian can recommend dental hygiene products and techniques that you can use. It's easier than you might think.

TOYS

Scottie puppies love to play and enjoy sharing that playtime with their human family members. Remember that a Scottie's jaw is very powerful and even his baby teeth are formidable weapons. Soft rubber toys are dangerous for a Scottie. Many die each year from ingesting pieces of the toys, or the various noisemakers that are often part of such toys.

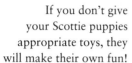

If you don't give your Scottie puppies appropriate toys, they will make their own fun!

If you want to give your dog a rubber toy, be sure you give the *extra hard, solid rubber* kind. Check these toys constantly and throw them away the moment you notice any breaks or cracks in the rubber. No matter what any manufacturer says, there is no rubber toy that a Scottie cannot eventually destroy.

"Buda Bones," "Nylabones," artificial fleece toys, or sterile bones (purchased at the pet store) make good toys. If, however, you see your dog chewing and eating the toy, discard it immediately! "Boomer Balls" make excellent toys for dogs and most Scotties seem to enjoy them. These balls are made in three sizes (small, medium and large) and are virtually indestructible. Most Scotties like them very much, and are equally enthusiastic about volley balls, soccer balls and basketballs. Unfortunately, these latter must be kept very firm or they will fall prey to the teeth of your enthusiastic Scot.

VACCINATIONS

Your new puppy should be current on his shots when he joins your family. Opinions vary on how often and at what age puppies should be vaccinated. Most veterinarians use a combined shot that protects the puppy against distemper, hepatitis, leptospirosis, parvovirus, coronavirus and parainfluenza. Some breeders prefer separate shots for parvovirus. The most important thing to remember about vaccinations is this: Your puppy received protective antibodies from his mother when he nursed during the first day or two of life. The strength of that immunity depends on many factors. If he received lots of maternal antibodies, then those antibodies not only protect him from disease, but they also fight off the effects of the first few vaccinations he receives. By age twelve to fourteen weeks, however, all of the vaccines, except parvovirus, should have stimulated an immune response in your puppy. He will need at least one parvovirus shot between eighteen and twenty weeks to insure immunity from this serious disease.

WORMS

It is not at all unusual for dogs to get internal parasites, commonly referred to as worms. Puppies get roundworms from their mother's milk. Your dog can get hookworms or whipworms from soil where other infested dogs have defecated and tapeworms from ingesting that most persistent of canine parasites—the flea. Worming used to be nearly as dangerous as the parasites themselves. Dog advice columns from the thirties describe dosing dogs with carbon tetrachloride, a highly toxic substance. The theory then was to give the dogs a low dosage of poison, high enough to kill the worms but not high enough to kill the dog! Fortunately, today's vermicides are very safe and effective.

Loose, bloody or foul-smelling stools can be an indication of worms. Coat and skin problems can also be caused by worms. If you suspect that your dog has worms, take your vet a small sample of the dog's stool for microscopic examination. If your dog is infested with tapeworm, there will be no sign in the fecal examination, but you will see small, white segments in the dog's stool or clinging to the hairs around the anus. When the segments dry, they look somewhat like grains of rice.

One of the most dangerous internal parasites is heartworm. Originally confined to the sunbelt, heartworm is now spread by mosquitos throughout the United States. There are a number of different heartworm preventatives. Some of these oral medications are given monthly, while others must be given daily. If you live in the north, it is not necessary to give heartworm medication year round (unless you are planning a winter vacation in the south with your dog). Before the first warm spell in the spring, take your dog to the veterinarian for a blood test. Once your veterinarian has checked your dog for heartworm, you must faithfully administer the medication until after the first hard freeze of the following winter. If you live where hard freezes are infrequent, it is safer to keep your dog on heartworm medication throughout the year. *Either way, you should have your dog tested for heartworm at least once a year, as even the best preventative is not 100% effective.* Consult your veterinarian for help in choosing the best medication for your schedule and lifestyle. *ABOVE ALL, DO NOT GIVE A PRODUCT CALLED "FILARIBITS PLUS." THIS HAS PROVEN TO BE TOXIC FOR SOME SCOTTISH TERRIERS. EVEN IF YOUR VETERINARIAN RECOMMENDS THIS PRODUCT, DO NOT USE IT. YOU MAY BE KILLING YOUR PUPPY.*

EXTERNAL PARASITES

The most common external parasites likely to affect your Scottie are fleas, ticks and *cheyletiella*. Fleas are not a minor problem to your Scottie. Under a microscope, a flea's jaws look like a backhoe. Not only is the bite very painful, but most Scotties are violently allergic to the flea's saliva. Flea bites can quickly become infected and turn into a serious health problem. *Fleas are not inevitable.*

In the past twenty years, numbers and types of products for flea control have grown rapidly as researchers attempt to provide total flea control without compromising the well-being of the dog, family members or the environment. Successful flea control can be achieved but only by formulating a treatment program designed specifically for the dog *and* the premises where he lives. Such a program must include the dog, the house, and the yard where the dog exercises.

Veterinarians are often frustrated by clients who refuse to accept that their dog has fleas. Intradermal testing for flea antigen reactivity is one way of demonstrating that the dog has been exposed to fleas. A simpler test is to roll your Scottie on his back and examine the skin around the dog's lower abdomen. While fleas themselves are often hard to see, particularly on a Scottie with a thick coat, they always leave small, brownish-colored specks in their environment. These specks look like dried blood and are, in fact, excreted by fleas who have ingested blood from your dog. The presence of this "flea dirt" is a sure sign of flea infestation.

The other objective raised by pet owners to flea control is the danger of using toxic substances in and around their home. The search for total non-toxic flea control has stirred much interest in "natural" remedies. Most of these, such as brewer's yeast, garlic or vinegar in the dog's water, will have little effect on fleas that have grown resistant even to many pesticides. Effective products with low toxicity are already on the market, however, and new ones are waiting in the wings. If you consult your veterinarian and use common sense, you *can* develop an effective program of flea control that is relatively safe for your pet, your yard and the other members of your household.

Finally, a word about flea collars. Flea collars only keep fleas away from the dog's neck. The one place that a flea collar *is* useful is in your vacuum cleaner bag. Cut a two- or three-inch segment from the collar and place it in the bag. It will kill any fleas that hatch from eggs you have vacuumed. Replace the flea collar segment about every three monts.

Ticks are another dangerous parasite because they carry a number of diseases. Certain species of ticks have been found to carry Lyme disease, which causes a painful inflammation of the joints and may later lead to arthritis.

If you find a tick on your dog, carefully pull the tick off the dog with twee-zers. Be sure that the head of the tick does not remain imbedded in the dog's skin as that may become infected.

Still another annoying, but less dangerous, external parasite is cheyletiella. This small skin mite lives on squirrels, rabbits, chipmunks and dogs. If your dog has cheyletiella, he will develop a dandruff-like condition and may scratch a great deal. If you are one of the unfortunate people who is sensitive to cheyletiella, you will break out with a very itchy rash, usually around your stomach, chest, forearms or ankles. Fortunately, cheyletiella usually responds to anything that kills fleas. A couple of baths (two weeks apart) in a good flea shampoo will usually rid your dog of this mite. Some veterinarians have successfully used Ivermectin, a heartworm preventative, to kill cheyletiella.

Chapter 8

Your Scottish Terrier's Health

Scotties, like all living creatures, are subject to congenital, hereditary and acquired health disorders. With the advent of antibiotics and vaccines, most of the serious health problems your dog will face are genetic. Many nongenetic health problems can be avoided or postponed, however, by providing for your dog's basic needs.

FINDING A VETERINARIAN

Ideally, you should find a veterinarian you feel you can work with before you buy your Scottie puppy. If you do not already know of one, ask your puppy's breeder. If the breeder is not local, call some of the members of your local kennel club and ask them about veterinarians in the area. Interview the veterinarian before you make your selection. Talk about the health problems specific to Scottish Terriers and, if the vet does not seem current on these problems, he or she should exhibit a willingness to learn about them.

Ask to look around the facility. The vet's office, workrooms, surgery room and kennel should be clean, and they should smell that way. Ask the veterinarian about emergency care and weekend calls. Many vets today use emergency clinics which vary widely in the quality of their care and the prices they charge. You may prefer a veterinarian who shares the night calls with the other doctors in the practice.

If you intend to breed, you will need a veterinarian who has a real interest in canine reproduction. Until recently, this was a rather neglected area of veterinary study, but there are a growing number of theriogenologists. These are vets who deal regularly with infertility, whelping problems, fading puppies, and who will usually be on call for whelping and other related emergencies.

PREVENTIVE CARE

It should go without saying that your puppy should have regular inoculations and wormings. Your adult Scottie should be checked at least once a year by the veterinarian. The annual checkup should include inoculations, a stool check, a heartworm test, and a teeth-cleaning. Your vet should examine the dog's eyes, ears and throat, and listen to the heart and lungs with the stethoscope. Finally, the vet should physically examine the dog with close attention to the bladder, the prostate (in males), and the uterus (in unspayed bitches).

FOOD

The number and variety of dog foods available today is often overwhelming to the new dog owner. Pet food and supplies often occupy an entire aisle at the supermarket. If you purchased your puppy from a breeder, ask the breeder for a recommendation. Otherwise, pick a good quality, brand-name, dry kibble and feed that to your dog. Feed the dog regularly—the same amount of food at the same time every day. Unlike people, dogs thrive on routine. If your dog is a finicky eater, do not start adding a lot of supplements to the food to make him eat. If you wish to add a *small* amount of canned food to his meal, mix no more than a tablespoon of meat with some warm water and pour it over the dry food. If your dog has not finished eating in twenty minutes, pick up the food and throw it away. As noted in the previous chapter, no healthy dog ever voluntarily starved himself to death. Your dog will always eat enough to survive and usually a lot more. Like people, lean dogs are healthier than fat ones.

EXERCISE

Scotties can adapt quite well to a sedentary life but do much better if they are regularly exercised. They do not need much—a brisk one-mile walk each day will not only improve your dog's physical well-being but will also provide him with interesting new smells, sights and experiences.

CLEANLINESS

Many skin problems can be avoided by keeping your dog clean. Regular brushing and bathing of furnishings will eliminate matted hair and dead skin cells. These provide a breeding ground for bacteria and mites that can attack the dog's skin.

COMPANIONSHIP

Dogs are social animals and need companionship. Like people, dogs develop mental aberrations and behavior problems when they are alone too much.

If you cannot be home with your dog during the day, share your evenings and weekends with him. If you cannot, then you should reconsider dog ownership until you can give it the time it should have.

COMMON HEREDITARY DISORDERS

Scottie Cramp

Scottie Cramp is the most widespread hereditary disorder in the breed and it is also the most benign. Affected dogs are normal at rest and exhibit normal ability to walk and run at the beginning of exercise. With continued exercise, or additional exciting stimuli (such as the sight of a squirrel), the dog's gait begins to change. The forelegs may move out to the side and forward rather than straight forward, in a movement called winging. The spine in the lumbar area may arch and the rear legs begin to overflex. If the excitement or exercise continues, the dog begins to exhibit a "goose-stepping" gait as the extensor and flexor muscle groups become more resistant to movement. If the dog is running, he may somersault and fall. Severely affected dogs may find their ability to walk or run completely inhibited. *This is not a seizure. There is no loss of consciousness.* As soon as the dog stops running or the squirrel runs away, the symptoms disappear almost immediately.

The severity of symptoms in affected dogs varies widely as does the amount and type of stimulation necessary to elicit clinical signs. Common stimuli of cramping episodes include running, fighting, courtship and breeding and fear. The symptoms appear to be caused by a buildup or depletion of some chemical compound in the dog's central nervous system, most probably serotonin. Serotonin is one of several chemicals that transmit nerve impulses from the brain to the muscles. In layman's language, the signal from the brain telling the dog how to run gets garbled in transmission on its way to the various muscles. The Scottie's muscles are not cramping and he is not experiencing pain. He has just temporarily lost the ability to coordinate his movements.

Scottie Cramp can be seen in puppies as young as six to eight weeks, although it often takes the eye of an experienced breeder to spot it. An affected puppy often learns to anticipate the onset of cramping and abruptly stops running or playing. By the time such a puppy is grown, he may never exhibit any signs at all. Similarly, an affected dog with a very laid-back personality is less likely to exhibit symptoms than his more hyperactive kinsman.

Although Scottie Cramp is a permanent condition, it does not worsen with age. The vast majority of dogs affected with Scottie Cramp make perfectly wonderful companions, able to share virtually all activities with their families. Treatment is unnecessary in nearly all cases. Where required, diazepam, at a dosage from 0.5 mg/kg to 1.5 mg/kg, reduces the clinical signs of cramp in an acute episode. Diazepam may also be given to reduce chronic, recurrent problems. Vitamin E, at doses above 125 IU/kg given once a day, is effective in elevating the threshold for eliciting symptoms. Vitamin E does not reduce the severity of the cramp, should it occur, but it does reduce the likelihood that an episode will occur. Consult your veterinarian before treating your affected Scottie with vitamin E, however, since it is possible to overdose your dog on this fat-soluble vitamin.

Von Willebrand's Disease

Von Willebrand's Disease (VWD) is the name given to a group of similar inherited bleeding disorders that occur in humans, pigs, dogs and rabbits. VWD is usually less clinically severe than hemophilia and is inherited as an autosomal trait. This means that it can be transmitted equally by and to both sexes.

VWD was first reported in a Scottish Terrier in 1972. By 1979, Dr. W. Jean Dodds had invited the Scottish Terrier Club of America to participate in her research on canine VWD. At that time, the incidence of this disorder in Scotties was estimated at 35 percent. By 1984, that figure had dropped to 18 percent, largely due to the cooperative efforts of scientists and responsible breeders.

Scotties are believed to have a form of VWD resembling type III VWD in humans. In this type of VWD, heterozygous dogs (dogs who carry one defective gene and one normal gene) are asymptomatic, that is to say, their blood clots in a normal period of time. Homozygous dogs (dogs who carry two defective genes), however, may exhibit any or all of the following symptoms:

Excessive bleeding when the nails are cut too short

Severe bleeding during surgery

Bleeding from the nose or gums, particularly during teething

Bleeding from the vagina or penis

Hematomas on the surface of the body, limbs or head

Internal bleeding

Lameness from bleeding into the joints

Stillbirths or neonatal deaths with evidence of hemorrhage at autopsy

Chronically infected and bloody ears

Prolonged bleeding during the heat cycle or after whelping

Bleeding in stools or urine

Dogs who are carriers of Von Willebrand's Disease may safely be spayed and neutered. They are perfectly suitable as companions. Twenty-five years ago, VWD was so prevalent in Scottish Terriers that many breeders had to use carrier dogs and bitches or face the extinction of their breeding programs. That is no longer the case today and carriers of this disorder should normally be spayed and neutered.

There is at present a blood test to detect carriers of Von Willebrand's Disease. The test, however, is not completely reliable. Researchers are currently working on the development of a DNA-based test which will enable breeders to positively identify and eliminate carriers of VWD from the Scottish Terrier gene pool.

Never buy a Scottish Terrier puppy from a breeder who is unfamiliar with VWD. A reputable breeder will absolutely guarantee that your puppy is not affected by this terrible disorder.

Cushing's Syndrome

Cushing's syndrome is a collection of symptoms caused by an excess of a hormone called cortisol. There are three main causes of Cushing's syndrome. About 80 percent of cases are caused by a tumor on the pituitary gland. Such tumors are usually benign, but secrete a hormone called adrenocortical stimulating hormone (ACTH). ACTH, in turn, stimulates the adrenal gland to produce excess cortisol. Another 10 percent of cases are caused by a tumor on the adrenal gland. The remaining cases are usually induced by veterinarians who over-prescribe corticosteroids to treat itching skin. It is, as yet, unknown whether there is an inherited predisposition to Cushing's syndrome in Scottish Terriers. It occurs often enough that breeders should consider its appearance in a pedigree when planning a mating.

The most definitive symptom of Cushing's syndrome is a huge increase in the amount of water drunk and a corresponding increase in the frequency and amount of urine produced. Left untreated, a dog with Cushing's syndrome gradually gains weight and experiences coat loss. The skin often darkens and appears thin. Muscle tissue atrophies, causing the dog's head to look skull-like.

Cushing's syndrome can be hard to diagnose. There is a number of tests that your veterinarian may wish to run. Generally, however, if your Scottish Terrier has the following four symptoms, he very likely has Cushing's syndrome:

The dog is drinking copious amounts of water and urinating frequently.

The dog has an elevated SGPT.

The dog has an elevated alkaline phophatase level.

The dog's ratio of urinary cortisol to urinary creatinine is greater than 24.

Cushing's syndrome is usually treated with a drug called Lysodren which inhibits the adrenal glands' ability to respond to the excess stimulation. The administration of Lysodren must be closely monitored as it can cause vomiting and diarrhea. The following protocol has been very successful in establishing the correct dosage. The affected dog's food should be diminished gradually over a one-week period until he finishes his meal in less than one minute. At that time, the dog is placed on a twice daily dosage of Lysodren at 50 mg/kg. This dosage is continued until a significant decrease in thirst is noted *and* the dog walks away from its food. At that time, the dog may be placed on a weekly dosage of 25-50 mg/kg. Dogs with sensitive stomachs may need to have their weekly dosage divided in half and given the drug twice per week. Water intake must be continuously monitored to ensure that the dosage is correct.

Since most dogs respond so well to Lysodren, surgery is rarely recommended. Radiation therapy, used in humans, is very expensive and rarely available for dogs.

Hypothyroidism

Hypothyroidism is an underproduction of hormones by the thyroid gland. It is more common in dogs than its opposite, hyperthyroidism. It is also causes more problems for dogs than hyperthyroidism which, unless tumor-related, seems to cause very few symptoms.

Symptoms of hypothyroidism include:

Abnormal loss of coat (often bilateral and symmetrical), poor coat condition, fading of coat color

Chronic skin disorders and infections, skin allergies, dry or scaling skin

Weight gain

Infertility

Fatigue, lethargy

Intolerance of cold

The thyroid gland, located in the neck, is a part of the complex endocrine system that includes the pituitary gland and the hypothalamus. The hypothalamus stimulates the pituitary gland to produce a hormone (thyroid stimulating hormone or TSH) which in turn stimulates the thyroid to produce Triiodothyroine (T3) and Thyroxine (T4). Thyroid hormones affect many body functions, including metabolism, growth and maturation, and reproduction. Hypothyroidism may be caused by a break in any part of this endocrine chain of events. It may also be caused by inadequate diet or liver malfunction.

It is important to determine the exact cause of your dog's hypothyroidism before embarking on a course of treatment. Your veterinarian must run a full thyroid panel and have the blood tested at a laboratory which uses canine thyroid values. Once you have the test results, your vet can prescribe the correct hormone replacement therapy.

Some people may advise you to give your show Scot a little thyroid medication to improve the coat. Do not be tempted to start thyroid treatment without proper veterinary supervision. The balance of the endocrine system is critical to your dog's health and you can cause the thyroid gland to atrophy by giving medication improperly.

Epilepsy

Epilepsy is a disorder characterized by recurrent seizures with no active underlying disease process occurring in the brain. It may be caused by a number of conditions, including low blood sugar, brain tumor, heat stroke, poison, nutritional deficiency and distemper. Classic or inherited epilepsy is often referred to as idiopathic, meaning of unknown cause.

Seizures take many forms and not all involve loss of consciousness. In the most typical form, the dog will salivate excessively. There is usually dilation of the pupils and stiffening of the limbs. The dog may arch its back and paddle its legs. Frequently, the dog's temperature will spike up three to five degrees. Urination or defecation may accompany or follow the episode. Seizures usually last only a minute or two, but severely affected dogs may have longer and more frequent episodes.

Most pet owners will recognize this typical seizure but there are other forms of seizures not so easily recognized. These partial seizures may include such behaviors as muscle twitching, chewing and lip smacking and snapping at the air.

If your puppy has a seizure before age nine months, or if your dog suddenly begins to have severe, frequent seizures, the cause is more likely to be infection, poison, metabolic disorder, nutritional imbalance or the presence of a tumor. Classic epilepsy usually begins after the dog is between three and five years of age and is characterized by intermittent seizures.

If your dog has a seizure, take him immediately to your veterinarian. Do not be disappointed if your doctor takes no action upon the first visit. Diagnosis is complicated and your vet will need to know the answers to the following questions (taken in part from "Diagnostic Approach To Seizures," *Veterinary Medicine,* July, 1993):

1. What does the pet look like when it is seizing?
2. What is the duration and frequency of the seizures?
3. Are there any localizing signs?
4. Has the pet ever had an illness resulting in a fever?

5. Has the pet ever been severely overheated?

6. Has the pet been exposed to toxicants?

7. Has the pet sustained any type of trauma?

8. Is the pet's vaccination status current?

9. Has the pet recently been in a kennel or pound?

10. Has the pet shown any signs of illness?

11. Do any of the pet's littermates have similar problems?

12. What is the pet fed and how often is it fed?

13. Does the pet roam?

Keeping good records of your Scottie's behavior before, during and after seizures can speed up your vet's ability to determine the cause of the seizures. Many epileptic dogs require no treatment at all. If seizures are infrequent and mild, they present less danger to a Scottie than the side effects of the medication used to control them. The drug of choice for dogs whose seizures are more acute or frequent is phenobarbital. Dilantin (diphenylhydantoin) and primidone (mylepsin or Mysoline) may also be used if phenobarbital is ineffective. All of these drugs can be toxic to the liver. If your Scottie must use one of them, his liver function should be closely monitored.

In recent years, there seems to be an increase of reported seizures in Scottish Terriers. While some of the increase may be due to environmental hazards, inherited epilepsy has definitely made inroads into the Scottie gene pool. Before you buy a puppy, ask the breeder about incidences of seizures in his or her breeding program.

Craniomandibular Osteopathy

Craniomandibular Osteopathy (CMO) is an inherited disorder usually characterized by an abnormal growth of the bone of the lower jaw. The growth may also occur in other parts of the cranium and, rarely, in the radius and ulna. CMO may appear in puppies as young as three weeks and as old as eleven months, but age of onset is usually between four and seven months. A puppy with CMO usually pulls away, flinches or screams with pain when his mouth is examined, depending on the severity of the disease. Other early symptoms are lethargy, fever and unwillingness to eat. An acutely affected puppy may be unable to open his mouth but mild cases may be misdiagnosed as teething problems or virus symptoms. An accurate diagnosis of CMO requires X-ray confirmation.

CMO is nearly always treatable. Mild cases usually respond to aspirin. Acute CMO cases may require the use of steroids such as prednisone or prednisolone. Fortunately, CMO is a self-limiting disorder, so an affected

Scottie will seldom require long-term medication in any form. As the dog matures, the abnormal bony growth abates and is often undetectable in the adult dog, even by radiography.

CMO is believed to be caused by a simple recessive gene. Although affected puppies nearly always outgrow their condition, most of them suffer greatly while they are sick. Dogs affected with CMO and dogs who are carrying the defective gene should always be spayed or neutered.

Skin Problems

There seems to be a common belief that terriers in general, and Scottish Terriers in particular, are subject to many skin problems. It is probably true, but it does not have to be. Most Scottish Terriers bred by reputable fanciers have no greater incidence of skin problems than dogs in general. Skin problems are varied in type, severity, cause and susceptibility to cure. Many are symptoms of underlying medical conditions while others reflect environmental problems. For example, hypothyroid dogs and dogs with Cushing's syndrome nearly always have skin problems. As soon as the medication restores the balance of the endocrine system, the skin also returns to normal. Scotties infested with fleas or mites nearly always develop skin problems, too. Once the parasites are eliminated, however, the skin problem abates as well.

Some skin problems are serious and chronic. Sadly, many veterinarians prescribe steroids for itching without identifying the underlying cause. The results are quick and positive so the client is happy. Unfortunately, these results are seldom permanent and the dog begins a cycle of itching, scratching, steroid use, and a brief period of clear skin. Gradually, the steroids disable the dog's immune system. Bacteria and fungus begin to attack wherever the dog's system is weakest. The skin grows worse and the cycle begins again until the dog's condition is critical.

Many skin conditions are related to autoimmune disorders; that is, for some reason, your dog's immune system attacks the skin. Autoimmune-mediated skin problems are usually chronic and expensive, requiring constant monitoring by your veterinarian. One form of autoimmune-mediated skin problem that can usually be treated successfully is food allergy. Dogs who are allergic to one or more ingredients in their regular dog food often respond very well to a diet of lamb and rice dog food. You may see no results until your dog has been on the new food for two or three months so you must be patient.

Parasite-related skin problems nearly always clear up when the parasite is removed. Fleas, mites and fungus can all affect your dog's skin. The most common mites are demodectic mange (which responds well to an Upjohn product called Mitaban), sarcoptic mange (usually treated with Malathion) and cheyletiella or walking dandruff (any product that will kill fleas will also kill this mite). Fungal infestations can be persistent but most respond to over-the-counter antifungal ointments. More serious infestations are usually treated with an oral medication called Fulvicin.

Cancer

Scottish Terriers have a substantially higher risk of developing cancer than all other dog breeds combined, although there are many breeds with even higher risks. The most frequent cancer diagnosed in Scotties is lympho-sarcoma, followed by bladder and other cancers of the lower urinary tract, malignant melanoma and gastric carcinoma. On the positive side, Scotties are at less risk of developing tumors of the testis, ovary, perianal gland, mammary gland, kidney, nervous system or thyroid. While bladder and gastric cancers are more likely related to environmental carcinogens, there is a clear familial risk for malignant melanoma in Scottish Terriers. As in humans, early detection is still the most beneficial factor in curing those forms of cancer that respond to treatment.

Benign Prostatic Hypertrophy

In simple terms, benign prostatic hypertrophy (BPH) means noncancerous enlargement of the prostate. It is the most common prostate disease in dogs, affecting sixty percent of all male dogs over the age of six years, although most exhibit no symptoms. The cause is still unknown, although some researchers believe that it is linked to some imbalance in the endocrine system. In Scotties, BPH can be somewhat more serious since the breed has been found to have 40 percent larger prostates than other breeds of similar size. Affected dogs may experience decreased stool diameter, straining to pass stool, or dripping undiluted blood before or after urination. Enlarged prostates are so common in Scotties that many veterinarians who specialize in canine reproduction recommend regular examination of the prostate using ultrasound. This technology enables the veterinarian to diagnose the condition in its early stages. Unless your male Scottie is an important stud dog, you can prevent this problem by neutering him as early as possible. If the dog is crucial to your breeding program, the growth rate of his prostate can sometimes be slowed by antibiotic treatment or regulated Proscar therapy administered under the *close* supervision of a specialist.

Chapter 9

Showing Your Scottish Terrier

WHAT IS A DOG SHOW?

American dog shows have their roots in British livestock judging. Farmers compared their prize animals to the livestock of other farmers and looked for superior breeding stock to introduce into their own herds. Since most dogs of that era worked for their living, it was only natural for dogs to join the competition. Cattlemen and shepherds compared herding and guard dogs, while hunters compared their retrievers and pointers. During the Victorian era, as more dogs moved into the household, exhibitors began to give more weight to the appearance of their purebred exhibits.

Today's exhibitors show their dogs to judges, usually former breeders or professional dog handlers, approved by the American Kennel Club on the basis of their knowledge of specific breeds. Every breed has a written Standard describing a perfect specimen of that breed. The judge compares each dog to that Standard and selects as winners the dogs most nearly resembling his or her own interpretation of that breed's Standard of perfection.

There are three types of conformation dog shows held in the United States. The first and most prevalent is the all-breed show. These shows normally offer classes for all breeds of dogs recognized by the American Kennel Club. After a winner has been selected in each breed, that dog or bitch competes in the Group to which the breed is assigned. For example, the Best of Breed Scottish Terrier competes in the Terrier Group. The seven Group winners then compete for Best in Show.

The second type of dog show is a Specialty show. A Specialty show only offers classes for a single breed. The Scottish Terrier Club of America, for example, holds two Specialty shows each year for Scottish Terriers. All Scottish Terrier Specialty clubs also offer Sweepstakes in conjunction with their shows. Sweepstakes are open to dogs and bitches aged six months to

189

For Scottie lovers, the National Specialty held with the Montgomery County KC show in Ambler, Pennsylvania in October is the most important and exciting show of the year.

All breeders bring their best dogs to Montgomery.

eighteen months with classes being divided by sex and age. Sweepstakes judges are usually breeders, and the winners receive part of the entry fees as prizes. Sweepstakes are intended as a showcase for future stars. No points toward a championship are awarded at Sweepstakes, but the competition is usually very keen and Sweepstakes wins are highly coveted. All wins at Specialty shows are considered especially prestigious and breeders will often hold their best dogs in reserve, sometimes for months, to compete at these events.

The third type of show is the Group show where only dogs of one Group compete. The American Kennel Club has placed all recognized breeds of dogs into seven Groups: Sporting, Hound, Working, Terrier, Toy, Non-Sporting and Herding. For many years, with very few exceptions, the Group show format was not allowed by the AKC. The Montgomery County Kennel Club where the Scottish Terrier Club of America holds its fall Specialty is one such Group show. Now, however, Group shows are springing up across the country.

HOW DOES A DOG BECOME A CHAMPION?

To become a champion, a dog must first be registered with the American Kennel Club. Registered dogs may be exhibited at shows licensed by the AKC and thereby earn points toward their championships. The following classes are normally offered in each sex at AKC shows: Puppy, Twelve-to-Eighteen Months, Novice, Bred-By-Exhibitor, American-Bred, and Open. Puppy classes are normally for puppies aged six months and under twelve months, but some shows offer two Puppy classes: six to nine months and nine to twelve months. The Novice class is for dogs over six months, born in the United States, Canada, Mexico or Bermuda, which have not won three first prizes in the Novice class, a first prize in Bred-By-Exhibitor, American-Bred or Open Classes, nor one or more championship points. This class is rarely used by Scottish Terrier exhibitors either at all-breed, Group or Specialty shows.

Dog (male) classes are judged before bitch (female) classes. Each dog who wins a class then competes with the other class winners for Winners Dog. The Winners Dog is awarded points toward his championship. The dog placed second in the class from which the Winners Dog came competes with the remaining class winners for Reserve Winners Dog. No points are awarded for Reserve, but on the rare occasion when the Winners Dog is later disqualified for some reason, the Reserve Winners Dog may be awarded championship points. After the dogs are judged, the same procedure is used in the bitch classes.

The Winners Dog, Winners Bitch and all champions entered and present then compete for Best of Breed. After the Best of Breed winner has been selected, the judge selects between the Winners Dog and the Winners Bitch for Best of Winners. If either the Winners Dog or Winners Bitch wins Best of Breed, Best of Winners is automatic. Finally, the judge selects the Best of Opposite Sex winner. If a dog wins Best of Breed, then the Best of Opposite Sex will be a bitch or vice-versa.

Provided competition is present, a dog or bitch going Winners may earn from one to five points per show. The number of points available is based on the number of dogs of the same sex defeated by the Winners Dog and the Winners Bitch. These numbers are set annually by the AKC and are based on the numbers of dogs and bitches shown in each of eight regions during the previous year. To determine the point value of the Winners award at any show, simply consult the catalog which will include the applicable point rating.

Adjusted ratings are also published annually in the April issue of the *Events Calendar* segment of the *AKC Gazette*.

Entries with a point value of three, four or five are called majors. To become a champion, a dog must win fifteen points under at least three different judges with at least two majors as part of the total; that is, he must win at least three points at a time, at two different shows under two different judges. A dog may not become a champion winning one or two points at a time until it reaches a total of fifteen. The purpose of this stipulation is to ensure that each dog that becomes a champion has had to defeat a representative number of dogs.

WHY SHOW YOUR DOG?

Nearly every successful exhibitor of Scottish Terriers started out showing his or her pet Scottie, just for the fun of it. The exciting thing about showing dogs as a hobby is that there are so many levels at which you may succeed. The novice exhibitor usually makes his debut at a puppy match, sort of an informal dog show where new exhibitors and new show dogs can learn the intricacies of conformation judging. After the first ribbon at a match, the happy exhibitor can look forward to the excitement of winning the first championship point at a real dog show, the achievement of the first championship, the first Specialty win, the first Group win and, with luck and persistence, the first Best in Show.

Each level of success requires more work, more time and more money— but the sport has room for every level of commitment. People from all walks of life and social backgrounds come together at dog shows drawn by their common love of their chosen breeds. And no matter what degree of success you attain, having fun with your Scottie should always be your goal.

Unless you have purchased a show dog, the odds are long against your Scottie being good enough to become a conformation champion. If you bought him from a reputable breeder as a pet, you have probably signed a spay-neuter agreement. Spayed and neutered dogs may not be shown in conformation. They may, however, participate in obedience, agility and earth dog trials.

FINDING A SHOW PUPPY

Your first decision should not be where to buy a show puppy. The first question you must answer is, "Do I want to breed Scottish Terriers?" If you plan to become a breeder, then the old maxim applies: Buy the best bitch you can afford. After all, this bitch is not only going to be a show dog, she is also going to be the foundation of your breeding program. She should be an outstanding example of the breed *and* she should be well-bred. Top quality show bitches are rare in the best of kennels and are seldom for sale, so be prepared to wait for a puppy. When one is available, you can expect that she will be costly. You can also expect to sign a contract obligating you to show the bitch, breed her and return a puppy to the breeder.

Your first bitch should be a quality animal with a linebred pedigree. That means that her parents will be related to each other through a common ancestor. Linebreeding is only as good as the quality of the common ancestor, so look for the names of top winners and top producers in the pedigree. There are many theories about tail-male or tail-female breeding (doubling up on the dogs on the top line of the pedigree or the bitches on the bottom line). The fact is that breeding is still as much art as science. You will, at first, have to depend on your mentor/breeder to guide you.

Your first bitch should be at least five months old or older. Some breeders may tell you that they can pick the good ones at birth, still wet and just out of the sack. A good breeder, however, will wait at least until your bitch has her second teeth. By then, the wise breeder should have a pretty good idea about the bitch's conformation and temperament as well. If you stay in dogs a long time, you will accumulate many wonderful memories. Few will compare with the introduction to your first Scottie show bitch!

On the other hand, if you want to enter the world of dog shows more cautiously, you may want to buy a well-bred male show puppy. Consider the following: First, you can usually find a first-class show quality male for sale without waiting. Breeders hoard their good bitches, but most have a surplus of good males. Second, for the same or less money that you pay for a barely finishable bitch, you can get a quite good quality male. Third, breeders are often reluctant to sell good bitches to novices who may drop out of dogs before the bitch is bred. Fourth, bitches are harder to finish than dogs. Breeders keep their best bitches and show them themselves or put them out with professional handlers. The novice often has a hard time competing with these more experienced groomers and handlers. The bitch entry is usually larger than the dog entry and the inexperienced can get lost in the crowd. Fifth, bitches are subject to the vagaries of their heat cycle which can often affect their willingness to show and the quality of their condition and coat. A male who likes to show usually does so consistently. Finally, breeders often want a puppy back when they sell a bitch. The novice exhibitor who wants to drop out may find that he is tied to a contract requiring the production of a litter or two. If you enjoy the experience of showing your male, you may then wish to take the plunge and buy a bitch. You will have the credentials to convince a breeder that you are serious and will do the right thing for one of his or her prized bitches. On the other hand, if this hobby is not for you, you still have a delightful pet without any cumbersome strings attached.

FINDING A BREEDER

The ideal way to locate the right breeder is first to educate yourself about the breed. Start by reading everything you can find about Scottish Terriers. Many books on the breed are readily available at your public library and bookstores.

Subscribe to the Scottish Terrier Club of America official magazine, *The Bagpiper*. You may obtain the address of the Scottish Terrier Club of America through the American Kennel Club, 51 Madison Avenue, New York, NY 10010. Another helpful magazine, mentioned several times in this book, is *Terrier Type*, P.O. Drawer A, La Honda, CA 94020. Appendix C of this book includes a bibliography of books on the Scottish Terrier. Many of the out-of-print books may be found using the book-finding services listed in the *New York Times Review of Books*.

Call the American Kennel Club at 919/233-9767 for locations and dates of all-breed dog shows in your area. Write the Corresponding Secretary of the Scottish Terrier Club of America (through the AKC) for a list of the dates and locations of the regional and national Specialty shows. Go to as many Specialties as you can, particularly the STCA shows. Each year the STCA hosts two national Specialties. The largest is held in conjunction with the Montgomery County Kennel Club show, in Ambler, Pennsylvania, in early October. The spring Specialty is held in a different part of the country each year. In addition, twenty of the twenty-two regional Scottish Terrier Clubs hold at least one Specialty show each year.

Most Scottie breeders show their very best dogs at the Specialty shows. Go and watch carefully. Study the exhibitors and their dogs. See which dogs attract your eye and see which dogs the judge selects. Introduce yourself to the Scottie people—they are generally a gregarious lot who enjoy nothing so much as talking about their Scots. You will hear lots of opinions—Scottie fanciers tend to hold very definite opinions. Listen and learn, but do not be in too big a hurry to buy a puppy

If there are no regional Specialty clubs near you, ask the STCA Secretary to give you the names and addresses of reputable breeders in your region. Visit as many breeders as you can, ask lots of questions, and above all, do not let yourself be rushed into a decision you may later regret.

While the quality of your first puppy is important, the reputation of the breeder you choose to buy from is even more important. There are four key questions you should ask yourself in choosing a breeder:

1. Does the breeder have quality stock? If so, their dogs will *consistently* be successful in the show ring.

2. How long has the breeder been in the fancy? You don't want to be taught by someone who has just bred their first big winner. Long-time successful breeders have perspective. They will help you keep yours when you need it most.

3. Has this breeder provided foundation stock for other successful breeders? Some lines exhibit a consistency and prepotency over many generations. It is easier to start a breeding program with such a foundation.

4. What sort of relationship does the breeder have with other novices? Look for a breeder who has a history of nurturing new fanciers—someone who will teach you about the Scottish Terrier's history, conformation, temperament, grooming and breeding; someone who will introduce you to the world of dog shows with all its rules, written and unwritten; someone who will give you the tools for success and then stand back and let you succeed; and someone who is willing to entrust a total novice with a good dog or bitch. This is crucial. Some breeders are so controlling that the novice is never allowed to really do anything independently. Others take your money, hand you the bitch and bid you farewell. One ensures that you never develop any confidence and the other ensures that you never learn any skills from him or her. Your relationship with this breeder will strongly influence your future in Scottish Terriers. As your abilities grow, he or she will gradually stop directing you. Your relationship will evolve into a friendship between equals.

Beware of the breeder who always has show puppies and the breeder who is eager to sell you a starter bitch. Show puppies are exceptional and they do not appear in every litter. If a breeder always seems to have a show puppy available, he or she is probably not as selective as one should be. Remember, as a novice exhibitor, you will need a better bitch to show than your more experienced competitors. They will groom their dogs more artfully and handle them with more skill than you. Your bitch will need to be so outstanding that her virtues will compensate for your inexperience.

As to the starter puppy, that is a code-word meaning, not good enough for my breeding program, but better than nothing, which is what you have now. If you are going to start your breeding program with this bitch, you do not need a starter —you need a foundation bitch. A good breeder will need some time to select the right one for you.

BUYING A BITCH

Most breeders today will require that you sign a written contract when you buy your bitch. This is as much for your protection as the breeder's. Do not be offended and do not hesitate to ask questions about the terms of the agreement. A standard contract should include the following:

1. A guarantee that the bitch is or will be of show quality and what measures the breeder will take if the bitch does not develop as expected.

2. A guarantee that the bitch has no health problems or genetic defects that would preclude her from being suitable for breeding.

3. A guarantee that the breeder will provide advice, guidance and, where possible, training to the buyer.

4. The purchase price and terms of payment.

5. A guarantee that the buyer will provide a healthy environment for the bitch.

6. A guarantee that the buyer will make a reasonable effort to show or have the bitch shown to her championship. If the buyer intends to use the services of a professional handler, many breeders will insist on having some input regarding which handler is selected.

7. Breeding terms. Nearly all breeders ask for a pick puppy from the bitch's first litter as part of the purchase price. This part of the contract needs to be very specific. What happens if the litter consists of a single puppy? Who determines which puppy is pick puppy? At what age must the puppy be chosen? Does the buyer have to take the puppies to the breeder or vice versa?

8. Terms for selling pet-quality puppies on spay-neuter agreements.

9. Terms for returning the bitch if the buyer cannot or does not wish to keep her.

10. Miscellaneous terms. Breeders may include terms such as requiring notice before spaying or prohibiting the buyer from reselling or leasing the bitch.

PREPARING FOR SHOW

Show preparation for a Scottish Terrier requires hours of regular grooming each week. Nearly all the hair is plucked rather than clipped or scissored. Therefore, grooming must be done in stages well in advance of the first show.

Before you start grooming, you will need certain basic equipment:

A grooming table with an arm and collar attachment

Oster A-5 clippers with a #10 blade and a #15 or #30 blade

Sharp scissors

Sharp thinning shears

Metal comb

Pin brush

Stripping knives

Nail clippers or file

Shampoo for dogs with harsh coats

Resco show leads (³/₁₆") Cordo Hyde, black for blacks or brindles, tan for wheatens)

Some kind of tack box to hold all your equipment

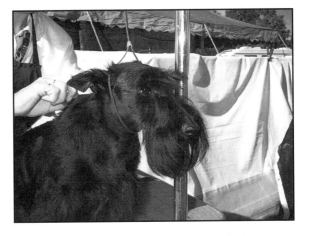

Scotties need lots of training to become accustomed to grooming. The noose is very helpful in controlling young dogs while they learn.

Few Scotties love being groomed but all are happy when it's over.

Quality grooming equipment is expensive, so get help from an experienced groomer before you select your tools. Some people find it easier to accumulate their equipment slowly after purchasing the basic items. Whether you acquire everything at once or piecemeal, remember that buying less than the best is a false economy. Fine grooming tools are a long-term investment.

The basic concept of terrier trimming is to pull out the dead hairs from the outercoat (called stripping or plucking) on a regular basis, so that a new coat is always coming in. Dead undercoat is removed by raking. The hair on the top of the skull, the neck, the body and the tail is stripped. The throat and the cheeks are usually clipped with a #10 blade up to a horizontal line level with the corner of the eye. The hair on the ears is also clipped, usually with a #15 or #30 blade. The leg hair is shaped by plucking and then neatened with thinning shears and scissors. Eyebrows and beard are also shaped with thinning shears. Nothing could sound easier and be so challenging.

Up until the 1970s, the novice exhibitor could expect little help from his competitors. The Scottish Terrier Club of America changed all that when it established a program whereby experienced exhibitors would teach grooming seminars in various locations around the country. The regional clubs took up the challenge and nearly all now offer some form of training to novice groomers. A few clubs have made videotapes of their seminars and sell them for a small fee.

No breed book could be sufficiently comprehensive to teach all the skills needed to trim a Scottie for show as the art is practiced in today's fancy. There is, however, a grooming manual available from the Scottish Terrier Club of America that is still the best on this subject.

Today's exhibitors are more than willing to help share their grooming skills. Most ask for little more than a promise from you to share what you have learned with future novices.

TRAINING FOR SHOW

Conformation dogs do not require nearly as much training time as obedience dogs. They must learn to walk on a lead, to stand on the table for examination by the judge, and to spar.

Before you can take your puppy to a training class, she should know how to walk on a lead and to ride in the car. When you are going on short errands, put her crate in the car and let the puppy accompany you. She may experience some car sickness until she gets used to it. Put some shredded newspaper in the crate to absorb any moisture. Refer to Chapter 7 for advice on lead training.

When your puppy has learned to walk on the lead and ride in the car, take her to the nearest conformation training class. Most kennel clubs offer such classes. At training class, your puppy will be exposed to different kinds, sizes and colors of dogs, new sounds and smells, and unfamiliar people. She must learn to stand for examination on a table and on the ground. She must also learn to walk in the gaiting patterns normally used in competition (the down-and-back, the triangle and the L) without sniffing the ground. If you do not live near a club that offers such training, your bitch's breeder should be able to refer you to someone in your area who will teach you and your puppy. Your teacher need not be a Scottie fancier—you can learn the basics from any experienced exhibitor or judge.

MATCHES

Nearly every show-giving club puts on at least one puppy match each year. Puppy matches are informal dog shows and are ideal training grounds for novice exhibitors and new puppies. A friendly member of your local kennel club will be glad to keep you apprised of the dates and locations of puppy matches in your area.

PERFORMANCE EVENTS

In addition to conformation judging, many dog shows offer obedience, agility, tracking, and earth dog events in which you and your Scottie may participate. While Scotties are not inclined to take orders, they enjoy working and playing with their family members. A good trainer can help you make training fun for your Scottie. Agility and earth dog events seem particularly suited to the Scottish Terrier temperament.

PHILOSOPHY FOR EXHIBITORS

In 1934, Dorothy Gabriel, Santa Scottish Terriers, wrote *The Scottish Terrier—Its Breeding And Management*. It offered some guidance to the novice exhibitor that was concise, eloquent and as true now as then. This book is hard to find today but her words should be repeated and heeded:

> I am hoping that the foregoing chapters may be an assistance to you, budding Scottish Terrier Fancier, along the hilly road to success. Although the Fancy seems grossly overcrowded, as in other things, there is plenty of room at the top. Some flash into the limelight at the beginning, breeding a champion in their first litter, but usually it is absolutely sheer and phenomenal luck and seldom lasts, and is no proof of their knowledge of the breed.
>
> In many cases of failure, trimming is often the great stumbling block. It is not the slightest use expecting to trim correctly straight away, and more than useless expecting a dog badly and carelessly put down, to get well in the money.
>
> You must remember that you are not competing against other novices only, but against experienced and often professional owners. It may seem as if this is asking a lot of you, and to your (often) disgruntled eyes appearing unfair. You must remember, however, that these experienced people

were once novices like yourself, and that hard work and sticking power have made them what they are. In dogs you cannot hustle things, you must know how to play the waiting game. Scottish Terrier people are a crowd of friendly souls. No beginner need be afraid they will not make friends quickly. Not only make them, but get a helping hand over the many difficulties for the asking.

Novice's luck is well known, and the start may be merry and bright. Sooner or later the bad streak comes, but the combination of getting your back into it, and the love you will by then have for your dogs, will help you through.

Hard work and sticking power are the whole root of dog breeding, which added to the ability of being able to play the game and do the straight thing, will ultimately lead to success.

The day will come, however, when you realize that much as you care for your dogs, there is one—*the one*—that no money can buy—no persuasion make you part with—that nothing can separate you from—till the hour of its passing—Then you will find—it's your own affair, But . . . you've given your heart to a dog to tear.

The key to obedience training a Scottie is to enjoy the time with your dog and make sure he enjoys it as well.

There is nothing the Scottie cannot do when *he* wants to.

Chapter 10

Breeding the Scottish Terrier

The principles involved in breeding purebred dogs were established long before anyone had heard of Gregor Mendel or DNA. Early man wanted dogs to assist in different forms of work. Herdsmen wanted herding dogs, hunters wanted hunting dogs, farmers wanted dogs to guard against predators, human and animal. While they may not have imagined the existence of genes, early breeders followed the rule that *Like begets Like*, that is to say, the offspring of parents will resemble those parents.

Breeders figured out fairly quickly, however, that like did NOT always beget like. In Scotties, for example, you can breed a black dog to a black bitch and get wheaten puppies. We know now that the wheaten color is caused by a recessive gene and that each black parent would have to be carrying one recessive wheaten gene and one dominant black gene. When a trait made a surprise appearance in early days, breeders kept the dogs displaying a favorable trait and eliminated those exhibiting undesirable ones. Remember Captain Mackie's encounter, described in Chapter 1, with the tipsy tod hunter whose dogs all had white feet. The old Scotsman was not particularly interested in having white-footed dogs. That trait just happened to be selected along with the traits that made his dogs fine killers of vermin. Offspring of the original sire who did not inherit their father's talents were eliminated from the breeding stock regardless of their color. As the sire's sons and daughters were interbred, a distinct TYPE of dog was established. Over time, successful TYPES evolved into specific breeds.

A purebred Scottish Terrier, then, is a dog whose genetic material has been manipulated through many generations of breeding, selectively eliminating genes for long legs, drop ears, short muzzles, white coats, and so on, and preserving those genes that produce the breed-specific characteristics. Purebred dogs can only be maintained by working within this small, selective gene pool. The breeder's perpetual enemy and ally, however, is Mother Nature.

In one way, Nature's goals are the same as the breeder's. Early breeders wanted to create dogs to fill a variety of niches: herding, hunting, guarding. Nature, too, wants her creatures to evolve to fill niches but her technique is much different. Natural selection depends on numbers and diversity. If Mother Nature were going to create breeds of dogs, she would have them reproduce in huge numbers, each generation containing a certain number of genetic mutations. The successful mutants would thrive and reproduce and the unsuccessful ones would die and become extinct. This technique worked well in the wild, particularly before the arrival of Nature's most successful mutation, *Homo sapiens*.

Nature resists the concept of a limited gene pool. It is constantly tinkering and nothing in our current technology can prevent nature from meddling with our perfect dogs. That means, for the present and the immediate future, all breeders will experience genetic defects in their dogs. Those defects may be caused by recessive genes that have been accidentally selected along the way or they may be mutations.

The spread of Scottie Cramp is a good example of how a defect establishes itself in the gene pool of a breed. The following explanation appeared in a letter from Norman Hankinson, the son of the great Bert Hankinson, kennel manager for J. Deane Willis (Bapton) in England, Walter Sterne (Earlybird) and Francis G. Lloyd (Walescot) in the United States, before starting his own breeding program under the kennel name "Scotshome."

By way of background, Mr. Hankinson wrote that after World War I A. G. Cowley (Albourne) owned virtually all the good Scotties in England:

Bearing all that in mind, we come to 1932. That year, at Somerset Hills, Jock McGowan [Mine Brook] showed a dog which had, I believe, been imported by Prentice Talmadge, who had brought Bentley Cotsol Lassie and Albourne Adair to America. Prentice seldom paid his bills, and Jock usually ended up owning his dogs. This dog, Albourne Wattadorg of Mine Brook, 782025 (Albourne Jonathan ex Albourne Black Bess), whelped June 26, 1929; Breeder A. G. Cowley, was registered with Jock McGowan as owner, and was, I believe, later sold to Dr. Ewing. The dog went Winners, Best of Winners, and was defeated for Best of Breed by Van Dine's Heather Reveller. Henry T. Fleitman was the judge. What made the event noteworthy was that Jock walked in, put the dog on the block, never moved it during Open and Winners, and repeated the performance for Best of Winners and Best of Breed. (In those days, shows were a little apt to become the personal fiefs of prominent handlers. For a few years, Jock "owned" Somerset Hills, just as Len Brumby, Sr. "owned" Westbury. This would explain how a dog could compete for four awards without moving one leg—and it also explains why Scottie wins in the 1930s offer no indication of worth.) There were then, and probably still are, no secrets in the dog game, and it was already known, when Jock pulled the stunt, that the dog could not walk two feet without losing control of its hindquarters.

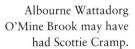

Albourne Wattadorg O'Mine Brook may have had Scottie Cramp.

That was the first instance of this condition to come to our notice, and it was so isolated that it was regarded as being an individual, rather than an inherent, weakness. It was 1935 or 1936, perhaps, when we next heard of the condition. Some people named Taylor, a naval lieutenant and his wife, came east from San Pedro to Long Island, and Mrs. Taylor told us that they had a young bitch which, after a certain amount of exercise, or when excited, would undergo a convulsive contraction in which the hind feet were drawn almost to its ears . . . [The bitch] was a product of West Coast breeding, as I remember it. We were not at all pleased when the condition appeared in our stock in 1938–39 or thereabouts.

The only common factor in all this would be Albourne breeding. In the early 1920s, Cowley's stock had been quite good—Albourne Adair certainly did the American-bred Scotty a lot of good . . . Albourne Wattadorg, appearing in 1932, was the first example of this condition to come to our attention. By the mid-and-later 1930s, Heather Necessity breeding had been jammed into the breed to such an extent that Albourne blood—far too much of it—was all over the place, and this is the only factor which, to my mind, would account for the wide and rapid geographical spread of the condition.

The only means of preventing worse defects from infiltrating is for breeders to acknowledge each problem as it arises, work together to eliminate it and then wait for the next genetic surprise.

SHOULD YOU BREED?

There is only one good reason to breed your Scottish Terrier bitch and that is to improve the breed. All other reasons—your family wants one of HER puppies; you want your children to experience the miracle of birth; every female creature should reproduce at least once; you need some extra disposable income—are specious.

The facts are these. The number of good homes available for all dogs, including purebred Scottish Terriers, has declined. Single-parent families or families where both parents work outside of the home have less time to spend with a pet that requires as much time as a dog. Accordingly, to produce a litter of puppies when you only want one puppy is wasteful. The miracle of birth can be pretty awful when things go wrong. It can be horribly traumatizing for young children to watch their pet deliver a deformed puppy or to hear her cry in pain. Studies have shown that spayed bitches have fewer health problems and live longer than intact bitches and that these benefits start earlier if the bitch is spayed early. Finally, breeding a litter can be horrendously expensive. Most breeders consider themselves unusually lucky if their financial loss on a litter is within their budget.

If you want to become a reputable and successful breeder, you must learn to look at your beloved companions with a critical eye. This is much easier said than done. The most common failing of unsuccessful breeders is their inability to be critical of their own dogs. Dorothy Caspersz offered this advice to breeders:

> Constant enquiry in your own mind and never-ending dissatisfaction with the result of your own efforts are the short cuts to success, if short cuts there be; but to attain success you must not be disheartened even though disappointed, nor must your self-confidence lead to self-satisfaction, for when a breeder begins to think he has nothing to learn he is on the high-road to collapse.

You must also be prepared for the many setbacks that inevitably accompany success. Imagine breeding successfully for many years and then discovering that while you were intentionally selecting certain good qualities, you have also been reproducing some serious genetic defect. Perhaps you may produce a top winning Scottish Terrier dog only to find that he is sterile or a great bitch who must be spayed before she is bred. The proportion of disappointment, even heartbreak, to success is wildly weighted against you.

IS YOUR BITCH SUITABLE FOR BREEDING?

You may love your bitch dearly but that does not make her a good candidate for motherhood. Your bitch is suitable for breeding if she has no health problems, she has a good temperament, she has outstanding conformation and the dogs in her pedigree also meet those standards.

Pedigree is particularly important since your bitch may produce traits she has inherited but does not display. Years ago, a young couple persuaded an experienced breeder to breed their bitch to her champion stud dog. The bitch was not a great beauty but she had a lovely temperament and an obedience title. Her sire's pedigree was known to the breeder and included some good dogs. The dam's pedigree comprised dogs unknown to the breeder. The young owners were so eager that the breeder overruled her own good judgment. The sire, in addition to being a champion, was a particularly sweet-natured dog who lived in a home with a two-year old child. This pair produced a litter of eight puppies, all of whom were home-raised and well socialized. Each inherited some traits from their parents as might be expected. They had better ears than their mother and broader heads than their sire. Unfortunately, they also inherited something else from one of the unknown ancestors—three of the puppies had such bad temperaments that they ultimately had to be put down.

As a general rule, if you got your bitch from a pet shop or a backyard breeder (someone who does not meet the criteria established below for a successful breeder), she is not a good candidate for breeding. Unless you bought her from a reputable breeder who is actively encouraging you to breed the bitch, she is not a good candidate for breeding. Unless she herself is a champion or of championship quality or is the daughter of champions, she is not a good candidate for breeding.

PREPARING TO BREED

Most breeders will want you to show your bitch to her championship before trying for a litter. This is fine as long as you do not wait too long before breeding her. Current veterinary thought on this matter is in agreement with the old breeders—do not wait too long to breed your bitch for the first time. How long is too long? Most theriogenologists (veterinarians who specialize in canine reproduction) suggest that a Scottie bitch be bred for the first time at her third or fourth heat. Certainly you are asking for trouble if your bitch has not produced a litter before her fourth birthday.

Your breeder/mentor will most probably select the stud dog the first time you breed your bitch. Many factors go in to making this decision. Generally speaking, the breeder will pick a stud from the same line as the bitch. The closer the relationship between the sire and the dam, the more likely it is the puppies will inherit the qualities of the parents. The risk, of course, is that while you are mating dogs with genes to produce desirable qualities, you may also unknowingly be doubling up on genes that produce problems. When that happens (and at some time in your breeding career it will) you must be prepared to backtrack through your pedigree as much as possible and eliminate dogs carrying those undesirable traits from your breeding program. The breeder must know the merits and defects of both dog and bitch and must know the origins of those merits and defects. Breeding is a blend of the genetic material of both parents. It is impossible to predict the results with certainty but a knowledge of the pedigrees of the prospective mates improves the likelihood of producing superior puppies.

For a maiden bitch, it is likely that the breeder will select a stud dog with a proven record. If you want to improve on your bitch's tail set, for example, you will want to select a dog who has consistently produced high tail sets. Despite all we have learned in the last quarter century about genetics, no one has yet accounted for that characteristic known as prepotency. For some unexplainable reason, certain dogs and bitches have the capacity to reproduce their outstanding qualities regardless of the merits of their mate. Likewise, some great show dogs have proven themselves disappointing as producers.

Finally, be prepared for disappointment. If it were easy to breed outstanding dogs, every exhibitor would have a kennel full of them. Your goal should be to gradually improve the quality of your dogs and not to breed a Best in Show dog in every litter.

THE STUD CONTRACT

Once you have selected a stud dog, contact the owner and make arrangements for the breeding. Many stud dog owners use a written contract. If yours does not, make sure that you both understand and agree on the following terms:

1. The stud dog owner guarantees that the dog is in good health and is fertile. If he is a proven sire, the contract should say so.

2. The stud dog owner guarantees that he will keep your bitch from having access to any dogs OTHER than the selected stud dog.

3. What provisions are to be made in the event the bitch does not conceive, or conceives and produces a single puppy, or conceives and produces stillborn puppies or live puppies who die at an early age. In years past, it was customary for the stud dog owner to give one free return service if the bitch failed to conceive. The bitch had to be bred her next season and to the same stud dog. Today, many breeders will give a return service if the litter consists of a single puppy, or if all of the puppies die at a young age.

4. The stud dog owner guarantees to execute the AKC papers necessary to register the litter.

5. The stud fee. Stud fees were traditionally set at the price of one pet-quality puppy. Most breeders will take a puppy in lieu of a stud fee. In such a case, the contract should specify which puppy will be given to the stud dog owner, at what age, and what provisions will be made if the bitch fails to conceive. It is customary in such cases to require the owner of the bitch to repeat the breeding at the bitch's next season.

6. Miscellaneous terms. Some stud contracts require that pet quality puppies be sold on a spay-neuter contract. Others include provisions for establishing legal jurisdiction in the event of a contract dispute.

BREEDING YOUR BITCH

There are many good books that cover the breeding and whelping of dogs in great detail. Read as many of these as possible before whelping your first litter. Talk to as many dog breeders as you can, particularly Scottish Terrier breeders. Nothing can substitute for experience, but the more information you have, the less likely you are to be surprised. Finally, if you can convince a fellow breeder to help you with the whelping, do it. You will need the encouragement and, should something go wrong, you will need someone to help you get your bitch to the veterinarian's office.

Your bitch should be in absolutely peak health before you breed her. If she is overweight, you reduce the odds of her conceiving at all and, should she conceive, you increase the odds of a difficult whelping. A brisk daily walk of a mile and a half will keep her in good muscle tone and prepare her for the rigors of motherhood.

When she is due to come in season, start checking her vulva for signs of swelling. Some bitches keep themselves very clean and you may not see the first signs of color. You may have to check her with a white tissue each day until color is visible. On that day, call the owner of the stud and make the necessary arrangements for the breeding. Most bitches will be ready to breed sometime between the tenth and thirteenth day after color is first seen, but this can vary. Most stud dog owners use a variety of techniques to determine when to breed, including:

1. Behavior of the stud dog and the bitch when they are placed together. The stud dog should become excited and attempt to mount the bitch. If the bitch is ready, she should be playful and stand for the male with her tail turned over to one side.

2. Color of the discharge. As the bitch approaches her peak fertility, the color of her discharge will change from red to straw-color to nearly clear.

3. Vaginal cytology. Some breeders will take a smear from the bitch's vagina using a sterile swab and examine the cells under a microscope. The epithelial cells from the lining of the vagina change shape and their nuclei dissolve as the peak breeding time approaches. Also, the small cells normally present in the background of a vaginal smear will disappear.

4. Hormone testing. Lutenizing Hormone (LH) is the hormone that triggers ovulation. During the heat cycle, LH serum, normally present in small quantities, increases significantly for a brief twenty-four to forty-eight hour period. That LH surge is normally accompanied by a rise in the level of progesterone. There are several blood tests that your veterinarian can perform in his office to detect this rise in progesterone. Ovulation occurs two days after the LH surge and the eggs then require another two or three days to mature. Once mature, the eggs live for forty-eight to seventy-two hours. This is the peak breeding time.

CARE OF THE MOTHER-TO-BE

Your bitch should be healthy and free of internal and external parasites prior to mating, but if you subsequently find that she is not, consult your vet. The first thirty days are critical ones for the rapidly growing fetuses, for that is when the major organs are being formed. Vermicides; flea powders, dips, and sprays; certain antibiotics; and medications given at the wrong time could cause abnormalities in the puppies or cause the bitch to lose her litter.

Keep her weight down. Obesity can make her pregnancy more difficult and is a decided detriment to easy whelping. A proper diet and regular, non-violent exercise are essential. Pregnancy, however, is not the time to start a strenuous exercise regimen.

At the fourth or fifth week of the gestation period, begin switching your bitch from her regular diet to a "growth" diet. The easiest way to do this is to use the "Puppy" version of her regular kibble. You may also add one multivitamin supplement. Several good commercial formulations are available. Oversupplementation can be dangerous to the health of your bitch and to her puppies as well. Discuss any questions with your veterinarian or another breeder.

Many breeders firmly believe that a daily supplement of raspberry leaves aids in easy whelping. These can be obtained in bulk or pre-packaged from most health food stores, where the leaves are sold as raspberry tea. While there is no scientific evidence to support belief in the efficacy of raspberry leaves as an aid to easy whelping, many breeders use them. They are not harmful to the bitch and if they do help, so much the better. If you decide to use them, a generous tablespoon of raspberry leaves in the bitch's daily ration is sufficient.

With the switch to puppy food, it will be necessary to increase only slightly the amount of food you give the prospective mother until the second half of her pregnancy. From the fifth to the seventh week, increase her food by half; and from the seventh week on, by half again. These amounts vary with the individual bitch, of course, and will depend on various factors; i.e., her size, weight, appetite, and apparent size of litter. Use good judgment in feeding; you do not want your bitch to be grossly overweight when she whelps. By the fifth or sixth week, if you are not already doing so, divide the amount you are giving her into at least two meals.

It is often difficult to determine whether your bitch is pregnant until the sixth, or even seventh, week. Puppies can be detected by ultrasound at about three weeks into the pregnancy. Many, but not all, pregnant bitches have a slight clear or milky discharge from the vulva. This is normal, but a dark, foul-smelling discharge means trouble. By the sixth week, a pregnant bitch should be noticeably heavier and slower and will be developing a "bosom." If you're still not certain, puppies can be detected by X ray, but not until very late in the pregnancy. Do not have an X ray done on your bitch any earlier than the fifty-fifth day.

This is also the time to notify your vet of the date you are expecting puppies. Find out if he or she will be available at that time and if you may call at any time after hours in case of an emergency. Make a second call a few days before the puppies are due, as a reminder. A good veterinarian is essential to a successful breeder. Fewer vets seem to be providing evening services, relying instead on emergency clinics or an on-call system using rotating veterinarians. If you intend to be a breeder, you will need a vet who will see you at night. Emergency clinics provide a wonderful service, but they are very expensive. The worst option is the on-call system since you may not get the best veterinarian available in the event that surgery becomes necessary.

The Whelping Box

Have a whelping box ready well in advance of the puppies' arrival. A box approximately 36" x 36" works quite well. Three of the sides should be eight to ten inches high and the fourth side should be adjustable. While the puppies are very small and relatively inactive, it can be kept low so that the bitch can more easily get into the box. Later, when the puppies become more venturesome, it can be raised to keep them from crawling out.

A guard rail in the box is a must! This prevents puppies who might crawl between the mother and the side of the box from being squeezed or smothered accidentally. It provides a protective crawl space all the way around the inside of the box—high enough for the puppies to crawl under but low enough to keep the mother's body from the sides of the box as she leans against it. The rail can be made either from dowels or flat boards and should provide protected space about three inches high and two or three inches wide around the inside of the box. Introduce your bitch to the box a few days before she is due to whelp. Lay a few sheets of newspaper in the bottom. Fold some of the double sheets in half and shred into half-inch strips. As her time nears, she will start nesting; i.e., scratching and tearing the papers.

Whelping

At about the fifty-ninth day, start taking your bitch's temperature with a rectal thermometer mornings and evenings. When the temperature starts to decline from its normal 101.5 degrees, check it more frequently. It may fluctuate up and down for one or more days before hitting the final low. Once it reaches 98 degrees, however, whelping time is probably less than twenty-four hours away. Unfortunately, you cannot depend too much on temperature as a guide. The temperature of some bitches will fluctuate several times prior to the delivery date, and some bitches will not experience any temperature drop at all.

As that time nears, the bitch will show increased signs of restlessness and discomfort. She will probably scratch up the papers in the whelping box, pant heavily, change position frequently and appear decidedly worried. Never leave your bitch alone at this stage. You can save many a puppy simply by being present when emergency measures are required. Your presence will also reassure the bitch.

Sooner or later the restlessness is followed by the first signs of labor. The length of time varies in each case. The initial contractions are mild and not always apparent. The later ones are much stronger and quite evident. They involve straining of the muscles of the lower flank in an effort to bring down and expel a puppy and last about one or two seconds. When they start coming fairly close together at regular intervals, delivery should be imminent. If the bitch labors hard for more than one hour without producing a puppy or has only mild contractions for more than two hours, she may need professional help. If you suspect this is the case, insist that your vet see her. All breeders would prefer for their bitches to deliver naturally, but for reasons yet undetermined, a growing number of Scottie bitches are unsuccessful whelpers. Accordingly, if you want live puppies, once the bitch has been in hard labor for an hour without producing a puppy, you should insist that your vet perform a Caesarian section.

One more word of caution: Some veterinarians use an injectable drug called oxytocin, sometimes referred to as a pit shot, to contract the uterus and to expel puppies. While this drug can be effective, it cannot work if there is a puppy stuck in the birth canal. Giving a pit shot under these circumstances will not only injure or kill the puppies, but can cause the uterus to rupture as well.

Textbooks say that puppies are usually born head first, but about half of Scottie puppies are delivered breech, i.e., backwards. Just before the bitch delivers the puppy, you will feel a large, firm mass at the vulva. Part of the sac which covers the puppy may protrude in a bubble effect. Do not puncture this. If the sac appears to be intact, let the bitch attempt to deliver the puppy herself. This may take ten minutes or longer. If the bitch seems to be having trouble expelling the puppy, you must help her. Using a dry, clean towel or two or three layers of gauze, grasp the protruding part of the puppy firmly. With each contraction, give a steady, firm pull downward. Wait for the next contraction before repeating this action. Try not to let the puppy slide back between contractions. Never jerk or yank, and always pull with the contractions. Once the head and shoulders are through, the rest is easy.

The breech birth is more difficult because it is harder to get a good hold on the puppy and the chance of injuring it while trying to pull it out backwards by the feet is greater. When the sac around the puppy is obviously broken, there is greater need for haste in getting the puppy out so that it can start breathing. In most cases, however, the delivered puppy is completely encased in the sac. The umbilical cord is attached to the sac and to the placenta ("afterbirth"). In delivering the puppy, try not to let the cord break away from the placenta until it, too, has been expelled. Grasp the cord with a piece of gauze and, with your hands close to the bitch's vulva, pull gently but firmly.

This should bring out the placenta. There should be one placenta for each puppy, and it is essential to keep track of them all. The mother will want to eat these before attending to anything else, but do not let her.

Remove the puppy from the sac immediately. Tie off the cord close to the body with dental floss in a tight double knot. This helps to stop any blood seepage and encourages the cord to dry up faster. At this point cut the cord with sterile scissors about one-half inch from the body, and, starting at the head, wipe the puppy with a clean towel or washcloth, then rub it briskly until it is fairly dry and breathing normally. If the puppy is quite limp and still, continue rubbing it vigorously. Remove what mucous you can from the nose and mouth. If there still are no signs of life, open the pup's mouth and very gently blow a little air into its lungs a few times. Continue the brisk rubbing and don't give up on an apparently dead puppy for at least fifteen minutes.

During the whelping, have a small cardboard box containing an electric heating pad covered with a soft towel ready. Set the controls at a temperature that will provide gentle warmth (usually "low"). Check the box frequently to insure that the puppies are not too hot. The newly whelped puppies should be put in this box as soon as they have been cleaned up so that they can dry quickly and keep warm until their mother is ready for them. You may have to put this box in another room out of the mother's sight and hearing if the puppies are crying and distracting her.

If the total whelping time is relatively short—no more than two or three hours, the puppies can stay in this box until the mother is finished whelping and until the whelping box has been cleaned up. Look in on them often, however, being sure to check the temperature of the heating pad each time. If the whelping is a long, drawn-out affair, however, give the puppies a chance to nurse between deliveries. Put them in with their mother for a short time, after sponging off her nipples with warm water and a mild soap. Encourage her to smell and lick them, then place them on nipples, making sure that each one is nursing. Most puppies will nurse automatically. In some cases, however, you have to squeeze a little milk out of a nipple and put the puppy's mouth around it. Be careful not to hurt the puppy in doing this. After the puppies have nursed, return them to the heating pad. They should stay in this box until the bitch has delivered her last puppy and the whelping box has been cleaned up for them.

After the bitch has whelped the last puppy, let her relieve herself, then sponge off and towel-dry her hindquarters. Give her some warm milk or broth and some soft food. Clean up the box and put down a piece of heavyweight artificial fleece cut to fit the box exactly. Do not put towels or lightweight rugs in the box, for the mother may unwittingly lay on a puppy that has crawled under one. The fleece is ideally suited for this purpose. It's heavy enough so that it stays flat. It absorbs moisture, yet does not feel wet, and it washes easily. Its thick, deep pile allows puppies to get their legs under their bodies and up on them sooner, and virtually eliminates the problems of "swimmers" and "flat-chest syndrome." Some bitches continue to dig after their puppies are born, kicking up the fleece and sometimes covering the puppies. If your bitch does this, you may not be able to leave even the fleece in the whelping box.

When the whelping box is ready for the puppies, put them in with the mother and make sure each one has nursed on a nipple. It is important the babies get some of the dam's first milk, called "colostrum," within twenty-four hours of birth, for this contains immunoglobulins and other substances that give the puppies immunity from any disease to which the mother is immune.

If your bitch has had a C-section, particularly if this is her first litter, she will probably not accept her puppies right away. It can sometimes take as long as three days before she realizes that she is a mother. In the meantime, never leave her with the puppies unattended. Keep them in the same box you used for them during the whelping and only put them in with her to nurse. Even the mildest bitch may exhibit bizarre reactions to new puppies after a section—she may attack and even kill the puppies if you do not watch her carefully. Normally, after a day or two, the bitch begins to show more normal maternal behavior.

CARING FOR NEWBORNS

Make certain the puppies are warm enough and totally free of drafts. Newborn puppies cannot control their body temperatures and must be kept at a floor-level temperature of ninety degrees for the first ten to fourteen days. Studies show that puppies reared in temperatures below eighty-five degrees develop impaired immune systems. You can keep the temperature evenly warm by using an electric panel under a portion of the floor of the box or by an infra-red lamp placed from three to five feet above the puppies.

The temperature in the box will vary, depending on changes in both indoor and outdoor temperatures, so the distance between lamp and puppies must be adjusted several times a day to maintain a constant ninety degrees. Too much heat, especially coupled with high humidity, can be lethal! Be sure to leave an area in the box that is not totally affected by the heating device you use so that the mother or her pups can escape to it if they become too warm. If the puppies are huddled together and whimpering, they probably are not warm enough; if they have placed themselves as far as possible from the heat source and are crying loudly, they most likely are too warm. After two weeks, it should be safe to lower the temperature.

Look in on the new family frequently and be sure to leave a small light on at night for a couple of weeks. Keep the whelping box clean. Check the puppies regularly to see that the mother is cleaning them and that each is nursing properly. For the first couple of weeks, the puppies will not be able to eliminate without stimulation from the mother. You will notice the bitch routinely licking her puppies, causing them to urinate and defecate.

If the stools are normal, the bitch will eat them in order to keep her box clean. If she is not licking the puppies, you may have to stimulate them yourself by rubbing their anal region with a cotton ball and some mineral oil. The dam's rear quarters will need sponging and towel-drying at least daily until her discharge stops.

Weigh puppies every day for the first two weeks. This cannot be emphasized too strongly. After the first day or so, the puppies should be gaining about an ounce per day. Failure to gain weight is the first and most easily observable symptom that your puppies are not thriving. If you wait until you can visually observe the loss of weight or failure to grow, you will probably lose the puppy. *If, over a forty-eight-hour period, a puppy has not gained or is losing weight, that puppy is in trouble and needs help immediately even if the puppy is nursing and appears normal in all other respects.*

If a puppy is not thriving, you must keep it from becoming chilled and start supplementary feeding with a formulation that simulates bitch's milk. The puppy will need to eat at least six times a day. Use a bottle, eye dropper, syringe, or stomach tube. Hold the puppy fairly upright and be careful not to give too much formula at one time. If you feed too fast, some of the formula could come back up and go into the lungs, which could cause the puppy to drown, strangle or develop inhalation pneumonia. If the puppy is too weak or seems vigorous, yet is not nursing, or is nursing without results, you have no option but to tube feed. Your vet or an experienced breeder can show you how to use the stomach tube. If the pup fails to gain within the next twenty-four hours, see your veterinarian immediately.

POSTNATAL CARE OF THE DAM

Watch the dam closely for the next two or three days. Take her temperature at least three times a day and, if it is more than one full degree above normal, call your vet. If the temperature is more than 103 degrees, do not delay in getting her to the vet. There may be a retained placenta or other source of infection.

After the puppies have arrived, gradually increase the mother's food. She will need larger amounts as the puppies grow and take more food from her. It is very important that she has as much food as she will eat. If she does not get this extra nutrition, she will draw upon her own resources in feeding her puppies and, in doing so, may seriously deplete the supplies she needs to maintain her own system. Should this happen, the consequences could be very severe. Many breeders still recommend supplementation with vitamins and minerals at this time. All of the latest research on canine nutrition indicates, however, that a bitch should be fed increased quantities of a balanced "Puppy" diet instead of vitamin supplements. If your bitch is one of the rare ones who gains weight while nursing, cut back slightly on the amount of food you give her. Your goal is to give her sufficient food to nurse her litter without becoming malnourished herself. If you have been doing so, continue to give the bitch her raspberry leaves until the puppies are weaned.

The bitch will also need plenty of liquid while she is nursing. Fresh water should be available at all times. Once the puppies start crawling around, however, arrange the water so that they cannot possibly crawl into it and drown.

Should you elect to remove dewclaws, do so between the third and fifth days, but only if the pups are thriving. Otherwise, do not subject them to even this small amount of stress. Puppies' nails grow very fast and become barbs in no time. These can be very painful to the dam as the puppies push their little paws against her tender breasts when nursing. Keep them trimmed down. Your own nail clippers work better for this than dog nail nippers.

WEANING

Three to four weeks is a good age to start weaning puppies, but you may wish to wait until the puppies reach five or six weeks. Some bitches will continue to nurse as long as you let them, while other bitches are ready to turn the puppies over to your care as soon as those sharp, little puppy teeth appear! If you wean your puppies young, you will need a formula to aid in the changeover from mother's milk to kibble. You may mix your own formula or use one of a number of commercial formulas.

Pyrex pie plates or small flat Corning Ware dishes make good food dishes for small puppies. The puppies should be brought up to the plate one at a time and encouraged to lap. It may be necessary to push some of the little heads down gently so that their mouths come in contact with the liquid. The puppies will lick their whiskers and in no time will be lapping away like veterans. Occasionally one encounters a puppy that seems determined not to lap. Do not give up—the puppy cannot nurse forever and will eventually begin to lap.

In starting out, give the formula to the puppies twice a day, preferably before they have filled up with mother's milk. Once they are lapping well, start feeding them four times a day, adding puppy kibble ground fine in a blender and a little Heinz or Gerber's strained chicken or beef to two of the meals. Be sure to use low-sodium or unsalted baby food or your puppies will be taking in too much salt. Once you have started to wean the puppies, cut back sharply on the amount of food you have been giving the mother. This will reduce the milk supply and will help to prevent caked breasts.

About the fourth or fifth day of the weaning period, start taking the dam away from her puppies at night and at intervals during the day, increasing the length of the intervals until she is no longer with them. This will help to ensure healthy appetites when you feed the puppies. Do not be alarmed if the mother occasionally regurgitates her partly digested meal in front of her puppies. This is normal and is Nature's way of providing the soft food puppies need in the early weaning period.

By the seventh or eighth day you can start adding cooked, ground beef or a good quality canned beef to the morning and evening meals and hot water instead of the formula for mixing with the dry food. If the dry food you regularly use is in the form of small pellets, you can discontinue grinding it.

If you wait until the fifth or sixth week to wean your puppies, you may skip the formula stage and start weaning them on a mixture of finely ground puppy kibble, warm water and a very small taste of Heinz or Gerber's low salt baby chicken or beef. Make the food very mushy until the puppies get the idea of how to eat it. You can gradually reduce the amount of water in the food until the texture is the same as the adult food you are using.

At the start of the second week of the weaning process, the puppies should be fed four times daily. Water should be available at all times. Naturally, the amounts of food should be increased as puppies get older. By the time the litter is eight weeks old, each puppy should be getting at least two cups of the mixed food a day.

If your puppies are healthy and eating well, supplementation should not be necessary. If, however, they need a little extra help, there are several good commercial vitamin products available. Your vet or another breeder can recommend one or two and you should give these to the puppies according to the manufacturer's instructions.

Puppies should be fully weaned by the time they are five or six weeks old—certainly no later than seven. If the mother is still feeding them by this time, you are doing her a disservice. When the pups are weaned, the dam's breasts should be almost normal and she should have no milk. It is important to check her breasts often during this period. If they become hot, hard, and swollen (caked), put hot compresses on them several times a day. If the condition persists, your vet should see her.

You should not keep the puppies in the whelping box much longer than four weeks, particularly if the litter is large. The puppies should have an area for exercise and a box or pen to sleep in. Do not keep them in a dark, isolated location, for this type of environment encourages timidity and shyness. Let them meet your friends and have as many safe, personality enriching experiences as possible. This is the best kind of socialization you can give them. Needless to say, any place you keep the puppies must be clean, warm, dry, and draft-free.

If yours are summer puppies, take them outdoors occasionally for their exercise. Do not do this before they are five weeks old and then only on warm days when the ground is dry. Supervise them and don't let them overdo. Start putting winter puppies out on nice days for two or three minutes at a time when they are six or seven weeks old and gradually increase the time outdoors, weather permitting.

Worming

Puppies will have worms more often than not, so early worming is recommended. With wormers like Parantel Pamoate (Nemex II) and Panacur, which are extremely safe and effective, most worms are simple to eliminate, and you can start worming puppies as young as two weeks.

Vaccinations

The colostrum that the puppy receives from its dam contains antibodies that protect it against all the diseases to which the bitch is immune. These antibodies are a mixed blessing, however, for, while they protect the puppy for an indeterminate number of weeks early in its life, they also can neutralize the effectiveness of the vaccines given a little later on. Since the level of maternal antibodies varies from puppy to puppy and cannot safely be predicted, it is important to begin vaccination at an early age and continue at regular intervals until the likelihood of maternal antibody interference has passed. In the case of canine parvovirus (CPV), the last shot should be given at twenty weeks; coronavirus (CV), sixteen weeks; and in the case of other infectious diseases, such as distemper, hepatitis, and parainfluenza (DHP), twelve weeks. Research has shown that the CPV modified-live (ML) virus vaccines confer longer-lasting immunity and greater levels of protection than the CPV killed virus vaccines and that, once the maternal antibodies have disappeared, two doses of the CPV-killed virus vaccine are needed to give immunity, as opposed to one dose of modified-live. Vaccination programs, especially for CPV, can vary from area to area, so you should set up your program in cooperation with your vet. A rumor has persisted, mostly among breeders, that vaccinating for several diseases at one time can "overload" the immune system. However, a large body of published research totally discredits this notion, showing that dogs respond individually to every component of a polyvalent vaccine as if each had been given separately.

Swimmer Puppies

Puppies usually are up on their feet by three weeks. If you have one that is dragging its back legs and cannot get up, you probably have a "swimmer." This is not uncommon in short-legged, heavy-boned, and heavy-bodied puppies whose muscles do not always develop fast enough to support the weight of their bodies. It is very important to start working with such a puppy as soon as you suspect it may be a swimmer. Scottie puppies raised on paper or other smooth surfaces are more predisposed to this condition than those raised on rougher surfaces. There will be fewer swimmers when puppies are raised on the artificial fleece referred to earlier.

Treatment is fairly simple and inexpensive. Getting the swimmer on a surface that provides good traction, e.g., the fleece, is of paramount importance. Sometimes this is all that is needed, but usually more is required. Two very effective methods of treatment are the "hobble" and the "trough." The hobble is made of narrow strips of tape wound around both elbows or hock joints in a figure eight pattern with just enough space between them to force the puppy to keep its legs under it and, at the same time, permit it to move each leg independently. The trough is a thirty- to thirty-six-inch long board with six-inch sides set about four inches apart. Each end is open. The sides are just far enough apart to permit the puppy to crawl through, yet close enough to push its legs up under its body. Start the puppy at one end and coax it through to the other. If necessary, gently push it from behind while tapping your fingers in front of it. Soon it will get the idea and will need only to be started out at either end. See that the puppy goes through several times in the morning, at noon, in the evening, and at night.

Most "swimmer" puppies start to develop a flat chest about three weeks of age as the result of their inability to get up on their feet and in consequence of having all their weight centered on their chests. The condition is not too serious at this stage of development, but it is important to get the puppies' front and rear legs under them and the puppies up on their feet as soon as possible.

Flat-Chested Puppies

Flat chests are also sometimes seen in puppies as young as two or three days. In your daily check-ups of the newborns, examine all chests carefully, especially those of the puppies that lose or fail to gain weight. A puppy will sometimes jerk its head off a nipple after a few seconds' nursing, vigorously push itself away from the dam, and start to cry. It may or may not regurgitate milk from the mouth or nostrils. When this happens, check the puppy thoroughly, being especially careful to feel its chest to see if it has flattened out. If you are not sure, compare it with the other puppies. The difference will be quite apparent. *At this stage, the flat chest poses a serious threat to the puppy's life,* for it puts pressure on the esophagus, partially blocking the tube that carries the food to the stomach. When the puppy gets hungry and starts to nurse, the milk goes down the tube as far as the stricture. Some of it trickles through to the stomach; the rest of it backs up and is either aspirated into the lungs or expelled through the mouth and nose. This often results in inhalation pneumonia. Immediate attention is necessary if the puppy is to survive. First it must have nourishment by tube feeding. The puppy may also require antibiotics to combat pneumonia. Next, the puppy's front legs must be taped so that its chest is not resting on a flat surface. The two front legs can be taped so that the puppy has to lie on its side but can still move around and change sides. A better way, however, is to make a hobble for the front legs, as for a swimmer, so that when the puppy is lying face down, its chest is being supported between its two front legs. Needless to say, newspaper is the worst possible surface for such a puppy. The artificial fleece is ideal.

Teething

Scottie puppies start getting their second teeth when they are about four months old. The new canines (the four fangs) often erupt before the old ones are shed. If this happens, the baby canines should be pulled when the new teeth are about one-fourth inch. If left in, these stubborn baby teeth could cause the new teeth to be pushed out of alignment.

Ears

Ears are nearly always up by three or three-and-a-half months. If they are not, play it safe and give them an assist. First, clip or trim as much hair as you can from the front, back and edges of the ear. Get as close as you can to the skin. Next, cut four strips of three-fourths-inch black, plastic tape. Lay one strip along the outer edge of the back side of the ear so that slightly less than half of it protrudes over the edge. Lay a second strip on the front side of the ear in the same position as the first strip. Press the tape down firmly and seal the two protruding edges. Do the same to the inner edge of the ear. This should hold the ear up. If not, ask an experienced breeder what he or she does in similar circumstances. You may wish to experiment with these approaches or have your vet tape the ears for you. Usually two or three days are all it takes—seldom more than a week. Do not leave the tape on for more than three days without checking the skin for irritation.

Eyes

Puppies' eyes usually open between the tenth and fourteenth day. If they are unduly slow in opening, or if you observe a puffiness in the corners or pus seeping through the edges, they need immediate veterinary care, for infection is present.

Remember the Two Most Important Rules:

1. A COLD PUPPY IS A DEAD PUPPY. MONITOR THE TEMPERATURE CLOSELY IN THE WHELPING BOX.
2. A PUPPY THAT IS NOT GAINING WEIGHT IS IN TROUBLE. ACT IMMEDIATELY IN ORDER TO SAVE THIS PUPPY'S LIFE.

Your Responsibilities as a Breeder

You have brought these puppies into the world and your responsibilities have just started. You must carefully screen prospective buyers to ensure that you place each puppy in a suitable home. You must be available to the purchaser to answer questions over the life of the dog. You must educate yourself about your breed so you can answer those questions intelligently. If, for some reason, the buyer cannot keep the dog, you must be willing to take the dog home and keep it until you can place it in a new home. If you cannot place or sell your puppies, you must keep them yourself. If you are not prepared for this much responsibility, breeding is not for you.

Chapter 11

Evolution of the Standard

Since the Scottish Terrier emerged as a distinct breed during the latter half of the nineteenth century, the breed Standard has undergone a number of important changes to result in the modern document by which our Scots are evaluated at home and in the show ring. It is of interest to make a "side-by-side" comparison of the following British and American Standards from different periods to achieve a perspective on how the breed developed into the modern version of the Scottish Terrier as we know it today.

BRITISH STANDARDS

THE MORRISON STANDARD (1880)

As published in The Scottish Terrier *by Dr. William A. Bruette, 1934.*

General Appearance—Is that of a thick-set, compact, short-coated, active terrier, standing about nine and a half inches high, with body of moderate length and averaging about sixteen to seventeen pounds weight for dogs and two pounds less for bitches. Ears and tail uncut; although in reality no higher at the shoulders than the Skye or Dandie Dinmont, it has a

STANDARD OF POINTS OF THE HARD-HAIRED SCOTTISH TERRIER CLUB (SCOTLAND).

As printed in the first Scottish Terrier Stud Book, *1887*

General Appearance (10).—The face should wear a very sharp, bright, and active expression, and the head should be carried up. The dog (owing to the shortness of his coat) should appear to be higher on the leg than he really is; but at the same time he should look compact, and possessed of great muscle in the hindquarters. In fact a Scottish Terrier, though

THE MORRISON STANDARD (1880)

leggier appearance from the fact that the coat is much shorter than in these two varieties. The head is carried pretty high, showing an intelligent face.

Temperament—An incessant restlessness and perpetual action, accompanied by an eager look, asking plainly for the word of command; a muscular form, fitting him for the arduous work; and sagacity, intelligence and courage to make the most of the situation, qualify the Scottish Terrier for the role of "friend of the family," or "companion in arms," in a sense unsurpassed by any other dog, large or small.

Head—Is longish and bald, and is full between the eyes. It is free from short or woolly hair and is smaller in the bitch than in the dog.

Muzzle—Is a most important point and should be long and very powerful, tapering slightly to the nose, which should be well-formed and spread over the muzzle, and black in colour; there must be no approach to snippiness. The teeth should be perfectly level in front, neither being under or over shot, fitting well together.

Eyes—Are small, well sunk in the head, bright and expressive, with heavy eyebrows.

STANDARD OF POINTS OF THE HARD-HAIRED SCOTTISH TERRIER CLUB (SCOTLAND).

essentially a terrier, cannot be too powerfully put together, and should be from about 9 in. to 12 in. in height.

Skull (5)—Proportionately long, slightly domed and covered with short hard hair, $3/4$ in. long or less. It should not be flat, as there should be a sort of stop or drop between the eyes.

Muzzle (5)—Very powerful and gradually tapering towards the nose, which should always be black and of good size. The jaws should be perfectly level, and the teeth square, though the nose projects somewhat over the mouth, which gives the impression of the upper jaw being longer than the under one.

Eyes (5)—Set wide apart, of a dark hazel colour; small, piercing, very bright and rather sunken.

THE MORRISON STANDARD (1880)

Ears—Are very small and free from long hair, feather, or fringe; in fact, as a rule, rather bare of hair and never cut.

Neck—Is short, thick and very muscular, well set between the shoulders and showing great power.

Chest and Body—The body gives an impression of great strength, being little else than a combination of bone and muscle. The chest is broad and deep; the ribs flat—a wonderful provision of nature, indispensable to dogs often compelled to force their way through the burrows and dunes, on their side. The back broad; the loins thick and very strong. This is a feature calling for special attention, as a dog in any degree weak in hind quarters lacks one of the main features of the breed and should on no account be used as a studdog. The body is covered with a hard, weather-resisting coat, about two inches long.

Legs—The forelegs are short and straight with immense bone for a dog of this size. Elbows well in, and not outside. The forearm particularly muscular. The hind legs are also strong; the thighs being well developed and thick; the hocks well bent and, below, straight.

Feet—Are small but firmly padded to resist the stony, broken ground. Nails

STANDARD OF POINTS OF THE HARD-HAIRED SCOTTISH TERRIER CLUB (SCOTLAND).

Ears (10)—Very small, prick or half prick, but never drop. They should also be sharp pointed, the hair on them should not be long, but velvety and they should not be cut. The ears should be free from any fringe at the top.

Neck (5)—Short, thick, and muscular; strongly set on sloping shoulders.

Chest (5)—Broad in comparison to the size of the dog, and proportionately deep.

Body (15)—Of moderate length, but not so long as a Skye's, and rather flat-sided; well ribbed up and exceedingly strong in hind quarters.

Legs and Feet (10)—Both fore and hind legs should be short, and very heavy in bone, the former being straight or slightly bent, and well set on under the body, as the Scottish Terrier should not be out at elbows. The hocks should be bent, and the thighs very muscular; the feet strong, and thickly covered with stout hair, the fore feet being larger than the hind ones, and well let down on the ground.

THE MORRISON STANDARD (1880)

STANDARD OF POINTS OF THE HARD-HAIRED SCOTTISH TERRIER CLUB (SCOTLAND).

strong, always black. Although free from feathering, the legs and feet are well covered with hair to the very toes.

Tail—Should not exceed seven or eight inches, covered with the same quality and length of hair as the body and is carried with a slight bend.

The Tail ($2^1/_2$)—should be about 7 in. long, never docked, carried with a slight bend and often gaily.

The Coat (15)—should be rather short (about 2 in.), intensely hard and wiry in texture, and very dense all over the body.

Size (10)—About 16 lbs. to 18 lbs. for a bitch, and 18 lbs. to 20 lbs. for a dog.

Colours ($2^1/_2$)—Steel or iron-grey, brindled or grizzled, black, sandy, and wheaten. White markings are objectionable, and can only be allowed on the chest, and that to a small extent.

Faults.

Muzzle—Either under or over hung.

Eyes—Large or light-coloured.

Ears—Large, round at the points, or drop. It is also a fault if they are too heavily covered with hair.

Coat—Any silkiness, wave, or tendency to curl is a serious blemish, as is also an open coat.

Size—Any specimens over 20 lbs. should not be encouraged.

Note: General Appearance follows Colour in the original standard. Order has been changed for ease of comparison.

STANDARD OF POINTS OF THE HARD-HAIRED SCOTCH TERRIER

As Adopted By The Scotch Terrier Club (England), 1888. As printed in Wm. McCandlish's The Scottish Terrier, *4th edition*

Skull (Value 7¹/₂)—Proportionately long, slightly domed, and covered with short, hard hair about ³/₄ in. long, or less. It should not be quite flat, as there should be a sort of stop, or drop, between the eyes.

Muzzle (7¹/₂)—Very powerful, gradually tapering toward the nose, which should always be black and of good size. The jaws should be perfectly level and the teeth square, though the nose projects somewhat over the mouth, which gives the impression of the upper jaw being longer than the under one.

Eyes (5)—A dark brown or hazel colour; small, piercing, very bright, and rather sunken.

Ears (10)—Very small, prick or half prick (the former is preferable), but never drop. They should also be sharp-pointed, and the hair on them should not be long, but velvety, and they should not be cut. The ears should be free from any fringe at the top.

SCOTTISH TERRIER CLUB OF ENGLAND STANDARD (1933)

As printed in the 1936 Scottish Terrier Club of England Handbook

Head—Without being out of proportion to the size of the dog, it should be long, the length of skull enabling it to be fairly wide and yet retain a narrow appearance. The skull is nearly flat and the cheekbones do not protrude. There is a slight but distinct drop between skull and foreface just in front of the eye. The nose is large, and in profile the line from the nose toward the chin appears to slope backwards. The eyes are almond-shaped, dark brown, fairly wide apart, and set deeply under the eyebrows. The teeth large, the upper incisors closely overlapping the lower. The ears neat, of fine texture, pointed and erect.

Forehand—The head is carried on a muscular neck of moderate length, showing quality, set into a long, sloping shoulder, the brisket well in front of the forelegs, which are straight, well boned to straight pasterns, with feet of good size, and well padded, toes well arched and closeknit. The chest fairly broad and hung between the forelegs, which must not be out at elbows nor placed under the body.

STANDARD OF POINTS OF THE HARD-HAIRED SCOTCH TERRIER

SCOTTISH TERRIER CLUB OF ENGLAND STANDARD (1933)

Neck (5)—Short, thick, and muscular; strongly set on sloping shoulders.

Chest (5)—Broad in comparison to the size of the dog, and proportionately deep.

Body (10)—Of moderate length, but not so long as a Skye's, and rather flat-sided; well ribbed up and exceedingly strong in hind quarters.

Body—The body has well-rounded ribs, which flatten to a deep chest, and are carried well back. The back is proportionately short and very muscular. In general, the top line of the body should be straight; the loin muscular and deep, thus powerfully coupling the ribs to the hindquarters.

Legs and Feet (10).—Both fore and hind legs should be short and very heavy in bone, the former being straight, and well set on under the body, as the Scotch Terrier should not be out at elbows. The hocks should be bent and the thighs very muscular; and the feet strong, small, and thickly covered with short hair, the forefeet being larger than the hind ones.

Hindquarters—Remarkably powerful for the size of the dog. Big and wide buttocks. Thighs deep and muscular, well bent at stifle. Hocks strong and well bent, and turned neither inward nor outwards. The tail, of moderate length to give a general balance to the dog, thick at root and tapering towards the tip, is set on with an upright carriage or with a slight bend.

The Tail (2½)—should be about 7 in. long, never docked, carried with a slight bend and often gaily.

The Coat (15)—should be rather short (about 2 in.), intensely hard and wiry in texture, and very dense all over the body.

Coat—The dog has two coats; the undercoat short, dense and soft; the outercoat harsh, dense and wiry; the two making a weather-resisting covering for the dog.

Size (10)—From 15 lbs. to 20 lbs., the best weight being as near as possible 18 lbs. for dogs, and 16 lbs. for bitches, when in condition for work.

Size—The ideally-made dog in hard show condition would weigh from 17 pounds to 21 pounds.

STANDARD OF POINTS OF THE HARD-HAIRED SCOTCH TERRIER

Colour (2¹/₂)—Steel or iron grey, black-brindle, brown-brindle, grey-brindle, black, sandy, wheaten. White markings are objectionable, and can only be allowed on the chest and to a small extent.

General Appearance (10)—The face should wear a very sharp, bright, and active expression, and the head should be carried up. The dog (owing to the shortness of his coat) should appear to be higher on the leg than he really is; but at the same time he should look compact, and possessed of great muscle in the hindquarters. In fact a Scottish Terrier, though essentially a terrier, cannot be too powerfully put together, and should be from about 9 in. to 12 in. in height.

Special Faults.

Muzzle—Either under or over hung.

Eyes—Large or light-coloured.

Ears—Large, round at the points, or drop. It is also a fault if they are too heavily covered with hair.

Legs—Bent, or slightly bent, and out at elbows.

SCOTTISH TERRIER CLUB OF ENGLAND STANDARD (1933)

Colour—Black, wheaten, or brindle of any colour.

Movement—In spite of its short legs the construction of the dog enables it to be very agile and active. The whole movement of the dog is smooth, easy, and straightforward, with free action at shoulder, stifle and hock.

General Appearance—A Scottish Terrier is a sturdy thick-set dog of a size to get to ground; placed on short legs, alert in carriage, and suggestive of great power and activity in small compass. The head gives the impression of being long for a dog of its size. The body is covered with a close-lying, broken, rough-textured coat, and with keen intelligent eyes and sharp prick ears, the dog looks willing to go anywhere and do anything.

STANDARD OF POINTS OF THE HARD-HAIRED SCOTCH TERRIER

SCOTTISH TERRIER CLUB OF ENGLAND STANDARD (1933)

Coat—Any silkiness, wave, or tendency to curl is a serious blemish, as is also an open coat.

Size—Specimens of over 20 lbs. should be discouraged.

NOTE: The order of the paragraphs in the 1933 Standard has been changed for ease of comparison between the two standards. General Appearance is actually the first paragraph, while Coat is placed between Colour and Movement.

SCOTTISH TERRIER CLUB OF ENGLAND STANDARD (1950)

SCOTTISH TERRIER BREED STANDARD

(As modified by the The Kennel Club) As printed in the 1951 Scottish Terrier Club of England Handbook

Copyright of The Kennel Club (1987) As printed in the 1987 Scottish Terrier Club of England Handbook

General Appearance—A Scottish Terrier is a sturdy thick-set dog of a size to get to ground, placed on short legs, alert in carriage and suggestive of great power and activity in small compass. The head gives the impression of being long for a dog of its size.

General Appearance—Thick set, of suitable size to go to ground, short legged, alert in carriage and suggestive of great power and activity in small compass. Head gives impression of being long for size of dog. Very agile and active in spite of short legs.

The body is covered with a close-lying, broken, rough-textured coat and, with keen intelligent eyes and sharp prick ears, the dog looks willing to go anywhere and do anything. In spite of its short legs, the

Characteristics—Loyal and faithful. Dignified, independent and reserved, but courageous and highly intelligent.

Temperament—Bold but never aggressive.

SCOTTISH TERRIER CLUB OF ENGLAND STANDARD (1950)	SCOTTISH TERRIER BREED STANDARD

construction of the dog enables it to be very agile and active. The whole movement of the dog is smooth, easy and straightforward, with free action at shoulder, stifle and hock.

Head and Skull—Without being out of proportion to the size of the dog, it should be long, the length of skull enabling it to be fairly wide and yet retain a narrow appearance. The skull is nearly flat and the cheek bones do not protrude. There is a slight but distinct drop between skull and foreface, just in front of the eyes. The nose is large—and, in profile, the line from the nose towards the chin appears to slope backwards.

Head and Skull—Long without being out of proportion to size of dog. Length of skull enabling it to be fairly wide and yet retain narrow appearance. Skull nearly flat and cheek bones not protruding. Foreface strongly constructed and deep throughout. Skull and foreface of equal length. Slight but distinct stop between skull and foreface just in front of eye. Nose large and, in profile, line from nose towards chin appears to slope backwards.

Eyes—Should be almond-shaped, dark brown, fairly wide apart and set deeply under the eyebrows.

Eyes—Almond-shaped, dark brown, fairly wide apart, set deeply under eyebrows with keen, intelligent expression.

Ears—Neat, of fine texture, pointed and erect.

Ears—Neat, fine texture, pointed, erect and set on top of skull but not too close together. Large, wide-based ears highly undesirable.

Mouth—Teeth large, the upper incisors closely overlapping the lower.

Mouth—Teeth large with perfect, regular scissor bite, i.e. Upper teeth closely overlapping the lower teeth and set square to the jaws.

Neck—Muscular, of moderate length.

Neck—Muscular and of moderate length.

Forequarters—The head is carried on a muscular neck of moderate length, showing quality, set into a

Forequarters—Head carried on muscular neck of moderate length showing quality, set into long sloping

| SCOTTISH TERRIER CLUB OF ENGLAND STANDARD (1950) | SCOTTISH TERRIER BREED STANDARD |

long sloping shoulder, the brisket well in front of the forelegs, which are straight, well boned to straight pasterns. The chest fairly broad and hung between the forelegs, which must not be out at elbows nor placed under the body.

shoulder, brisket well in front of straight, well boned forelegs to straight pasterns. Chest fairly broad and hung between forelegs which must not be out at the elbow nor placed under body.

Body—The body has well-rounded ribs, which flatten to a deep chest and are carried well back. The back is proportionately short and very muscular. **In general,** the top line of the body should be straight; the loin muscular and deep, thus powerfully coupling the ribs to the hindquarters.

Body—Well rounded ribs flattening to deep chest and carried well back. Back proportionally short and very muscular. Topline of body straight and level, loin muscular and deep, powerfully coupling ribs to hindquarters.

Hindquarters—Remarkably powerful for the size of the dog. Big and wide buttocks. Thighs deep and muscular, well bent at stifle. Hocks strong and well bent and neither turned inwards nor outwards.

Hindquarters—Remarkably powerful for size of dog. Big, wide buttocks, deep thighs and well bent stifles. Hocks short, strong, turning neither in nor out.

Feet—Of good size and well-padded, toes well arched and closeknit.

Feet—Good size, well padded, toes well arched and close knit, forefeet slightly larger than hindfeet.

Tail—Of moderate length, to give a general balance to the dog, thick at the root and tapering towards the tip—is set on with an upright carriage or with a slight bend.

Tail—Moderate length giving general balance to dog, thick at root and tapering towards tip. Set on with upright carriage or slight bend.

Gait/Movement—Smooth and free, straight both back and front with drive from behind and level gait throughout.

SCOTTISH TERRIER CLUB OF ENGLAND STANDARD (1950)

Coat—The dog has two coats. The undercoat short, dense and soft. The outercoat harsh, dense and wiry. The two making a weather-resisting covering to the dog.

Colour—Black, wheaten or brindle of any colour.

Weight and Size—The ideally-made dog in hard show condition could weigh from 19 lbs. to 23 lbs. Height at shoulder 10 to 11 inches.

SCOTTISH TERRIER BREED STANDARD

Coat—Close lying, double coat; undercoat short, dense, and soft; outer coat harsh, dense wiry, together making a weather-resisting covering.

Colour—Black, wheaten or brindle of any shade.

Size—Height at withers 25.4cms–28cms (10–11 ins); Weight 8.6–10.4kgs, (19–23 lbs).

Faults—Any departure from the foregoing points should be considered a fault and the seriousness with which the fault should be regarded should be in exact proportion to its degree.

NOTE: Male animals should have two apparently normal testicles fully descended into scrotum.

AMERICAN STANDARDS

STANDARD OF POINTS OF THE SCOTTISH TERRIER CLUB OF AMERICA

1900

Skull (Value 5)—Proportionately long, slightly domed and covered with short hard hair, ³/₄ in. long or less. It should not be flat, as there should be a sort of stop or drop between the eyes.

STANDARD OF POINTS OF THE SCOTTISH TERRIER CLUB OF AMERICA

As accepted by the Club, February 12, 1925

Skull (5 points)—Long, of medium width, slightly domed and covered with short hair. It should not be quite flat as there should be a slight stop or drop between the eyes.

STANDARD OF POINTS OF THE SCOTTISH TERRIER CLUB OF AMERICA (1900)

Muzzle (5)—Very powerful and gradually tapering towards the nose, which should always be black and of good size. The jaws should be perfectly level, and the teeth square, though the nose projects somewhat over the mouth, which gives the impression of the upper jaw being longer than the under one.

Eyes (5)—Set wide apart, of a dark hazel colour; small, piercing, very bright and rather sunken.

Ears (10)—Very small, prick or half prick, but never drop. They should also be sharp pointed, the hair on them should not be long, but velvety and they should not be cut. The ears should be free from any fringe at the top.

Neck (5)—Short, thick, and muscular; strongly set on sloping shoulders.

Chest (5)—Broad in comparison to the size of the dog, and proportionately deep.

Body (15)—Of moderate length, but not so long as a Skye's, and rather flat-sided; well ribbed up and exceedingly strong in hind quarters.

STANDARD OF POINTS OF THE SCOTTISH TERRIER CLUB OF AMERICA (1925)

Muzzle (5 points)—In proportion to the length of the skull, with not too much taper toward the nose. Nose should be black and of good size. The jaws should be perfectly level and the teeth square, although the nose projects somewhat over the mouth giving the impression that the upper jaw is longer than the lower.

Eyes (5 points)—Set wide apart, small and of almond shape, not round. **Color** to be dark brown or nearly black. To be bright, piercing and set well under the brow.

Ears (10 points)—Small, prick, set well up on the skull, rather pointed but not cut. The hair on them should be short and velvety.

Neck (5 points)—Moderately short, thick and muscular, strongly set on sloping shoulders, but not so short as to appear clumsy.

Chest (5 points)—Broad and very deep, well let down between the forelegs.

Body (15 Points)—Moderately short and well ribbed up with strong loin, deep flanks and very muscular hindquarters.

STANDARD OF POINTS OF THE SCOTTISH TERRIER CLUB OF AMERICA (1900)

Legs and Feet (10)—Both fore and hind legs should be short, and very heavy in bone, the former being straight or slightly bent, and well set on under the body, as the Scottish Terrier should not be out at elbows. The hocks should be bent, and the thighs very muscular; the feet strong, and thickly covered with stout hair, the fore feet being larger than the hind ones, and well let down on the ground.

The Tail (2½)—should be about 7 in. long, never docked, carried with a slight bend and often gaily.

The Coat (15)—should be rather short (about 2 in.), intensely hard and wiry in texture, and very dense all over the body.

Size (10)—About 16 lbs. to 18 lbs. for a bitch, and 18 lbs. to 20 lbs for a dog.

Colors (2½)—Steel or iron-grey, brindled or grizzled, black, sandy, and wheaten. White markings are objectionable, and can only be allowed on the chest, and that to a small extent.

General Appearance (10)—The face should wear a very sharp, bright, and active expression, and the head should be carried up. The dog

STANDARD OF POINTS OF THE SCOTTISH TERRIER CLUB OF AMERICA (1925)

Legs and Feet (10 Points)—Both fore and hind legs should be short and very heavy in bone in proportion to the size of the dog. Forelegs straight or slightly bent with elbows close to the body, as Scottish Terriers should not be out at the elbows. Stifles should be well bent and legs straight from hock to heel. Thighs very muscular. Feet round and thick with strong nails, forefeet larger than the hind foot.

Tail (2½ points)—Never cut and about seven inches long, carried gaily with a slight curve but not over the back.

Coat (15 points)—Rather short, about two inches, dense undercoat with outer coat intensely hard and wiry.

Size (10 Points)—About ten inches at the shoulder and weight about 18 or 20 pounds for both sexes. The correct size must take into consideration height fully as much as weight.

Color (2½ Points)—Steel or iron gray, brindled or grizzled, black, sandy, or wheaten. White markings are objectionable and can be allowed only on chest and that to a slight extent only.

General Appearance (10 Points)—The face should wear a keen, sharp and active expression. Both head and tail should be carried well up. The

STANDARD OF POINTS OF THE SCOTTISH TERRIER CLUB OF AMERICA (1900)

STANDARD OF POINTS OF THE SCOTTISH TERRIER CLUB OF AMERICA (1925)

(owing to the shortness of his coat) should appear to be higher on the leg than he really is; but at the same time he should look compact, and possessed of great muscle in the hindquarters. In fact a Scottish Terrier, though essentially a terrier, cannot be too powerfully put together, and should be from about 9 in. to 12 in. in height.

dog should look very compact, well muscled and powerful, giving the impression of immense power in a small size.

Faults

Faults

Muzzle—Either under or over hung.

Eyes—Large or light-coloured.

Ears—Large, round at the points, or drop. It is also a fault if they are too heavily covered with hair.

Eyes—large, round or light colored. Light bone. Out at elbows. Ears round, drop, or too large. Coat soft, silky, or curly. Jaw over or undershot. Over or undersize.

Coat—Any silkiness, wave, or tendency to curl is a serious blemish, as is also an open coat.

Size—Any specimens over 20 lbs. should not be encouraged.

Disqualification
Evidences of the use of a knife or other instrument to correct any defects. (The removal of dew claws being excepted.) [Written by Mackenzie]

It should be the spirit and purpose of the judge in deciding the relative merits of two more more dogs to consider the approximation of nature to the standard rather than the effect of artificiality. [Written by Ewing]

Paragraph order has been changed for ease of comparison.

OFFICIAL STANDARD OF THE SCOTTISH TERRIER	STANDARD OF POINTS OF THE SCOTTISH TERRIER CLUB OF AMERICA

(Adopted by the Scottish Terrier Club of America in April, 1947, and approved by the American Kennel Club, June, 1947)

(Adopted by the Scottish Terrier Club of America in June, 1993, and approved by the American Kennel Club, November, 1993)

GENERAL APPEARANCE—The face should wear a keen, sharp and active expression. Both head and tail should be carried well up. The dog should look very compact, well muscled and powerful, giving the impression of immense power in a small size.

GENERAL APPEARANCE—The Scottish Terrier is a small, compact, short-legged, sturdily-built dog of good bone and substance. His head is long in proportion to his size. He has a hard, wiry, weather-resistant coat and a thick-set, cobby body which is hung between short, heavy legs. These characteristics, joined with his very special keen, piercing, "varminty" expression, and his erect ears and tail are salient features of the breed. The Scottish Terrier's bold, confident, dignified aspect exemplifies power in a small package.

SIZE and WEIGHT—Equal consideration must be given to height, length of back and weight. Height at shoulder for either sex should be about 10 inches. Generally, a well balanced Scottish Terrier should weigh about from 19 to 22 pounds and a bitch, from 18 to 20 pounds. The principal objective must be symmetry and balance.

SIZE, PROPORTION AND SUBSTANCE—The Scottish Terrier should have a thick body and heavy bone. The principal objective must be symmetry and balance without exaggeration. Equal consideration shall be given to height, weight, length of back and length of head. Height at withers for either sex should be about 10 inches. The length of back from withers to set-on of tail should be approximately 11 inches. Generally, a well-balanced Scottish Terrier dog should weigh from 19 to 22 pounds and a bitch from 18 to 21 pounds.

OFFICIAL STANDARD OF THE SCOTTISH TERRIER	STANDARD OF POINTS OF THE SCOTTISH TERRIER CLUB OF AMERICA

HEAD—The head should be long in proportion to the overall length and size of the dog. In profile, the skull and muzzle should give the appearance of two parallel planes.

SKULL—Long, or medium width, slightly domed and covered with short, hard hair. It should not be quite flat, as there should be a slight stop or drop between the eyes.

The **SKULL** should be long and of medium width, slightly domed and covered with short, hard hair. In profile, the skull should appear flat. There should be a slight but definite stop between the skull and muzzle at eye level, allowing the eyes to be set in under the brow, contributing to proper Scottish Terrier expression. The skull should be smooth with no prominences or depressions and the cheeks should be flat and clean.

MUZZLE—In proportion to the length of the skull, with not too much taper toward the nose. Nose should be black and of good size. The jaws should be level and square. The nose projects somewhat over the mouth, giving the impression that the upper jaw is longer than the lower. The teeth should be evenly placed, having a scissors or level bite, with the former being preferable.

The **MUZZLE** should be approximately equal to the length of skull with only a slight taper to the nose. The muzzle should be well filled in under the eye, with no evidence of snipeyness. A correct Scottish Terrier muzzle should fill an average man's hand.

The **NOSE** should be black, regardless of coat color, and of good size, projecting somewhat over the mouth and giving the impression that the upper jaw is longer than the lower.

The **TEETH** should be large and evenly spaced, having either a scissor or level bite, the former preferred.

OFFICIAL STANDARD OF THE SCOTTISH TERRIER

STANDARD OF POINTS OF THE SCOTTISH TERRIER CLUB OF AMERICA

The jaw should be square, level and powerful. Undershot or overshot bites should be penalized.

EYES—Set wide apart, small and of almond shape, not round. Color to be dark brown or nearly black. To be bright, piercing and set well under the brow.

The EYES should be set wide apart and well in under the brow. They should be small, bright and piercing, and almond-shaped, not round. The color should be dark brown or nearly black, the darker the better

EARS—Small, prick, set well up on the skull, rather pointed but not cut. The hair on them should be short and velvety.

The EARS should be small, prick, set well up on the skull and pointed, but never cut. They should be covered with short velvety hair. From the front, the outer edge of the ear should form a straight line up from the side of the skull. The use, size, shape and placement of the ear and its erect carriage are major elements of the keen, alert, intelligent Scottish Terrier expression.

NECK—Moderately short, thick and muscular, strongly set on sloping shoulders, but not so short as to appear clumsy.

NECK, TOPLINE, BODY—The **NECK** should be moderately short, strong, thick and muscular, blending smoothly into well laid back shoulders. The neck must never be so short as to appear clumsy.

BODY—Moderately short and well ribbed up with strong loin, deep flanks and very muscular hind quarters.

The BODY should be moderately short with ribs extending well back into a short, strong loin, deep flanks and very muscular hindquarters. The ribs should be well sprung out from the spine, forming a broad, strong back, then curving down and inward to form a deep body that would be nearly heart-shaped if viewed in cross-section. The TOPLINE of the back should be firm and level.

OFFICIAL STANDARD OF THE SCOTTISH TERRIER

CHEST—Broad and very deep, well letdown between the forelegs.

TAIL—Never cut and about 7 inches long, carried with a slight curve but not over the back.

LEGS and FEET—Both forelegs and hind legs should be short and very heavy in bone in proportion to the size of the dog. Forelegs straight or slightly bent with elbows close to the body. Scottish Terriers should not be out at the elbows. Stifles should be

STANDARD OF POINTS OF THE SCOTTISH TERRIER CLUB OF AMERICA

The CHEST should be broad, very deep and well let down between the forelegs. The forechest should extend well in front of the legs and drop well down into the brisket. The chest should not be flat or concave, and the brisket should nicely fill an average man's slightly-cupped hand. The lowest point of the brisket should be such that an average man's fist would fit under it with little or no overhead clearance.

The TAIL should be about seven inches long and never cut. It should be set on high and carried erectly, either vertical or with a slight curve forward, but not over the back. The tail should be thick at the base, tapering gradually to a point and covered with short, hard hair.

FOREQUARTERS—The shoulders should be well laid back and moderately well knit at the withers. The forelegs should be very heavy in bone, straight or slightly bent with elbows close to the body, and set in under the shoulder blade with a definite forechest in front of them. Scottish Terriers should not be out at the elbows.

The FOREFEET should be larger than the hind feet, round, thick and compact with strong nails. The front feet should point straight ahead, but a slight "toeing out" is acceptable. Dew claws may be removed.

OFFICIAL STANDARD OF THE SCOTTISH TERRIER

STANDARD OF POINTS OF THE SCOTTISH TERRIER CLUB OF AMERICA

well bent and legs straight from hock to heel. Thighs very muscular. Feet round and thick with short nails, forefeet larger than the hind feet.

HINDQUARTERS—The thighs should be very muscular and powerful for the size of the dog with the stifles well bent and the legs straight from hock to heel. Hocks should be well let down and parallel to each other.

COAT—Rather short, about 2 inches, dense under coat with outer coat intensely hard and wiry.

COAT—The Scottish Terrier should have a broken coat. It is a hard, wiry outer coat with a soft, dense undercoat. The coat should be trimmed and blended into the furnishings to give a distinct Scottish Terrier outline. The dog should be presented with sufficient coat so that the texture and density may be determined. The longer coat on the beard, legs and lower body may be slightly softer than the body coat but should not be or appear fluffy.

COLOR—Steel or iron gray, brindled or grizzled, black, sandy or wheaten. White markings are objectionable and can be allowed only on the chest and that to a slight extent only.

COLOR—Black, wheaten or brindle of any color. Many black and brindle dogs have sprinklings of white or silver hairs in their coats which are normal and not to be penalized. White can be allowed only on the chest and chin and that to a slight extent only.

GAIT—The gait of the Scottish Terrier is very characteristic of the breed. It is not the square trot or walk desirable in the long-legged breeds. The forelegs do not move in exact

OFFICIAL STANDARD OF THE SCOTTISH TERRIER

STANDARD OF POINTS OF THE SCOTTISH TERRIER CLUB OF AMERICA

parallel planes; rather, in reaching out, the forelegs incline slightly inward because of the deep, broad forechest. Movement should be free, agile and coordinated with powerful drive from the rear and good reach in front. The action of the rear legs should be square and true and, at the trot, both the hocks and stifles should be flexed with a vigorous motion. When the dog is in motion, the back should remain firm and level.

TEMPERAMENT—The Scottish Terrier should be alert and spirited but also stable and steady-going . He is a determined and thoughtful dog whose "heads up, tails up" attitude in the ring should convey both fire and control The Scottish Terrier, while loving and gentle with people, can be aggressive with other dogs. He should exude ruggedness and power, living up to his nickname, the "Diehard."

NOTE: The gait of the Scottish Terrier is peculiarly its own and is very characteristic of the breed. It is not the square trot or walk that is desirable in the long-legged breeds. The forelegs do not move in exact parallel planes—rather in reaching out incline slightly inward. This is due to the shortness of leg and width of chest. The action of the rear legs should be square and true and at the trot, both the hocks and stifles should be flexed with a vigorous motion.

OFFICIAL STANDARD OF THE SCOTTISH TERRIER

PENALTIES—Soft coat, round or very light eye, overshot or undershot jaw, obviously oversize or undersize, shyness, timidity or failure to show with head and tail up are faults to be penalized. No judge should put to Winners or Best of Breed any Scottish Terrier not showing real terrier character in the ring.

SCALE OF POINTS
Skull 5
Muzzle 5
Eyes 5
Ears 10
Neck 5
Chest 5
Body 15
Legs and feet 10
Tail 2½
Coat 15
Size 10
Color 2½
General Appearance 10
TOTAL 100

STANDARD OF POINTS OF THE SCOTTISH TERRIER CLUB OF AMERICA

PENALTIES—Soft coat; curly coat; round, protruding or light eyes; overshot or undershot jaws; obviously oversize or undersize; shyness or timidity; upright shoulders; lack of reach in front or drive in rear; stiff or stilted movement; movement too wide or too close in rear; too narrow in front or rear; out at the elbow; lack of bone and substance; low set tail; lack of pigment in the nose; coarse head; and failure to show with head and tail up are faults to be penalized.

NO JUDGE SHOULD PUT TO WINNERS OR BEST OF BREED ANY SCOTTISH TERRIER NOT SHOWING REAL TERRIER CHARACTER IN THE RING.

SCALE OF POINTS
Skull 5
Muzzle 5
Eyes 5
Ears 10
Neck 5
Chest 5
Body 15
Legs & Feet 10
Tail 5
Coat 15
Size 10
General Appearance 10
TOTAL 100

Appendix A

Regional Scottish Terrier Clubs

A valuable service is performed by the regional Scottish Terrier clubs all across the United States. These clubs can be more attentive to the "grassroots" needs of their members and to how local customs and conditions affect the Scottish Terrier in their operating area. To contact the Scottish Terrier Club of America or any club on the following list, write the American Kennel Club, 51 Madison Avenue, New York, NY 10010 to request the name and address of the current Secretary, who will be happpy to help you in any way.

Greater Dallas Scottish Terrier Club

Greater Pittsburgh Scottish Terrier Club

Heart of America Scottish Terrier Club

San Francisco Bay Scottish Terrier Club

Scottish Terrier Club of California

Scottish Terrier Club of Chicago

Scottish Terrier Club of Greater Atlanta

Scottish Terrier Club of the Greater Baltimore Area

Scottish Terrier Club of Greater Dayton

Scottish Terrier Club of Greater Denver

Scottish Terrier Club of Greater Houston

Scottish Terrier Club of Greater Louisville

Scottish Terrier Club of Greater New York

Scottish Terrier Club of Greater Washington, D.C.

Scottish Terrier Club of Michigan

Scottish Terrier Club of New England

Scottish Terrier Club of Northern Ohio

Scottish Terrier Club of Tampa Bay

Scottish Terrier Club of Utah

Scottish Terrier Club of Western Virginia

Washington State Scottish Terrier Club

Recommended Reading

A. E. F. *Friendship's Offerings,* 1927.

Ash, E. C. *The Scottish Terrier,* 1936.

———. *Dogs: Their History and Development,* 2 vol., 1927.

Ashmore, Marion. *Lost, Stolen or Strayed,* 1931.

Barrie, Caswell. "The New Scottish Terrier Standard," *American Kennel Gazette,* (March 1925): 20–22, 151.

Barton, F. T. *Terriers: Their Points and Management,* 1907.

Bruette, Willliam. *The Scottish Terrier,* 1934.

Buckley, Holland. *The Scottish Terrier,* 1918.

Caspersz, D. S. *The Scottish Terrier Pedigrees,* with supplements, 1930, 1934, 1951, 1962. "What the Scottie Will Become," *American Kennel Gazette,* (July 1931): 25–27, 119. *The Scottish Terrier,* 1938. *The Scottish Terrier,* (Foyles), 1958. *The Popular Scottish Terrier,* 1956, 1962. Revised by Elizabeth Meyer, 1976.

Collins, Sewell. *The Rubaiyat of a Scottish Terrier,* 1897.

Dalziel, Hugh. "The Scotch Terrier," in *British Dogs,* 2nd ed., 1897.

Davies, C. J. *The Scottish Terrier,* 1906.

De la Roche, Mazo. *Portrait of a Dog,* 1930.

Deu, Edna, et al. "Stars in the Doghouse, (Deephaven Kennels)," *Country Life in America,* (April 1939): 55, 109–110.

Drury, W. D. *British Dogs,* ch. 39, 1903.

Elliot, K. (Della). *Notes on the Standard of the Scottish Terrier,* 1976. A comparative analysis as viewed in books on the breed by Caspersz, Kirk, and Marvin. Published in New South Wales.

Ewing, Dr. Fayette. *The Book of the Scottish Terrier,* 1932, and subsequent editions.

Gabriel, Dorothy. *The Scottish Terrier,* 1928, 1936.

Gilkey, Ann. *Grooming and Conditioning the Scottie, Terrier-Type,* February–July 1963.

Gray, D. J. Thompson. *The Dogs of Scotland,* 1887 and 1893 (Whinstone).

Green, James E. *The Scottish Terrier and the Irish Terrier,* 1894.

Haynes, William Sr. *Scottish and Irish Terriers,* 1912, 1925. *The Scottish Terrier,* 1915.

Hutchinson, Walter. *Hutchinson's Popular and Illustrated Dog Encyclopedia,* 1939.

Jesse, G. R. *Researches into the History of the British Dogs,* 1866.

Johns, Rowland. *Our Friend the Scottish Terrier,* 1932.

Jones, A. F. *American Kennel Gazette,* "Ballantrae's Reasons for Success," (March 1927): 13–17, 71; "Hillwood Turns to the Scottie," (February 1932): 9–13; "Bred by Science and Humanity" (Sporran Kennels), (July 1932): 7–11, 124; "Vigal is Building Slowly," (December 1932): 24–28, 157; "A Kennel without a Fault (Relgalf Kennels)," (July 1934): 7–11, 173; "Why Bricht's Aim is to Breed Scotties of the Highest Quality," (February 1936): 12–15, 99; "Championship, The Standard for Scotties of Miss Hull," (March 1936): 11–14, 79; "Raising Scotties That Win Is the Greatest Enjoyment to Owners of Barberry Knowe," (July 1936): 13–16, 153; "Scotties Started Relgalf on the Way to Fame," (August 1938): 27–31.

Kipling, Rudyard. *The Supplication of Black Aberdeen,* 1931. *Thy Servant A Dog,* 1930. *His Apologies,* 1927.

Kirk, T. Allen. *American Scottish Terrier Champions' Pedigrees,* 1962. *This Is The Scottish Terrier,* 1966.

Kirmse, M. A Derrydale Press book of etchings, mostly Scots, 1930.

Lee, Muriel. *The Official Book of the Scottish Terrier,* 1994.

Lee, Rawdon. *Modern Dogs (Terriers),* 1903.

Leighton, Robert. *The New Book of the Dog,* 1907.

L'Hommedieu, Dorothy K. MacGregor, 1941.

Lucas, E. V. *If Dogs Could Write,* 1929.

Marvin, John T. *The Book of All Terriers,* 1964, includes breed chapter.

———. *The New Complete Scottish Terrier,* 1982.

Mason, Charles H. *Our Prize Dogs,* 1888.

Matheson, Darley. *Terriers,* 1962, includes breed chapter.

Maxtee, J. *British Terriers,* 1909; *Scotch and Irish Terriers,* 1909, 1923.

McCandlish, W. L. Chapter on the breed in *Dogs by Well Known Authorities,* 1906; *The Scottish Terrier,* 1909.

Megargee, Edwin S. "The Ideal Scottish Terrier," *The American Kennel Gazette,* (January 1933): 17–20, 136.

Penn-Bull, Betty. *Scottish Terrier Coats,* Re-trimming the breed, n. d; *The Kennelgarth Scottish Terrier Book,* 1983.

Poultney, C. B. *Mr. Roddie Dhu,* 1935 (and sequels).

Robertson, James. *Historical Sketches of the Scottish Terrier,* 1899.

Scottish Terrier Breeders' and Exhibitors' Association Yearbooks (published annually).

Scottish Terrier Club of America Yearbooks, 1923, 1932, 1948, 1952 (supplement), 1959, 1961, 1965, 1972, 1986, 1991.

Scottish Terrier Club of England Yearbooks (published annually).

Sheilds, G. O. *The American Book of the Dog,* 1891. Includes a chapter on the breed by John H. Naylor.

Smith, Croxton. *Terriers, Their Training, Working and Management,* 1937. Includes chapters on the breed by McCandlish.

Stables, Dr. Gordon. *Our Friend the Dog,* 1883.

Suckley, M. and A. Dalgliesh. *The True Story of Fala,* 1942.

Van De Water, Frederick F. *Members of the Family,* 1942.

Van Dine, S. S. "Crashing the Dog Breeding Gate," *American Kennel Gazette,* (December 30): 29–32, 166. *The Kennel Murder Case,* 1932.

Watson, James. *The Dog Book,* 1906, 2 vol. Includes much early information on the breed in America.

Youatt, William. *The Dog,* 1846.